SCORSESE'S MEN

SCORSESE'S MEN

melancholia and the mob

Mark Nicholls

PLUTO PRESS AUSTRALIA

First published in 2004 by
Pluto Press Australia
7 Leveson Street
North Melbourne Victoria 3051
www.plutoaustralia.com

Copyright © Mark Nicholls 2004

Design and Typesetting by Egan-Reid Ltd.
Edited by Michael Wall
Printed and bound by Griffin Press

Australian Cataloguing in Publication Data
   Nicholls, Mark Desmond.
   Scorsese's Men : melancholia and the mob.

   Bibliography.
   Includes index.
   ISBN 1 86403 156 5.

   1. Scorsese, Martin—Criticism and interpretation. 2. Men in motion pictures.
   3. Sex role in motion pictures. 4. Machismo in motion pictures. 5. Masculinity
   in motion pictures. I. Title.

   791.436521

Cover photo: Martin Scorsese on the set of *The Age of Innocence*, 1992
© HowardJacqueline/Corbis Sygma

Internal photos: Kobal Collection.

For Ali

Acknowledgments

I am very grateful to a number of people who have supported me while writing this book. Particular thanks go to my friend and colleague Barbara Creed who has been outstanding in her encouragement and support for this project. I am especially grateful for the time she gave to reading and discussing my ideas and for the insights she provided from her vast knowledge and experience. Jeanette Hoorn has been a similarly encouraging and supportive colleague and friend and I am grateful for her generosity and many kindnesses. Thanks go to Sarah Crisp, Tony Moore, Michael Wall and all the staff at Pluto Press Australia, the Dean and Faculty of Arts at the University of Melbourne, Jaynie Anderson, Angela Ndalianis and all my colleagues at the School of Art History, Cinema Studies, Classical Studies and Archaeology, the staff at the Baillieu and Education Resource Centre Libraries at The University of Melbourne, Alan Braun and the staff at the American Film Institute Library in Los Angeles (Martin Scorsese Archive), Charles Silver at the Film Study Center of the Museum of Modern Art in New York, the staff of the British Film Institute Library in London, Cassandra Laing, Bill Jones and family, Tony Nagelman, Neil Mackinnon, Mark Pennings, Deb Thomas, James Panichi, Dennis Hunt, John Jackson, my research assistants Brigid Stapleton and Domenique Meyrick, and my students at The University of Melbourne who have contributed countless insights, especially those who have worked closely with me as editors of *Screenscape* and as part of *The Visconti Project*. In particular, I wish to express my gratitude to the late Saul Bass who kindly gave of his time for an extended interview on his work with Scorsese, Hitchcock and Preminger. Finally, the generous support and encouragement of friends and family especially my son, Oscar Wirtz, my mother, Joan, and my late father, Peter, has been invaluable. Above all, I thank my partner, Ali Wirtz, for her unfailing enthusiasm, support and encouragement which have been the major force behind the completion of this book. Her contribution to this book has been immense.

Contents

INTRODUCTION

Acute melancholia

He's suffering from acute melancholia together with a guilt complex. We know he blames himself for what happened to the woman. We know little of what went on before.

Vertigo (1958)

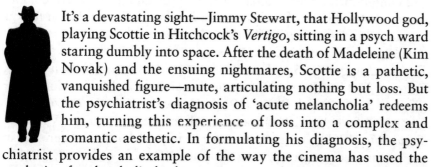 It's a devastating sight—Jimmy Stewart, that Hollywood god, playing Scottie in Hitchcock's *Vertigo*, sitting in a psych ward staring dumbly into space. After the death of Madeleine (Kim Novak) and the ensuing nightmares, Scottie is a pathetic, vanquished figure—mute, articulating nothing but loss. But the psychiatrist's diagnosis of 'acute melancholia' redeems him, turning this experience of loss into a complex and romantic aesthetic. In formulating his diagnosis, the psychiatrist provides an example of the way the cinema has used the aesthetic of melancholia both to reinstate male characters who admit defeat and to spare its audience the enduring nightmare of wounded masculinity.

When Martin Scorsese released *The Age of Innocence* (1993)—the film that inspired the writing of this book—popular discussion paid great attention to whether the film was part of, or a departure from, the Scorsese canon. What I still find arresting about *The Age of Innocence*

lies not in its comparison with the key Scorsese films, such as *Mean Streets* (1973), *Raging Bull* (1980) and *GoodFellas* (1990), but in the way the film articulates a profound sense of melanchoy surrounding its central male protagonist, Newland Archer. The expression of a deep melancholia in *The Age of Innocence* is central to its hero's experience of loss, which is celebrated as a sign of sensitivity. Unlike the horrific deprivation suffered by the hero of classical tragedy, for the male melancholic loss is both seductive and empowering. Rather than being crippled by the kind of moral punishment exacted upon the tragic hero, or the heroine of a melodrama, the male melancholic appears at the end of his narrative as if in a state of grace, strangely beautiful in his self-sacrifice. There is something exquisitely civilised about Newland Archer walking off into the distance of a Paris street, having denied himself a final reunion with the woman 'he wanted most'.

Over the past two decades there has been a solid body of critical writing devoted to the representation of masculinity in the cinema. Film theorists have explained masculinity in terms of a number of psychoanalytical concepts, including sadism, fetishism, masochism, hysteria, the Oedipus complex and masculine protest.[1] One area which has received little critical attention is male melancholia—a surprising omission given the extent to which it permeates the cinema.

Male melancholia is central to those films and genres that depict male characters in the conetxt of emasculation, masochism, repression and containment. Melodramas of the 1940s and 1950s have demonstrated the problems of male crisis and melancholia in relation to war trauma (*Random Harvest* (1942), *The Man in the Gray Flannel Suit* (1956)); alcohol, mania and impotence (*Written on the Wind* (1957), *Tarnished Angels* (1958), *Lost Weekend* (1945), *A Star is Born* (1951), *Cat on a Hot Tin Roof* (1958)); the demands of an overbearing father (*Written on the Wind*, *Picnic* (1955), *Home From the Hill* (1960), *The Long Hot Summer* (1958)); and the domestic grind (*There's Always Tomorrow* (1956), *Bigger Than Life* (1956)). Melancholia is present in the urban Oedipal struggles of film noir (*Double Indemnity* (1942), *Woman in the Window* (1944), *Scarlet Street* (1945), *Gilda* (1946), *Lady From Shanghai* (1948)) and in the masochistic narratives of the boxing picture (*Champion* (1949), *On the Waterfront* (1954), *Somebody Up There Likes Me* (1956)).

Representations of melancholia are not confined to Hollywood—indeed the figure of the male melancholic is central to European cinema.[2] The tradition and conventions of the European approach to melancholia has made for a European-influenced response among American and immigrant American filmmakers to the representation of melancholia in film. In the tradition of, among others, Alain Resnais (*Hiroshima Mon Amour* (1959), *Last Year at Marienbad* (1961)), Bernardo Bertolucci (*Il Conformista* (1970)), Jean Pierre Melville (*Le Samurai* (1967)), Luchino Visconti (*Il Gattopardo* (1963)), Andrei Tarkovsky (*Nostalghia* (1983)) and Volker Schlöndorff (*Un Amour de Swann* (1984)), North American (some émigré) directors such as Martin Scorsese, David Cronenberg, Francis Ford Coppola, Alfred Hitchcock, Orson Welles, Woody Allen, Douglas Sirk and Fritz Lang have all been influential in the formation of a cinema of melancholia. It is also important to note that certain actors have become identified with the melancholic persona, among which Robert De Niro, Jeremy Irons and Woody Allen (in a comic sphere) stand out.

These films and examples do not represent a comprehensive picture of melancholia in the cinema. I have included this list to suggest the range of films that engage with notions of male melancholia, and the gap in contemporary criticism on the subject. My aim is to establish the structures of melancholia and their significance in the representation of male desire in film. In order to focus on the workings of melancholia in the cinema, I have selected five films by Martin Scorsese which provide exemplary instances of the representation of male melancholia—*The Age of Innocence*, *Raging Bull*, *Taxi Driver*, *GoodFellas* and *Cape Fear*. Given the consistent presence of motifs of male melancholia in Scorsese's films, one would expect that critical analysis of his work would have brought to light this key area. This has not been the case. By selecting five films directed by a celebrated auteur and belonging to different genres (melodrama, boxing film, film noir, gangster, thriller), it is possible to demonstrate not only the wide-ranging significance of the narrative of male melancholia but also the lack of critical writing in this area.

Outside Scorsese's films there have been very few substantial discussions of male melancholia in the cinema in general. References to melancholia in film literature are almost always made in the discussion of other issues. Feminists interested in the cinema have considered melancholia in relation to issues of femininity, and this work has been extended by recent work on ghosts in the cinema.[3] Similarly there has been very little written about the films of Martin Scorsese in relation to melancholia despite the significance of melancholia in his output. Notions of melancholic 'memory' and 'desire' are raised in Lesley Stern's important work on Scorsese, but, while implicit to her reading of Scorsese's heroes, an extended consideration of male melancholia in Scorsese is not her central concern.[4]

Where melancholia has been invoked, it is frequently used to validate and protect certain forms of male desire, cinematic or otherwise, particularly against claims of misogyny. This is to present the male melancholic as a mentally complex, profound and tortured rebel-outsider. By invoking the so-called qualities of melancholia, discourses of patriarchy have enabled its favourite sons to circumvent the disturbing conundrums of difference posed by feminist critics. Such readings rely upon and perpetuate the dominant cultural paradigm which appropriates notions of 'femininity' to justify the myth of male melancholia as a state of noble suffering and validated impotence. Thus discussions of melancholia have traditionally cast this affliction as an aesthetic of disempowerment—effectively, as Tania Modleski has considered the practice in *Feminism Without Women*, appropriating 'femininity' while oppressing women.[5]

This aesthetic of impotence portrays the melancholic as wounded, emasculated, alienated and as the sufferer of a profound loss—all due to his pursuit of a moral vision that is antithetical to the repressive and corrupt mob culture which surrounds him. Like the heroine of a melodrama, the male melancholic is represented as engaged in a struggle which he can never win. Unlike the heroine, however, the melancholic appears to have the ability to lose his struggle and still retain power and privilege. Modleski affirms this idea when, reacting to signs of feminist optimism over the possibility of a crisis at the heart of contemporary masculinity, she advises caution:

> . . . we need to consider the extent to which male power is actually consolidated through cycles of crisis and resolution, whereby men ultimately deal with the threat of female power by incorporating it.[6]

Feminist film theorists such as Modleski and Pam Cook have discussed melancholia in relation to the representation of masculinity in specific films in order to question notions of masculinity as transparent and unproblematic. In particular they focus attention on a possible crisis in the representation of masculinity around issues of loss and feminisation. At the same time, they express concern about the way in which narratives about male melancholia may be manipulated in the interests of male power. Looking at Scorsese's *Raging Bull* in particular, Cook refers to the way in which the spectator can be seduced by the melancholic character's narrative of loss.[7] Reading the character of Scottie in *Vertigo*, Modleski describes Scottie's appropriation of feminine characteristics and an occupation of 'a *feminine* position' in order to augment his own power.[8] My main concern is to explore in depth the theoretical underpinnings of male melancholia through the films of Martin Scorsese. In doing so I aim to demonstrate how the Scorsesean male melancholic is able to adopt an emotional stance historically seen as feminine yet retain his privileged position of power and authority. As in *Vertigo*, this is a process widely adopted in the cinema, making perverse and guilt-ridden stalkers like Scottie into cute and universally adored melancholics.

My theory of male melancholia is based on five central features which are evident, in various combinations, in each of the five films under discussion. These are, firstly, that the melancholic experiences a sense of separateness from a corrupt and conservative group; secondly, that he undergoes the trauma of loss; thirdly, that he demonstrates a refusal to relinquish mourning of that loss, resulting both in the construction of a fantasy scenario (or 'crypt scenario') and in the fetishisation of that loss; fourthly, that he displays an ultimate desire for conformity with the group, which will be achieved through an overt show of self-sacrifice or renunciation; and, finally, that he benefits from the consolidation of personal authority and power through the workings of melancholia.

Unlike most writers on Scorsese, I have chosen not to present my analysis of his films in order of their production. This is partly to avoid any suggestion of this book being another of the 'life and works of the great man' variety. I have instead ordered the chapters according to the way the theme of melancholia unfolds in my analysis of the films. As already mentioned, *The Age of Innocence* inspired this line of inquiry, which is why I lead the discussion with this film. The other chapters are then presented according to the way each film further exemplifies one or more of my five central features of male melancholia, or variations on the general notion of melancholia.

Chapter 1 sets out a critical context for male melancholia, drawing on an analysis of a range of psychoanalytic and other critical texts. Chapters 2 and 3 present a close reading of Scorsese's *The Age of Innocence* and *Raging Bull*, demonstrating in both of these the five central features of male melancholia. I then proceed to identify even more roles for the male melancholic: in Chapter 4 he is seen as 'flâneur' in a reading of *Taxi Driver* (1975) inspired by the work of Walter Benjamin, and in Chapter 5 as a 'stranger/foreigner/tourist' in a reading of *GoodFellas*. Through an analysis of *Cape Fear* (1991) in Chapter 6 demonstrating the presence and power of the male melancholic's 'other' as a 'white trash' angst, the book locates the role of the Scorsesean male melancholic in the perverse body politic which houses him. Chapter 7 considers this thesis in his latest films. What follows then is a timely re-evaluation of the films of Martin Scorsese in terms of a masculinity which is wounded but ultimately triumphant. As Max Cady badgers Sam Bowden in *Cape Fear*, on the question of masculinity in this book, 'you're gonna learn about loss'.

CHAPTER ONE

The uses of melancholia:
better to have lost and loved than never to have lost at all

> You talkin' to me? Well who the hell else are you talkin'. . .
> you talkin' to me? Well I'm the only one here.
>
> Travis in *Taxi Driver*

 The image of Robert De Niro staring into the mirror as Travis Bickle in *Taxi Driver* is the best-known moment in Scorsese's films and an icon of the new Hollywood cinema. This scene has been celebrated, discussed and parodied for the simplicity with which it portrays the pent-up frustrations, rage and contained violence which, increasingly, seem part of the human condition. But Travis's ultimate act of violence, *Taxi Driver*'s connection with the 1981 attempted assassination of Ronald Regan by John Hinckley, and the frequent 'boys' own' descriptions of Scorsese's films have overemphasised a reading of this scene in terms of action and violence. Most of us have never held a hand gun, let alone practised in front of the mirror for a bloody shoot-out scene. But all of us, in childhood and beyond, have stood before the bathroom mirror projecting an ideal self, usually intended to address an

1

object of fear and fascination but really only addressing our feelings of an inadequate self.

For all the manic violence this celebrated scene may suggest, Travis's mirror rehearsal suggests not action but retreat. The scene seems to resonate with film fans more for its sensitive and complex resignation to this inadequate self than for its appeal to the action and violence we know ourselves to be incapable of. Placing himself as a morally superior 'man apart' from the corruption and confusion of the urban mob, Travis is playing out his fantasy scenario of destroying evil, saving the virtuous and redeeming the community. A bloody and violent self-sacrifice is central to his mission. Public validation of that mission is implicit. The mirror reminds us, however, that the fantasy scenario is a response to the inadequate self. Travis's routine thus looks less like a moment of empowering action than a melancholic marker of loss—that gap which, as Julia Kristeva puts it, sits at the centre of our being:

> The disappearance of that essential being continues to deprive me of what is most worthwhile in me; I live it as a wound or deprivation, discovering just the same that my grief is but the deferment of the hatred or desire for ascendancy that I nurture with respect to the one who betrayed or abandoned me. My depression points to my not knowing how to lose—I have perhaps been unable to find a valid compensation for the loss? It follows that any loss entails the loss of my being—and of Being itself. The depressed person is a radical, sullen atheist.[1]

Myths of melancholia

Since the Renaissance the *homo melancholicus* has been considered a man of genius, insight and creativity. This Renaissance view of melancholia has further empowered the already potent male individual in our culture and has had a profound influence over representations of masculinity in the cinema. And yet melancholia has been considered from various points of view. Pythagoras saw it as a case of too much black bile in the system. For Walter Benjamin, who both critiqued and embodied the condition, it was a social and personal struggle between rebellion and conformity. One characteristic, however, remains central to the depiction of the melancholic—his constant and legitimised role as 'a man apart'. As I have already noted with Travis, this 'man apart' tag is a central characteristic coveted by the Scorsesean melancholic and, in part, celebrated by film fans. In *Mourning and Melancholia*, Freud outlines some of the factors which support the melancholic's well-articulated desire for difference:

> The distinguishing mental features of melancholia are a profoundly painful dejection, cessation of interest in the outside world, loss of the capacity to love, inhibition of all activity, and a lowering of the self-regarding feelings to a degree that finds utterance in self-reproaches and self-revilings, and culminates in a delusional expectation of punishment.[2]

According to such displays as these the melancholic represents the dynamic between himself and his group by way of his 'keener eye for the truth than other people who are not melancholic'. These ideas are graphically portrayed in the way some of Scorsese's heroes, like Jake La Motta (Robert de Niro) in *Raging Bull*, court bloody self-punishment. The somewhat mysterious nature of the melancholic to those 'who cannot see what it is that is absorbing him so entirely' gives him a certain fascination. His very mysteriousness, and an air of insight and command, are derived from the stance of authority Freud observes in those who engage in self-criticism.[3] Shakespeare's Hamlet, in this sense, stands as a model suitable to the melancholic's sense of self-importance and, indeed, for his ultimate failure and self-delusion.[4] In Scorsese's films this is best represented by the disturbing charm of his melancholic heroes and the fascination they elicit from those around them. The attraction Betsy (Cybill Shepherd) feels for Travis in *Taxi Driver* is a perfect example of the way a perception of mysteriousness can be garnered from the male melancholic's performance of anything from dull incomprehension to psychosis.

Friday night drag queen
In *The Gendering of Melancholia*, Juliana Schiesari critiques historical interpretations of melancholia by revealing the way in which it further empower the male character by casting him as 'creative genius'; this is the very notion of genius that Newland Archer (Daniel Day-Lewis) pretends to possess in *The Age of Innocence*. By taking on notions of grief, suffering, loss and sensitivity, the male melancholic uses these traditionally feminine attributes in the service of his own cultural validation. At the same time he further displaces the role of women in

patriarchy. In terms of Schiesari's critique of Freud's *Mourning and Melancholia*, the profound sensitivity of the male provides the basis of a melancholic temperament, while it is left to the female merely to mourn.[5] By highlighting Freud's observations of the melancholic's display of a 'heightened sense of morality', Schiesari leads us to the melancholic's ultimate allegiance, namely a subjugation to his 'overdeveloped superego', seen both in his castigation of others and his own self-reproaches.[6] Accordingly, Schiesari draws our attention to Freud's example of Hamlet. This example places Freud's male melancholic within a cultural tradition which validates his expression of loss as a part of a cultural myth—the melancholic as Renaissance prince, artist and intellectual.[7]

This legitimisation is based upon a positive notion of melancholia formed by fifteenth-century philosopher Marsilio Ficino. Schiesari quotes Ficino on the melancholic's separation from the 'common crowd', his 'blessed lack' or personal expression of loss, all derived from his creative powers, and the general tendency of male melancholia to turn itself from a condition of loss into a 'privileged artifact'.[8] In this context, against the male display of loss, female loss is rendered insignificant. The male melancholic's superiority is grounded in his ability to play the game of marginalisation which 'grants him cultural legitimacy'.[9]

Freud and Benjamin both comment on the fact that in a well-known etching by sixteenth-century artist Albrecht Dürer, 'Melancholia' is female. Schiesari sees this as functioning 'as a metaphor of male sorrow'.[10] Scorsese continues this use of female characters to signify male sorrow, particularly in the example of the self-destructive ex-prostitute Ginger (Sharon Stone) in *Casino* (1995). The aim of this appropriation of femininity and sensitivity is to open up the possibilities of transcendence, and so complete the list of privileges sought by the male melancholic. As Schiesari points out, this is a desire for 'a transcendence of difference (whether social, sexual, ethnic or linguistic)' which not only serves the melancholic's assumption of 'moral conscience, artistic creativity, or heightened sensitivity', but also his desire to free himself from the 'rigid binarism' of patriarchal gender roles. Not that he seeks their undoing generally. He merely wants the privilege for himself. Seeking the power to control himself, and to mark the limits of his revolt, 'the melancholic thus stands both in reaction to and in complicity with patriarchy'.[11] In this manner the Scorsesean melancholic is something of a Friday night drag queen. We see in *Mean Streets* (1973), for example, that the melancholic Charlie (Harvey Keitel) longs for a life outside the constraints of the Mob organisation. He wants to be the 'other', to love the epileptic Teresa (Amy Robinson) and the anarchic Johnny Boy (Robert De Niro), but he only wants this escape when it suits him.

Rebel within the cause

Just as Jake La Motta struggles against the Mob in *Raging Bull* and Newland Archer takes on the might of the network of families in nineteenth-century New York, the idea of a reaction against patriarchy is central to the melancholic's self-image as a social rebel. Critical to this rebellion is his distaste for the corruption and oppression of his own tribe. In *The Origin of German Tragic Drama*, Benjamin points to 'greedy' and 'disloyal' characteristics of the melancholic under the 'black bile' diagnoses of the high Middle Ages. As Scorsese does in *Raging Bull*, Middle Ages philosophy associated excessive melancholia with bestiality. Benjamin quotes Sancho Panza in *Don Quixote* as a good example of this notion: 'Sir, sorrow was not ordained for beasts but men, yet if men do exceed in it they become beasts'.[12] Making a further connection between melancholia and misanthropy, Benjamin quotes Andreas Tscherning's poem of 1912, 'Melancholy Speaks Herself': 'I fear only that the world might be distrustful of me, lest I should want in some way to penetrate the spirit of hell'.[13] This might have been the lament of Scorsese's Jesus (Willem Dafoe) in *The Last Temptation of Christ* (1988).

Freud also sees this spirit of rebellion in the melancholic and points directly to the licence to express outrage at the world around him that is implied within his rebellion. Central to Freud's clinical portrait is his observation of 'the disturbance of self-regard' apparent in the melancholic. Freud clearly spells out the essence of the melancholic's delusions by giving him a level of insight and justification in his self-reproaches.[14] They provide the 'key to the clinical picture': 'we perceive that the self-reproaches are reproaches against a loved object which have been shifted away from it on to the patient's own ego'.[15]

The movement away from genuine self-reproach by melancholics seems to lie in their lack of humility and submissiveness. They make 'the greatest nuisance of themselves', acting as though slighted and as if 'treated with great injustice'. 'All this is possibly only because the reactions expressed in their behaviour still proceed from a mental constellation of revolt'.[16] Schiesari agrees with the link between the melancholic's self-criticism and his criticism of others. She suggests a revision of Freud's truthfulness/unfairness reading of melancholic self-reproach. Either the melancholic is genuinely self-reproachful or, if speaking too harshly of himself, he is really speaking harshly of others. For Schiasari, the step from seeing the melancholic's self-reproaches as covert critique of others to the view of him as "moralist' critic of society'—the 'disagreeable but justified rebel'—is a small one.[17] The idea of self-justification introduces ambivalence into the description of the melancholic. While he sees himself as a non-conformist, his assumption of what Benjamin scholar Max Pensky calls a 'half willing collaboration' places him also as a conformist. Like the licenced figure of the king's fool that we know from Shakespeare, the melancholic speaks the unpalatable truths that exist between the individual and society and is pardoned his transgression.[18]

The secret heart of woes[19]

In his comparison of melancholia with mourning, Freud argues that, unlike mourning, melancholic loss (or what Freud would call the 'object-loss of melancholia') is frequently 'of a more ideal kind' and remains unconscious. In *Life Lessons* Scorsese's contribution to the three part film, *New York Stories* (1989), the love affair between celebrated New York artist Lionel Dobie (Nick Nolte) and his assistant Paulette (Rosanna Arquette) is over before the film begins. Consistent with the unconscious nature of melancholic loss however, Paulette remains in the narrative and is the central object of Lionel's longing. Unlike mourning, which relies upon objective 'reality testing' to free the melancholic from loss, melancholia holds a puzzling obscurity for those around the melancholic who 'cannot see what it is that is absorbing him so entirely'.[20] This is precisely because melancholia lives not in the objective world of social reality but hidden in the unconscious. Following 'a real slight or disappointment', such as Paulette's rejection of Lionel, the melancholic libido fails to separate from the lost object or be placed upon a new object, withdrawing instead into the ego. In the ego the melancholic establishes an identification with the lost object. Loss of the object, the root cause of which is patently obvious to all, becomes 'ego-loss', which escapes what might be called public scrutiny.[21] As in Lionel's fantasy images of love making with Paulette, in Scorsese this hidden ego activity often takes the form of the melancholic's inner visions or distorted perceptions—his fantasy scenario. Thus the melancholic narrative can be played out under the direction of no external authority other than the melancholic's own narcissism.[22] In loosening the sufferer from its attachment to a lost love, melancholia may look like normal mourning, but the resemblance is superficial. Melancholia demonstrates none of the real work of mourning to free the sufferer from that loss. In fact, its attempts to do so are only ever half-hearted. Melancholia is both a painful wound and a treasured object, which preserves the struggle over the object by taking this struggle out of the objective sphere—the world surrounding the melancholic—and restaging it in the ego. The struggle remains for a prolonged period, if not indefinitely—'So by taking flight into the ego love escapes extinction'.[23]

In 'Mourning or Melancholia: Introjection versus Incorporation' Nicolas Abraham and Maria Torok elaborate upon this idea by taking up Freud's notion of the 'wound'. According to their reading of the situation, which distinguishes itself from Freud's by removal of its activity from the unconscious to the conscious mind, the melancholic works to 'hide, wall in and encrypt' this wound. This process is brought about 'when reality must be denied along with the narcissistic and libidinal import of loss'. As Newland holds onto Ellen (Michelle Pfeiffer) as a ghost of the past in *The Age of Innocence*, or Travis writes to his parents of his imaginary girlfriend and secret service job in *Taxi Driver*, this system preserves the object as a cherished memory of the melancholic's most precious possession.

Such a process or system does not, however, represent melancholia for Abraham and Torok; they observe the onset of melancholia only when the 'crypt' is disturbed and threatened with destruction. At this point the melancholic displays the overt sadness and despair at the base of his wound, as does Jake La Motta, memoralising the loss of his beloved brother Joey (Joe Pesci) in his night club routine and final dressing room mirror scene. The public display of grief is the proof of his devotion and demonstrates the extent to which, as Freud puts it, the shadow of the object has fallen on the ego. Abraham and Torok show how the melancholic's public suffering gives a voice to the lost object, which says, in effect, 'he endures all this because of me'. The melancholic's explanation is, 'Being a melancholic, I stage and let everyone see the full extent of my love object's grief over having lost me'.[24] This is essentially the project of *Life Lessons*' melancholic, Lionel Dobie. At the lowest point of their break-up, Lionel promises to do anything for Paulette to prove his love. When Paulette challenges him to kiss a nearby cop on the beat, the celebrated New York identity humiliates himself, taking on the guise of a crazed vagrant beggar—his own public display of loss. When he blows the cop a kiss and is waved on like street trash, he turns round to discover that Paulette has increased his humiliation by vanishing into the night.

Fetishist/collector/courtier

Discussing the way Freud highlights the loss of the object as 'controlled by a *what* rather than a *who*', Schiesari makes some key points about the nature of melancholic loss. Freud indicates that, while the melancholic finds fault with his own ego, the mourner sees it in the world, which 'has become poor and empty'.[25] Schiesari suggests that this tendency to find fault in the world is also the tendency of the melancholic who uses this sense of 'betrayal of and by the world . . . as a pretext through which the ego can represent itself'. The demonstration of loss thus becomes the method by which the melancholic ego authenticates the conflict between the inner and outer world. The object of loss is thus devalued 'for the sake of loss itself'. This idea accounts for the way the Scorsese melancholic so readily jettisons and forsakes his object of desire. In *GoodFellas*, Henry Hill (Ray Liotta) has few qualms about 'ratting out' his 'wiseguy' friends. As in the final image of the film—a romaticised portrait of Tommy (Joe Pesci) firing his gun at the audience—these Mob figures are worth more to Henry as objects of loss from a world of 'action' he will miss forever. Schiesari argues that the melancholic ego moves its attention away from the 'whom' (the love object) lost and towards the '"who" that presents himself as losing in melancholia', that is, the melancholic himself. The object of loss is totally devalued in favour of empowering the ego through the love of loss for its own sake.[26]

Later in her work Schiesari relates the concept of loss to the idea of a fetish by noting how loss itself becomes a fetish when the understanding of the 'what' of the object is itself lost. In this sense the fetishism of melancholia acts as the 'someone or something besides itself', the decoy for the narcissistic element requiring pity—the love that dare not speak its name. Melancholic loss, like a fetish, insists that it is *the* loss and denies the existence of any other. If, according to Schesari, melancholic loss operates like the fetish, it may be also associated with that 'recovery of meaning' in the 'proliferation of signs' which I shall discuss presently in relation to Julia Kristeva's work on melancholia. Just as Sam Bowden (Nick Nolte) derives a comforting sense of visual pleasure in his surveillance of Max Cady (Robert De Niro) and his violent excesses in *Cape Fear* (1991), the melancholic acts as a fetishist, denying castration, denying loss by piling-up objects of loss.[27]

In her introduction to an edition of Benjamin's essays, Susan Sontag writes of Benjamin's attachment to things (as opposed to people) as his perception of the way in which the melancholic interacts with the world.[28] Haunted by death, Sontag argues, the melancholic displays the full potency and ingeniousness of his contemplation of lifeless things. As Newland Archer is frequently found gazing upon Old Master paintings and similar *objets d'art*, the melancholic temperament heaps up such things, often as fragments or ruins or allegory—'The only pleasure the melancholic permits himself'[29]—and, in Benjamin's view, shares this tendency with both baroque and Surrealist sensibilities. Thus this melancholic, like Benjamin himself, stands as a collector immersing himself in the 'baroque cult of ruins' and the collectable fragmentation of 'the nihilistic energies of the modern era . . . A world whose past has become (by definition) obsolete . . .' The passion for seeking out and collecting books in Benjamin, and others of the melancholic temperament, is muted by its own fetishism. Sontag's addition to the following Benjamin phrase is telling: 'Collectors are people with a tactical instinct'—like courtiers'.[30] The tactical instinct of the courtier—the understanding of *comme il faut*, which may be said to derive itself from total immersion in the 'thingness' of rules, laws and precepts—threatens to undermine the very insight that such collecting aims to demonstrate. Through an immersion in things, the tactical instinct of the courtier takes the melancholic away from his desire for power, the desire to be the prince.[31] Like Charlie in *Mean Streets*, despite his desire to challenge the system, Newland Archer's fluency in the lifeless rules and rituals of nineteenth-century New York society is such that he will always be subject to its decrepit authority.

In *Melancholy Dialectics*, Max Pensky laments Freud's lack of speculation on the original bond between mother and child which might have led Freud to an understanding of melancholia which includes an 'understanding of the relation of the ego to its libidinal objects'. Such a consideration might well have drawn a conclusion, as has Pensky's reading of Kristeva, about the 'limit', 'impossibility' and failure of 'object-relations'. Melancholia, in the Kristevan sense, Pensky argues, occurs when union with the erotic object 'as an act of symbolisation' breaks down. The failure of this bond associates melancholia with meaninglessness and brings about a breakdown of 'depressed narcissist's' methods of securing relations with the outside world. The retreat of the melancholic from the realm of meaning, 'thus traces back to the originary libidinal wound: the loss not of the object, but of the thing, the mother (death)'. As Pensky reads Julia Kristeva in *Black Sun*, this sets the melancholic off on a journey where the recovery of meaning becomes his central concern. Being able to sublimate loss, meaning for the melancholic is found in his 'fascination with the rifts and discontinuities that remain in the proliferation of signs.'[32]

The unnamed Thing

The melancholic's breakdown—which marks loss, death or grief—reignites what Kristeva, in *Black Sun*, calls 'echoes of old traumas'. Such a reawakening points quickly to the essential narcissism of melancholic depression—the narrative of loss of being that it *really* plots. What is reignited is, of course, the old trauma of the loss of the 'unnamed Thing'—the mother, a largely and revealingly absent entity in the films of Martin Scorsese.

Like sacrifice, at least in Kristeva's reading of it which I discuss in relation to *Raging Bull*, the melancholia of this loss takes place at the threshold of language, that fetish system through which the subject tries, hopelessly, to find the lost mother and all that she signifies:

> The child king becomes irredeemably sad before uttering his
> first words; this is because he has been irrevocably lost,
> desperately separated from the mother, a loss that causes him
> to try to find her again, along with other objects of love, first
> in the imagination, then in words.[33]

This sadness represents a state of inhibition, and asymbolia (a failure of symbols). Although 'temporary sadness or mourning' and 'melancholy stupor' may be clinically different, both entertain an intolerance for loss of the object and both mark a failure of symbols to compensate for the melancholic's withdrawal from the world. Thus, at the loss of the object and the failure of symbols, the melancholic longs for the unnamed Thing. This is suggested, for example, in Henry's disapproving mother in *GoodFellas*, when he comes home looking like a gangster, or Charlie's mother's non-presence in *Mean Streets*, suggested by the kitchen notes and freshly laundered shirts she leaves behind for her son.

As Kristeva points out, 'primary identification' with the father *should* be the means through which the melancholic becomes reconciled with the loss of the Thing, and initiated into the realm of law, language and culture—that 'bond of faith' of the symbolic. This bond, however, is the very thing which 'disintegrates in the depressed person'. For the melancholic, 'primary identification proves to be fragile, insufficient to secure other identifications, which are symbolic . . .'[34] If melancholia thus suggests a postponement of the melancholic's entrance into the symbolic, how might this entrance be achieved ? How might the subject protect himself against disintegration? As Freud observed, melancholia's tendency is to turn itself around into mania. Kristeva points to the 'depressive affect'—a display of sadness and moodiness—to provide comfort against the sense of loss: Jake's violent gesture of self-sacrifice in the ring in *Raging Bull*, Travis's bloody massacre at the end of *Taxi Driver*. The 'triumph over sadness' is achieved by a shift in identification from the lost object to the 'third party—father, forma, schema':

> A requirement for a denying or manic position ('no, I haven't lost; I evoke, I signify through the artifice of signs and for myself what has been parted from me'), such an identification, which may be called phallic or symbolic, insures [sic] the subject's entrance into the universe of signs and creation.[35]

The conformist[36]
In his 1997 film, *Kundun*, Scorsese presented the 14th Dalai Lama as his most sophisticated melancholic to date. Possessed by an overwhelming sense of his people's oppression by the occupying Chinese, Kundun responds to the situation with a melancholia of a dialectical nature. Kundun's response is marked by its telling insight and a strong realisation of the complexity, and perhaps the futility of the world. Dominated by sorrow, guilt and self-reproach, however, his response also appears passive, ineffectual and not without blame. Central to Walter Benjamin's notion and embodiment of melancholia, as Pensky sees it, is its own dialectical nature.[37] In his introduction to his work on Benjamin, Pensky demonstrates this dialectic, and what he calls 'the exceedingly strange role of melancholy in Benjamin's work', by examining two texts by Benjamin written in the early 1930s: *Linke Melancholie* and *Agesilaus Santander*.[38] The juxtaposition of the two readings of these articles underlines Benjamin's use of melancholia in political terms to denote socio-political conformity and, by demonstrating his own tendencies towards melancholy, argues for a more complex understanding of melancholia as a mode of critical insight, a dialectic of 'pure opposition'.[39] Such a reading of melancholic expression is, therefore, instructive for our consideration of those Scrosesean melancholics, like Kundun, who tread the fine line between rebellion and conformity.

Linke (*Leftist Melancholy*) presents Benjamin's critique of Weimar author-intellectuals for producing texts which undermine and transform their support for the proletariat by producing 'weapon[s] of reaction'. Pensky observes that, in such reviews, Benjamin assumed the role of Weimar critic, assailing his contemporaries for the 'secret complicity between cultural expression and political domination' that they failed to grasp, thus forcing them to consider their political loyalties. Focusing upon the poetry of Erich Kästner,[40] in whose work Benjamin saw a conformist ambivalence, he accuses these leftists of being guilty of melancholia. In Benjamin's view, this is a mode mired in the concerns of bourgeois-leftism (linksbürgertum) which, as we see in Scorsese's well meaning but ineffectual melancholic, fails to mobilise against the despotism it describes, preferring to reflect upon 'the desperation and sadness of a bourgeoisie that, while "upset" by social injustice, has no interest in acting against it'. Accordingly such literary output works in secret to 'support an unjust regime by transforming revolutionary opposition into objects of aesthetic appreciation'.[41]

In this context, Pensky points out, Benjamin is interested in a stage or reincarnation of melancholia in the twentieth century. Characteristic of this is the appropriation of melancholia as the property of middle-class writers that enabled the expression of despair to be relocated as 'a force of political reaction'. Melancholy can easily infect and work against a political cause that it intends to support. Imbued with meaninglessness, resignation and negativity, 'melancholy politics' runs the risk of making 'a secret, half-willing collaboration with the forces it seeks to oppose'. In Kästner's poetry, Benjamin establishes 'the ancient links between melancholia and *acedia*', the passivity and inactivity that works against the author's revolutionary intentions. Benjamin's criticism thus stands as a call for action and struggle against the forces that work, subtly, to undermine the fight against despotism. In this context, as Pensky calls it, these forces are powered by 'the politics of melancholia'.[42]

Benjamin's 1933 piece, *Agesilaus Santander*, written in a period of painful self-reflection on Ibiza, stands as the single expression of his own melancholy character. In its occult obsession with Benjamin's own relation with a 'satanic angel', this 'history of saturnine melancholia' reveals, as Pensky points out, that its author and the critic of *Linke Melancholie* are the same person. More than the melancholic's mere hypocrisy, Pensky argues that this juxtaposition points to the dialectical nature of Benjamin's melancholic and critical vision. Melancholy is thus no '"mere" sadness' of a personal emotional condition, nor is it 'some essentiality, some real being, that could be referred to as directing or inspiring Benjamin's thinking 'from the outside''. It is a 'space' which provides a 'way of seeing' or insight between the melancholy subject and object, between 'Benjamin's "messianic" and "materialistic" gaze'. This is the melancholic vision which sees the objective world as 'a complex puzzle awaiting decipherment'. Nevertheless, such a vision or insight, with which Pensky aligns Kristeva's sense of the duality of melancholy objects, at best remains locked into its 'essential paradox'. Such a paradox can, perhaps, only compromise those values associated with struggle that Benjamin outlines in the *Linke*.[43]

In light of this dialectic, Pensky's brief history of melancholy ends, tellingly, with Wolf Lepienies'[44] observations of the melancholic as passive rebel. As 'a specific category of social rebellion', melancholia is, to Lepienies, 'a simultaneous rejection of both the means and ends of sanctioned social behaviour'. It marks the retreat of the despairing individual in the face of stifling social oppression. Believing all avenues of escape to be blocked, the melancholic retreats into a brooding condition of 'interiority' and 'a homesickness for the past and apathy for the present'.[45]

In the terms of Scorsese's *Kundun*, Benjaminian melancholia, for all its disruptive potential, looks very much like 'a safe journey and a safe return'. Despite his potential for 'messianic' insight, the male melancholic seems destined to pass from Freud's 'constellation of revolt' to 'the crushed state of melancholia'[46]—as a *Mean Streets* barfly reminds Charlie when he presents him with his own portrait—a swastika. In the end the male melancholic owes greater allegiance to his 'overdeveloped superego' than to 'the effects of a turbulent unconscious' as Schiesari puts it.[47] Ultimately his concerns are conservative and seek to uphold those values of the patriarchy in which he holds a privileged place. Thus, as Henry Hill forsakes his Mob friends and finds himself back in the realm of suburban drudgery, the Scorsesean melancholic so often gives up desire in order to be reconciled with the authority of his tribal group, effecting the melancholic's 'mundane vision'. His vision is, thus, *Trauerspiel* (sorrow play) rather than *Tragödie*. As George Steiner, points out, tragedy is mythic; it stages rites of sacrifice in which the silent hero, ethically superior to gods and men, attains transcendence. Grounded in history, *Trauerspiel* is earthy, carnal and its creators and characters 'cling feverently to the world'. A counter-transcendental entity, *Trauerspiel*, like Scorsesean melancholia, 'celebrates the immanence of existence even

Sam's Earthly paradise. Martin Scorsese and Robert De Niro on the set of Casino

where this existence is passed in torment. It is emphatically 'mundane', earthbound, corporeal.'[48] When Sam Rothstein (Robert De Niro) is blown up by a car bomb in *Casino* and spends much of the credit sequence flying through the fires of Hell, he does not transcend to an Olympian height, but is unceremoniously dumped back on earth, amongst the five cent gaming machines and cheap casino hustlers of Las Vegas.

CHAPTER TWO

The Age of Innocence:
a mean and melancholy history

> Whenever he thought of Ellen Olenska, it had been abstractly,
> serenely, like an imaginary loved one in a book or picture. She
> had become the complete vision of all that he had missed.
>
> *The Narrator*

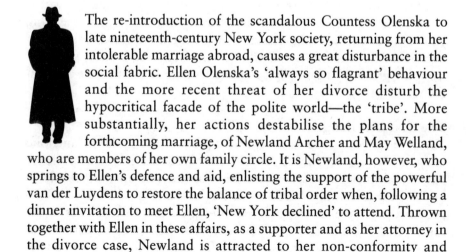 The re-introduction of the scandalous Countess Olenska to late nineteenth-century New York society, returning from her intolerable marriage abroad, causes a great disturbance in the social fabric. Ellen Olenska's 'always so flagrant' behaviour and the more recent threat of her divorce disturb the hypocritical facade of the polite world—the 'tribe'. More substantially, her actions destabilise the plans for the forthcoming marriage, of Newland Archer and May Welland, who are members of her own family circle. It is Newland, however, who springs to Ellen's defence and aid, enlisting the support of the powerful van der Luydens to restore the balance of tribal order when, following a dinner invitation to meet Ellen, 'New York declined' to attend. Thrown together with Ellen in these affairs, as a supporter and as her attorney in the divorce case, Newland is attracted to her non-conformity and

independence and falls in love with her, despite his impending marriage. There begins his struggle against propriety which culminates in their mad embrace and declarations of love. Just as he declares the impossibility of his marriage ('Do you see me marrying May now?') a telegram arrives from May, an insightful operator despite her seeming innocence, informing Ellen of the success of Newland's recent attempts to bring forward their marriage. This leaves Newland 'buried alive under his future'.

Newland now regards married life with May as a personal death. Even when separated from Ellen for a year or so, he loses none of his desire for her. Denial sharpens his passion. At their first reunion, Ellen confirms that her feelings are reciprocal, promising him that she will not return to her husband in Europe. 'That's no life for you', he remarks. 'It is', she replies, 'as long as it's part of yours'. Tribal forces, orchestrated by the silent and unseen hand of May, however, are at work to bring about their separation. As Newland's desire for escape with Ellen reaches its height, he and May hold their first dinner—a 'farewell' for the Countess Olenska. May towers over Newland as they discuss the 'success' of the party. Implicit in May's demeanour is the success of her subtle removal of Ellen (she has informed Newland of her pregnancy) from the tribe and the danger Ellen presented in her influence over Newland.

In Paris many years later Newland, fifty-seven and recently widowed, has the opportunity to meet Ellen again through the intervention of his son, Ted. In Ted's last conversation with May, before she died, she revealed the affair and her role in it. With Newland, she assured Ted and his brothers and sisters, they would be 'safe'. Ted repeats her words to his father: 'Because once, when she asked you, you gave up the thing you wanted most'. As the master of self-denial, Newland assures Ted that he did not need to be 'asked'. Perversely, moved by May's missive from the grave, Newland Archer refuses to see Ellen, the one thing in the world he most desired.

The next best thing

The Age of Innocence is a representation of the male melancholic imagination *par excellence*, and Newland Archer is Scorsese's most patent male melancholic. Far from being a search for an attainable love, his journey is a compulsive search for loss and an obsessive care to preserve that loss: he wants his desire to be unsatisfied. Loss is the centrepiece of his fantasy of separation from the regime he purports to detest—New York society. The search for unsatisfied desire, of course, can never end. A prisoner of its cycle, the male melancholic must give up that key object of desire—Ellen in Newland's case—through which he seeks loss as an escape. He exchanges it for the privileges of conformity with a regime which promises him the last and greatest pleasure of patriarchy—power. The melancholic's power is achieved through the denial of desire, in that desire is aligned with loss of control and with a state of jouissance (joy in the maternal realm) which both constitute a profound threat to patriarchy.

It is a mistake, however, to read the narrative of *The Age of Innocence* as moving Newland towards some primary sense of loss. This particular feeling of loss assailed him long before the current cycle of symbolic loss and plenitude began. It is the loss of the 'pre-symbolic', the maternal realm that haunts the male melancholic and provides the impetus for his endless journey to recover his lost object of desire. The various dramas of loss and recovery, fullness and emptiness that he acts out are merely part of a search for a state of melancholia that will satisfy his desire. They are, however, a poor substitute for that maternal bond. In this sense, Newland's final rejection of Ellen marks a 'good enough' state of desire he must accept. What he gives up at this point is nothing new; patriarchy has forbidden it long ago. What he accepts—and its presence is obvious throughout the narrative—is melancholia, which is the next best thing.

The Ghost and Mr Archer

The social threat Ellen represents creates the disturbance which opens the narrative. What Newland finds, or believes he finds, when he enters the opera box in which she is being paraded, is, in a sense, a dead body—the most abject of all things.[1] 'You have been away a very long time', says Newland, responding to one of her many slight breaches of *comme il faut*. Ellen replies accordingly: 'Oh, centuries and centuries. So long, I'm sure I'm dead and buried and this dear old place is heaven.'

Clearly she is not dead. It is more that to both Newland and the tribe, Ellen must be attributed with a taboo not unlike the taboo on the dead. Due to her foreign marriage, her unconventional habits, her consorting with undesirable persons and general reputation for immorality, Ellen is dead to proper society. In terms of Freud's theory in *Totem and Taboo*[1] she is, in the eyes of this elitist clan, 'of the wrong tribe' and carries the prohibitions associated with the incest taboo. She may not be touched and it is the job of the tribal organisation to convince Newland of it—that she is lost to him.

Newland's impression of the situation relies on the very idea that Ellen is dead or absent. It is certainly a condition of his ambivalence towards her that he should think her dead. Ellen's death is certainly prominent in his thoughts and desires. Just before the telegram announcement of the May/Newland marriage, for example, Grannie Mingott argues the case for Ellen's return to Europe. At this suggestion Newland bursts out with the cry that he 'would rather see her dead'. A year and a half later, following the marriage, the narrator describes Newland's detachment when hearing of Ellen, 'as if listening to reminiscences of someone long dead'. In the face of his temporary reversion to his 'old inherited ideas about marriage' after the 'madness' with Madame Olenska, 'Archer trained himself to remember it as the last of his discarded experiments. She remained in his memory simply as the most plaintive and poignant of a line of ghosts.'

In this regard Newland accepts Ellen's taboo status as established by the tribe. To him, however, she is only dead in the sense that death signifies a state of conceptual absence. His model of desire relies on such a seemingly permanent absence but not in so far as it puts her beyond the melancholic's touch. Nevertheless, his willingness to understand Ellen's 'death' is tempered by his reluctance to give up his attachment to the idea of loss, if not also of Ellen herself. Thus, either by 'taking flight into the ego'[2] or by creation of a 'crypt'[3] (see the discussion below) the male melancholic immerses himself in a fantasy obsession which hides his 'secret heart of woes'. The attempts made by the New York tribe to rally around May and block Newland's access to Ellen thus appear like Freud's agents of 'reality-testing' in *Mourning and Melancholia*. They fail to convince the patient, Newland, that the object of his desire no longer exists.[4] In the melancholic struggle over the object of desire, something other than normal mourning takes place and is restaged, not in conscious reality, but in the ego.[5]

The battle over Ellen is like a tribal war which dictates the terms of obedience for its members via an obsession with objects.[6] An analysis of key scenes between Newland and Ellen sheds light on the nature of this fantasy and of his melancholia. My argument is that the representation of melancholia in *The Age of Innocence* deals with two relationships: first and most importantly a relationship and dialogue with Ellen, staged in Newland's melancholic 'crypt'; and secondly with the tribal group, and how its assertion of certain signs and symbols informs Newland's complex state of melancholia.

The exercise of Newland's melancholia is demonstrated in some nine scenes with Ellen in which the incorporation the act of encrypting the lost object within the melancholic unconscious as outlined by Abraham and Torok,[7] is a dominant factor.[8] Furthermore, as in any doppelganger or shadow relationship, the dialogue between Newland and Ellen suggests an exchange and appropriation of each other's positions. As when the ego fuses with the lost object, in a free and arbitrary way, this exchange seems to contribute to the construction of Newland's identity as a melancholic. These scenes also make clear the essential characteristics of male melancholia: a pretension to creative insight, the assumption of genius and moral superiority, an outsider status, an acquaintance with loss and, importantly, an appropriation of the feminine in some form.

Part One: The Crypt
A man apart

The van der Luyden dinner party provides Newland with his first significant discussion with Ellen, and in it we see a number of motifs which mark their later encounters. As Newland wanders the room alone and finally sits, Scorsese's slow-motion camera emphasises Ellen's unconventional crossing of the room—'to get up and walk away from one gentleman in order to seek the company of another'—as if magically drawn to Newland. Marked by this breach of etiquette, the scene establishes Ellen's unconventionality, the attraction it has for Archer, and the way it constructs an intimacy between them. As the exchange makes clear, Ellen possesses the qualities of rebellion he desires for himself, qualities that May clearly does not possess. Accompanied on the soundtrack by the second movement of Beethoven's *Pathetique* sonata,[9] the couple talk. Their conversation comes around to that characteristic of the Countess's which Newland finds most appealing and moving—her grief and sense of sorrow. The suggestion of her past punishment at the hands of her husband adds a touch of tragedy to her tale of loss. Both Newland's melancholic expression and the *Pathetique* sonata are responses to, and aestheticisations of, expressions of his sorrow, the melancholic's habitual state. The melancholic relies upon such expressions as a source of identification with grief and an expression of his own highly valued sensitivity. Both operate to separate Newland from others and increase his intimacy with Ellen as its source. Certainly, his public association with Ellen's unconventional behaviour goes a long way towards satisfying his desire to be seen as similarly rebellious in the pursuit of his more noble cause—that of his own moral vision.

The scene of their meeting the next day repeats the motifs of the previous meeting—an initial unconventional act or comment, a lively and flirtatious banter, Ellen's expressions of sadness and need, all leading to their increased intimacy, and all emphasising Newland's 'noble cause'. Distinguishing himself from the ever-interloping Julius Beaufort, who has suggested Ellen's street to be unfashionable, and others like him 'who have nothing more serious to consider', Newland assumes the melancholic's favourite role of social and moral critic. Both here and in the later scene in which divorce is discussed he shows himself as critic but also reader of the New York social labyrinth and its smooth hypocrisies. 'Everything is labelled, but everybody is not', he informs her. In this he draws on his bourgeois and highly self-conscious sensibility to reveal his fascination with objects and signs, and to show that he can read and explain them. The need Ellen expresses gives him the opportunity to demonstrate the qualities of the critic from within; he is in possession of a superior moral code and the melancholic's 'keener eye for the truth'.[10]

Conversations with a lost object

Despite this ability, which he loves to exercise around Ellen, Newland still allows himself to engage in a game of exchange with her over positions of strength and weakness. The bewilderment he betrays when surveying her works of art suggests that Ellen introduces much to Newland's conventional world he does not comprehend.[11] Following his sycophantic assertion of the importance of the van der Luydens in New York society, Ellen's effortless observation about this importance fascinates him. In mocking condescension to his pretensions towards superior knowledge, she backs off: 'But of course you must tell me'. Intrigued by her insight, he laughs as he says 'No, it's you telling me'. Clearly Newland has much to learn from Ellen, and her ability to teach him is the source of his personal growth. As he says to her over a year later, 'You gave me my first glimpse of a real life and then told me to go on with a false one'.

This suggests an essential factor in the construction of the 'crypt of melancholia' which maintains its fantasy of desire by upholding a dialogue with the lost object of desire within the melancholic ego—in this case a dialogue which took place a year ago. The exchange and appropriation of each other's positions of strength and weakness over such social understandings, and later over aspects of advice, noble sacrifice, love, grief and finally loss, are more about Newland's own monologue rather than a dialogue with Ellen. The lively banter or heated exchanges that make up Newland's encounters with Ellen demonstrate the melancholic's tendency to give voice to his loss of the object, for whom he mourns. Hence his ability to slip in and out of positions of dominance. His final objective, it must be remembered, is the complete devouring ('Introducing all or part of a love object or a thing into one's body'[12]) of the lost object—a devouring to the extent that he may demonstrate, in his grieving, her loss as his own. In his display of loss the melancholic is always living in the shadow of the other.

We might accept the premise that these encounters are, at least on one level, dialogues between an ego (Newland) and a lost object of desire (Ellen). Accordingly we should not be surprised that the lost object in this narcissistic fantasy can be hostile, even if such an assumption is regularly inconsistent. Newland's faith in causes outside those sanctioned by his tribal group is such that this faith must be regularly tested. Just as Ellen threatens convention, so too she arouses Newland's interests in unconventionality. In their late-night business meeting Ellen challenges Newland's allegiances and motivations. Their initial smalltalk about painters and exhibitions sets the theme of the encounter, which will determine Newland's loyalties. Does he side with Ellen or with those who represent convention and custom? The question further serves to answer the growing suspicion, in Ellen, that Newland is in love with her.

Her mocking desire 'to become a complete American and try to be like everybody else' is of course repugnant to him—'I don't think you'll ever be quite like everybody else', he says. Her suggestion, however, is more likely calculated to determine how much Newland is going to try to be like everybody else. The tight shot/reverse-shot/close-up strategy Scorsese employs, as they discuss the Count's 'vile' letter, emphasises the intimacy and the severity of the situation. There is clearly something important at stake. Recalling that Newland has just failed to assure Letterblair of his own opposition to the divorce, his ambivalence towards the threat Ellen holds for him induces him to dissuade her from that course. Although seemingly indifferent to social dictates, in their encounters Newland expresses the very dread associated with taboo violation to Ellen. He constantly informs her of the way the New York *monde* reacts to her outrages. This is hardly the figure he likes to cut for himself, and she is left to determine his real position. Or rather, in accordance with his fantasies as played out in these scenes, he must have an opportunity to display his skills in rejecting the dictates of social conformity. His near use of the word 'unpleasant', scorned by Ellen in a previous scene, is interrupted by the camera's tilted point-of-view shot, moving into close-up from her ringless hand to her face. She says nothing but her look suggests castigation. In their previous meeting, Newland informed her that 'all the older women like and admire you, they want to help'. To which she replied 'I know, so long as they don't hear anything unpleasant'. Her look, here, like another she gives a second later when Newland implies agreement with the rumours about her, suggests anger and disappointment. Furthermore, in her look there is an element of interrogation of Newland's position on the situation:

> *Ellen:* What harm could accusations like that do me here?

> *Newland:* Perhaps more harm than anywhere else. Our legislation favours divorce but our social customs don't.

> *Ellen:* Yes. So my family tells me. Our family. You'll be my cousin soon. And you agree with them?

Newland has demonstrated that he does not agree with them. In standing up he implies this. Reeling from the blow of accusation contained in the words 'our family', however, he continues to excuse his position. He does this fearing the very freedom Ellen hopes to gain and the threat it poses to his desire to suffer the exquisite torment of loss. That is, to be the male melancholic. The fact that Ellen then so readily agrees to his suggestion surprises him for two reasons: it undoes something of his idealisation of her and it marks the failure of his secret desire. If she insists on the divorce, it suggests that she loves him. Newland marks his failure to bring her to this position, in his most passionate gesture towards her to date, by kissing her hands. 'I do want to help you', he says. In her reply, before he departs, she says, 'You do help me. Goodnight cousin.' Ellen both confirms his failure and at the same time plays the vital role of the object of desire denying the satisfaction of desire—which always, somewhat perversely, marks the most intensely romantic scenes in Scorsese's films. The cutting-off of desire suggests the farewell scene upon which the melancholic's fantasy relies. Scorsese's device, however, is to constantly repeat it, as the next scene does, by staging an equivalent farewell scene from Dion Boucicault's play *The Shaughraun*.

Newland loves the 'farewell scene'. As he tells Ellen, 'I usually leave the theatre after that scene to take the picture away with me'. Thus he is prepared to go to extreme lengths to preserve its effect and to cultivate it in his own life. A number of their encounters, including the theatre scene, are structured like farewell scenes, building up towards the final farewell near the end of the film. Ellen thanks Newland for his advice of the previous night, thus confirming that his efforts have ensured their separation. The melancholic relies heavily upon such scenes to remind him of the absence of and separation from desire; it is in this denial of desire that he derives utmost satisfaction.

In two ways Scorsese emphasises the isolation of Newland and Ellen from the rest of the group in Regina Beaufort's theatre box: firstly by means of an iris filter encircling them, and secondly by eliminating all noises on the soundtrack save their own voices. Having never mentioned the yellow roses Newland sent her, Ellen now alludes to them in the context of the play they have been watching. For Ellen they are the gesture of a lover made in lieu of the consummation of his passion. They also mark the confirmation of his perpetually restrained desire. Newland, perhaps mistaking her meaning, thrills at her mentioning it. According to his fantasy scenario, she is calling him her lover. At the mention of May's absence, Ellen offers Newland the opportunity to show what sort of lover he is: 'And what do you do while May is away?' 'I do my work', replies Newland, somewhat off balance. In a verbal gesture of similar effect to that of calling him cousin, as she did in the previous scene, Ellen shows her disappointment in the confirmation of her suspicions by thanking him profusely for his advice. Scorsese backs up the significance of this gesture with a lighting and sound change which returns the scene to 'normal'. In effect, Newland's object of desire has called him her love and he can only mark its impossibility—a fact he confirms by leaving the theatre, yet again, to take the picture away with him. On the next day, of course, he further marks the impossibility of his desire by searching the city for yellow roses. Victorian etiquette suggests that yellow roses ambivalently signify both passion and friendship. Accordingly they represent the highly satisfactory standing order of the unrequiting lover. Satisfying the pleasure of his search is not part of Newland's desire—his searches always have the effect of never arriving, never finishing. The roses can be found nowhere in the city, yet when presenting themselves in abundance two days later 'Newland Archer passed them by'.

Hide and seek

The encounters between Newland and Ellen so far set up a pattern which will play itself out to the end of the first half of the film, which is marked by Newland's marriage to May. It is a pattern of presence and absence, attraction and repulsion, which reflects the melancholic's desire based on palpable absence. The dynamic of presence and absence is explained in Freud's observations of a child's game in *Beyond the Pleasure Principle*.[13] The following scenes demonstrate the way Newland employs Ellen as 'toy' in a game of mastery. Through this game, by 'stage-managing' his denial of her, he gains compensation for his original experience of maternal loss. Ultimately building towards the moment when Archer must forsake Ellen and marry May, the game leans towards the predominance of absence.

Following the play, Newland writes to Ellen wanting to see her; she does not reply immediately but explains later that she has run away with the van der Luydens to Skuytercliff. Her letter hints that he should follow, and he does. When they meet she expresses an intimate happiness both at seeing him—'I knew you'd come'—and at his presence—'I can't feel unhappy when you're here'. In stark contrast to her mood of their previous encounters, Ellen seems to satisfy Newland's curiosities about her feelings for him. His response to the second statement is almost hostile, however: 'I shan't be here long'. Having come so far, with considerable effort, he is suddenly in a situation in which his game of catch-up around which he stages his romantic fantasies is being undermined by her loving appearance. His no doubt carefully rehearsed opening line, 'I came to see what you were running away from', provides him with the excuse he feels he needs to follow her and to force things to a result. He allows himself to believe that she is running away from him and uses this repulsion-energy to feed his game of presence and absence, and to follow her. He does not consider that she may be fleeing for reasons other than to drag him along behind her. Later in the Patroon house, standing at a distance from Ellen, he turns away from her and presses the question again: 'You must tell me what you're running from'. He receives no answer but imagines the answer he wants. In his fantasy he closes his eyes, as he did at the farewell scene of the play, seemingly to withstand the emotional assault as Ellen moves towards him and embraces him from behind. In this gesture she seems to answer him, 'I am running away because, as you suspected, I am in love with you'. As he turns to meet her embrace, the moment is revealed as imaginary. Ellen sits alone, cold and isolated in her chair, seemingly—due to the shot scale—smaller and further away than before. Noticing Beaufort approaching, Newland mocks himself and at the same time congratulates himself on his second, if somewhat tardy, insight into the connection between Beaufort and the Countess. The realisation, following his suspicion of desire in Ellen, allows him to reverse the poles of attraction and propel himself away from her. Later, in the same mood, he ignores her letter requesting a chance to explain her actions, and moves off in a state of negative desire towards May in Florida.

It is not that Newland merely misreads his encounters with Ellen. He may not believe her protestation of ignorance about Beaufort's arrival but he cannot have missed the fact that, following his brief fantasy of Ellen's embrace, she performs the embrace in reality, virtually repeating his own daydream version. She has clearly stated her desire for him. Her actions come too close to the satisfaction of desire for Newland, who accordingly latches onto a narrative of rivalry involving Beaufort rather than face the prospect of being involved in a relationship of reciprocated love. Rejecting these realities and temporarily invoking the melancholic's favorite bluff of pretending not to desire that which other men desire, Newland throws open the door to Beaufort: 'Hello, Beaufort! This way! Madame Olenska was expecting you.' This bluff not only serves to deny the satisfaction of desire but to mark his separation from the group as a man apart. His entire narrative is about the pretense that he is above common tribal desires, whereas in fact it is these desires which correspond to his own core desire—conformity with the group. Later that night, masochistically cocooned by the perfect safety of his newest delusions about Ellen, he can crumple up her note requesting a chance to explain, plan his flight to May, and mourn the future he is shoring up. Despite its foreboding aspects, there is comfort in the melancholic's crypt:

> That night he did not take the customary comfort in his
> monthly shipment of books from London. The taste of the
> usual was like cinders in his mouth, and there were moments
> when he felt as if he were being buried alive under his future.

Having taken the steps with May and which will further put Ellen out of reach, he can now allow himself an ardent wish to see her. Indeed she has been looking for him while he has been in Florida. Newland expresses this wish to Ellen following the scene with Grannie Mingott in which the details of his Florida visit are made clear. Newland is left standing between the two intrepid women looking like an embarrassed schoolboy. This short scene acts as a prelude to the last scene before Newland's marriage to May. It is an intense meeting with Ellen which summarises the various characteristics of their relationship. Furthermore, in its unusual changes of mood, the scene suggests something of its unreal nature as a reworking of Newland's fantasy scenario based on an original experience of profound loss.

The other woman

Standing before a mantle in almost mirror symmetry, Newland and Ellen accuse each other of disloyalty. In Newland's suspicion of Ellen's collaboration with Catherine to bring about her return to Count Olenska, Newland hints at Ellen's blocking of their consummation. Ellen returns the accusation, with rather more force, by mentioning Newland's collaboration with Catherine in order to advance his marriage to May. Defending himself by stressing May's nobility in allowing him 'Time to give her up for another woman', Newland sets himself up for a frustrating parody. By referring to 'this other woman' Ellen perpetuates the discussion of desire in the third person, although she clearly understands that person to be herself. Newland seems vaguely annoyed at this but does not point out the fact immediately. Instead he uses it to begin his advance, which is gratifyingly put down, 'Don't make love to me. Too many people have done that.' By maintaining the idea of 'this other woman' in the third person, the dialogue satisfies the melancholic's penchant for keeping desire and its naming in the abstract. Even at this late stage, his fantasy works hard to locate desire somewhere else. Furthermore, the location of that object of desire—as temporarily somewhere else and someone else other than Ellen—parodies the way in which his melancholy fantasy allows for the fluidity of roles and identity. This recalls the constant exchange of positions between Ellen and Newland that I mentioned earlier.

The most significant of these exchanges occurs in a discussion of self-sacrifice in this scene. Raising the idea that Newland would have married her had it been possible, Ellen begins an exchange of mutual accusation as to who had made it impossible. Both present their position as determined by the motive of acting for the sake of the other. Newland has encouraged Ellen not to divorce in order to save her from scandal. Ellen has agreed to it to save Newland and May from association with that scandal, from which, otherwise, she had no need to fear. A summary of this tit-for-tat exchange might have each of them saying: 'I expressed my love for you by denying myself the possibility of consummating it'. This is how the melancholic loves and how he fantasises that his object of desire loves. Seemingly at an impasse, the regime of denial breaks down, necessitating their embrace until this regime can be reinstated.

It is surprising that Newland does not lead the retreat but presses the realms of the possible: 'Do you see me marrying May now?' It is a bluff, however, standing as a response to what has been in effect an accusation of his greatest weakness—self-deprivation. Ellen, who has argued this all along, exposes his delusion: 'You say that because it is the easiest thing to say at this moment, not because it's true'. With his blocking of their union so solidly executed, he can afford to add another layer to his fantasy. At this point the mood of the scene appears to alter to suit this new layer, as Ellen's characterisation seems also to change. Having argued so persuasively that Newland has made their union impossible, she takes a new tack. In a long speech she outlines his goodness and nobility of character, which are those very things she has just used to argue against him. In the course of the scene her role—subject to Newland's fantasy—has changed again. Once again they have exchanged positions and Newland has attributed his strategy of desire to her while taking the role of innocent for himself. Ellen's speech might have been written for her by Newland. It stands both as Newland's own credo and as a justification of his conformist behaviour. It comes seemingly from the lips of the woman who, in this regard, he respects the most:

> Newland, you couldn't be happy if it meant being cruel. If we act in any other way I'll be making you act against what I love in you most. And I can't go back to that way of thinking. Don't you see? I can't love you unless I give you up.

The embrace pose they take up during the last speech is an unusually awkward one. On one level it suggests the embrace of two Victorian upper-middle-class lovers whose union cannot be. Beginning with the delicacy of foot kissing the scene ends amid the rippling flounces of Ellen's dress, keeping lips and eyes and cheeks at a safe distance. On another level it suggests the far greater intimacy and power of the foetal pose, with Newland half winding around and clinging to Ellen's lap/ womb as she curls around him in a yin-yang formation. It is a striking image of dominance and submission which makes literal the essence of the melancholic's loss. This is the loss he longs for on one hand, and runs from on the other.

The key to reading this pose is given by the visual suggestion of the tiger-skin rug on the floor under Ellen's feet. The embrace of the two lovers is by this motif associated with the cheek-to-cheek pose of the two protagonists in Frenand Khnopff's *L'Art, les caresses ou le Sphinx*, which hangs over the mantle. This striking image of Oedipus and the Sphinx/mother he must renounce establishes the scene. Newland stands to the left of the screen below a similarly dark-haired Oedipus; Ellen to the right of screen below a similarly fair-haired Sphinx. Like their representatives in the painting, Ellen and Newland come together in this scene in an embrace which, like the painting, emphasises a cheek-to-cheek pose. Both scenes stress not the destruction of the Sphinx by Oedipus, but his undeniable and obsessive attachment to the 'other' he must destroy. Thus the painting stresses the essence of Newland's desire for Ellen, and its impossibility, which are the key themes of the scene and of the film.

An understanding of this loss can be determined through Julia Kristeva's idea of the 'pre-symbolic Thing', namely the lost mother and all she signifies.[14] As discussed in Chapter 1, the breakdown of the melancholic subject's fluency with the symbolic culture (the realm of the father), brought on by what Kristeva calls the 'archaic attachment' to the mother causes the melancholic to have 'the impression of having been deprived of an unnameable, supreme good, of something unrepresentable, that perhaps only devouring might represent'.[15] Given the fragility and inability of primary symbolic identifications—such as with a father figure—to compensate for the loss, Kristeva considers the question 'How can one approach the place I have referred to?' An act of sublimation of loss suggests an approach, that is, a poetic expression or encounter that acts as the container through which melancholics may dedicate their sorrow and desire to the cause of the maternal attachment. In such an encounter, 'One can imagine the delights of reunion that a regressive daydream promises itself through the nuptials of suicide'.[16]

Newland Archer, of course, will never go this far. His dialogues with Ellen work as desperate attempts to effect that sublimation, allowing him a series of 'disappointing adventures and loves' and a space in which, through the agency of this encounter with Ellen, he may be 'alone with the unnamed Thing'.[17] A scene with Ellen some eighteen months after Newland's marriage to May seems to speak of the melancholic's pleading (via Ellen) with his mourned Thing begging it not to desert him. Assuring him, and his heavy sighs, that she will not go back to Europe, Ellen leaves Newland as the camera/edit fades her image from sight sooner than she can stroll off the set. The narration stresses the extremity of devotion to this constantly fading desire:

> He would see her again at the theatre or at a reception.
> Perhaps he might be seated next to her, perhaps they might
> have another time alone, somewhere, but he could not live
> without seeing her.

Following Ellen's constant assurances throughout the scene, Enya's *Marble Halls* playing on the soundtrack helps to point once again to the narcissistic component of the scene, undermining the integrity of his sublimation and his current allegiance to the pre-symbolic Thing. The haunting female voice seems to be mirroring the resonances of his fantasy: 'But I also dreamt which charmed me most that you loved me still the same'. However, Newland can never really approach such sublimation. His primary identification with the 'father in individual prehistory' allows him, in the end, to 'become reconciled with the loss of the Thing', although he refuses to relinquish mourning for that loss. Preferring to maintain his primary attachment, he cannot bring himself to assert the fragility of symbolic identification[18]

Part Two: The Empire of Signs

Newland is, of course, no artist and can only claim a connection with artistic expression by assuming the role of the middle-class connoisseur. Ellen asks him about his relationships with American painters: 'Do you live in their *milieu*?' He does not, but, as he tells her, whenever he is in London or Paris he never misses an exhibition. Newland's encounter with M. Rivière (once advised by Maupassant) at a Paris dinner party, and his subsequent discussion with May, indicate something both of Newland's yearning for a place within artistic circles and the suppression of such urges by the dictates of the tribal organisation surrounding him. May thinks Rivière 'a little common' and so Newland must conclude 'Then I won't ask him to dine'.

Newland's artistic pretensions, and their suppression, increase both his yearning for that euphoria known to the artist and his contempt for the community and his own integration within its repressive order. His contempt for the smooth hypocrisies of New York society, embodied in particular by Larry Lefferts and Julius Beaufort, expresses his desire for escape and isolation. He strives hopelessly to place himself above the petty machinations of the men and women surrounding him. The Scorsesean ego seems to be always in flight from that mirror reflection of self seen in those around it—as we see in relation to *Raging Bull* and *Taxi Driver*. As Adrian Martin has suggested, the Scorsesean hero cannot stand to be like himself when that self is so much like the common herd around him.[19] In a similar vein, in his consideration of Scorsese's films, Alain Masson has defined the 'flight from one's likeness' as 'a definition of liberty'.[20] In Scorsese this is the work of melodrama, because flight from such confines of the self are impossible.

Newland constantly expresses the desire to go to Japan or India, to escape in books, poetry, and good works for distressed divorcees. Part of his complex fantasy of desire is to fly to that country where words like 'mistress'—as he says to Ellen—do not exist. The silent society in which he lives shows no distress at the ease with which it colonises such notions, making the idea of escape impossible. When May leaves town for Florida, Paris, London or Newport she encounters the same people and her life is subject to the same scrutiny as in old New York. India for Newland promises release from such pressures. As Newland's friend, Philip, remarks, however, upon an invitation to go with him, 'You must have three weeks to do India properly'. In this sense, America is hardly part of the new world at all and Christopher Columbus did indeed discover it 'to go to the opera with Larry Lefferts', as Ellen suggests earlier in the film. No one closes off the avenues of escape more that Ellen, however. When Newland talks of that distant country, located behind the backs of their loved ones, Ellen is forced to admit 'I've been there and it's no place for us'.

The narrative of *The Age of Innocence* is centrally concerned with offering, then closing off, avenues of escape. Its aim is to halt the expression of unrestrained sexuality and to regulate and relocate maverick or threatening elements. The melodrama in general evokes the struggle for order in its subject matter in its own fundamental dialectic of signs. Order is negotiated in the film over a concern generic to the melodrama for the relative value of its signs and surfaces. Both its protagonists and audience engage in the dialectic by attempting to sort through the plethora of signifiers. This is to determine which signifiers, in fact, have substance. As Scorsese has commented, nothing sums up the film's obsessive presentation and spectacle more that Edith Wharton's own conclusion, 'They all lived in a kind of hieroglyphic world. The real thing was never said or done or even thought, but only represented by a set of arbitrary signs.'[21]

The fantasy scenario Newland has constructed with Ellen must be challenged to keep him, and it, special and secret. There is no use having a secret unless somebody guesses it. Like everything precious to Newland, his secret is only worth having if it is to be lost, if he can be forced to surrender it. Just as we read Newland's dialogue with Ellen as fantasy, it is tempting to cast the force outside it, the tribe, as an active agent of Freud's 'reality testing'. This brings the mourning subject (Newland) around to an acknowledgment 'that the loved object no longer exists and it proceeds to demand that all libido shall be withdrawn from its attachments to that object'.[22] Newland, as I have argued already, likes to cast himself as the passive victim of circumstance in order to achieve what he wants, but will not admit to. To read the group's opposition to his melancholic fantasy as a genuine threat is to be fooled by Newland's acting of the melancholic role. It is to ignore the fact that, in the end, his plan is largely achieved. It is also to overlook that opposition, a largely self-inflicted fantasy, is part of that satisfaction. The tribe is in decline—a state, as Kristeva says, 'particularly favorable to black moods'[23]—and has lost real power to regulate him; were it not in decline the narrative of melancholia and loss could never have taken place. If the tribe opposes Newland's fantasy, it does so as part of his own design to outline the terms of his desire and to get the thing he wants most—not Ellen but the loss of her. Like Jake La Motta in *Raging Bull*, Newland, in his fantasy, works in a collaboration of sorts with the tribe that he has constructed as his opposition. He does so to increase the stakes of his mock sacrifice.

An understanding of this collaboration and the observation of Newland's rebellion undercuts the notion of the 'secret heart of woes' which is so important to his melancholic self-image. Both *The Age of Innocence* and *Raging Bull* show how reliant the melancholic is on making a show of sorrow—hardly a secret process. The point of melancholia, however, is to allow the melancholic to display his secret with impunity, to turn it into a generally perceivable and controllable aesthetic of rebellion. The melancholic's collaboration with the tribe, as we shall see, is designed to let his melancholic display to go as if unnoticed for a time. This allows him the vital secrecy with which to adorn his fantasy scenario.

An aspect of the melancholic's design is to assume the patriarch's privilege over the arbitration of signs—the power to set the laws which regulate the social world. For Newland this is to assume, like the flâneur, such a superior understanding of his environment and its signs as to stand beyond their petty meaning. Newland must stand behind the taboo on Ellen or reject it. This plan has failed, however, before it starts. Newland cannot be the patriarch; he is one of the band of brothers, living under the threat of castration. His pretension to ownership over the power to determine the signs, a power similar to the determining of taboos, is immediately undermined by the impossibility of his ever rejecting the 'set of arbitrary signs' which his forefathers bequeathed him. Instead, as compensation, he elects to become the expert reader of signs. As fetishist, collector, connoisseur and courtier—see Chapter 1—he regulates and restrains his flight of fantasy with Ellen by his engagement and constant obsession with objects. Playing around in both the delusion and confusion engendered over the contemplation of lifeless ruins, he makes an art of making his adherence to the realm of symbols look like the search for the pre-symbolic Thing. The success of his narrative of symbolic classification is marked by his fantasised containment of Ellen

Containing Ellen Olenska. The van der Luyden's 'little dinner'.

in a situation of the lifeless object—as he says, 'I'd rather see her dead.'

The maintenance of tribal order, in this instance, is emphatically concerned with enforcing the taboo upon Ellen. The tribal drama here is about naming that taboo, about expounding upon its meaning and what its implications are, especially for Newland. The negotiation or struggle over the arbitrary signs is the method by which order is propped up in societies via the workings of melodramatic narratives. Such signs, the things of melodrama, lack the full force of taboo but are not to be taken as unrelated trifles. They are the distant cousins of the primary taboos whose transgression is punished with death. Their mobilisation and negotiation in the narrative demonstrates, by gentle suggestion, the full force of modern tribal organisation and how it works to regulate its more important taboos.

The set of arbitrary signs

The most visually striking aspect of Scorsese's film is the way it foregrounds New York society's obsession with objects. In the opening title sequence, directed by Saul and Elaine Bass, we are presented with a summary of the way tribal societies regulate themselves by deference to material objects. In its montage mixing words and sentences from nineteenth-century etiquette manuals, with Victorian lace, and time-lapsed blooming of flowers, we observe the way such objects operate in significationof deeper layers of meaning. Playing with the natural and the artificial, the title sequence begins with the signs of Victorian etiquette around the names of the movie's stars, these sentences -acting as a layer over the blooms. This layer of language is transformed into a gauze of lace, a specifically Victorian form of presentation/preservation of nature. As the blooms become more violent and explosive, the sequence moves towards the director's credit and the lace is replaced by the restoration of the text of the etiquette manual. As signs of *comme il faut* and meaning, they wax and wane in their communication, take on material form, layer, encompass and inhibit the expression of nature.

Finally merging with the bright yellow sunburst of daisies of the film's first scene, on the opera set of *Faust,* the title sequence represents, in shorthand,[24] how signs work in this culture to maintain order. It points to the way the system connives to put people and things into a signifiable form, in which they can be easily read and controlled. This is also the project of Newland Archer—to encapsulate the objects of his desire into readable forms of possession. As we observe in the transformation of the sentences into lace and back again, the dominance of signifiable/material form lies in its arbitrary legislation over meaning. The importance of reading and understanding is paramount, and confusions and mistakes in this regard can easily arise. As Newland discovers in May, material surfaces can hide deeper substance, and the fetishisation of parts can obscure the meaning hidden in the whole. A social threat arises when the tribe and one of its members are at odds over the way they read and subscribe to the system of signs. It is averted, however, when they are all reading the same way. This is, after all, their joint project and the substance of the melancholic's collaboration. He will temporarily challenge the reading of symbols in order to pursue and then relocate his desires within the existing system.

In representing Newland's arrival at the Beaufort ball and his solemn march towards the ballroom, Scorsese uses a familiar long-take strategy. He often employs this approach, notably in *GoodFellas* and *Mean Streets*.[25] As in these earlier examples, Scorsese's camera follows his melancholic hero without cutting—in this case for almost a minute and a half. The device suggests to the viewer that they are walking with the melancholic through his world. This has the effect of augmenting the way the sequence presents that world, its characters and something of its customs of behaviour. The viewer's introduction to Newland's world is made largely through the presentation of people and paintings. Regina Beaufort greets her guests standing just beneath a full-scale portrait of herself. As Newland makes his way, connoisseur-like, through the 'vista of enfiladed drawing rooms' the camera and its voice-over narration conspire to draw the association between the people's manners and the images of the same in paintings hanging, like mirrors, on the walls. Women, in particular, seem to be captured in this way. An older woman, whom Newland greets, sits reviving herself below a painting. This work contains an echo of her situation as it depicts a young woman fainting as two men leave the frame of the canvas, seemingly indifferent but responsible for her plight. Just as Regina is caught and contained by her own portrait, her husband Julius represents himself by proxy in a pictorial allegory of one of his many mistresses—'*The Return of Spring* the much-discussed nude by Bouguereau, which Beaufort had the audacity to hang in plain sight'. The long-take finally cuts to two elderly gentlemen chatting in the ballroom, bridging the rupture of this cut by echoing the two men in Tissot's *The Whisper*. Given the subjects of the paintings in this montage, the idea of social destabilisation is once again attributed to a woman and that threat echoing its potential in the tribe is foregrounded in the narration: 'This was a world balanced so precariously that its harmony could be shattered in a whisper'.[26]

The association between individuals, their activities and objects of artifice is not confined to paintings, however. As we see in the opening montage of the opera scene, the narrative presents individuals as the sum of their object parts—brooches, bracelets, camellias and clips. Larry Lefferts' opinion 'on the question of pumps versus patent-leather Oxfords' marks him as much as Catherine Mingott is later marked by Ellen's use of her carriage to visit the disgraced Regina Beaufort. The restrictive effect of such social symbols is made literal by Scorsese's method of framing characters within silver candlesticks as they sit at the first Archer dinner. The presentation of wedding gifts with the cards of their senders' names, reinforced by details of narration alluding to individuals, highlights the association. Just as the calling card can suggest a potency of presence, as in the assertion of prominence associated with a precious gift, so too does the object leave traces. The object solidifies and captures the name and thus works in the service of surveillance.[27] Lesley Stern elaborates on the connection between signs and rituals operating within the film. Through a discussion of the carriage scene and the opening titles, Stern points out the cohabitation of the passionate and the poignant, in the ritual life, with the dread of confinement—all contributing to a symbolic world 'suffocatingly circumscribed':

> Everything means something in this milieu, every gesture and utterance refers to something else, no detail is indifferent, and all details are circuitously connected. In this world so full of signs and coded messages flowers above all are denaturalised. Marguerite plucks the petals from the daisy, singing 'He loves me, he loves me not'. The flower is put to use, in other words; it is mobilised as a sign.[28]

As we shall see in the discussion below of the film's coda, it is in this scenario of object logic that Newland places Ellen. Given Catherine Mingott's comment that in Europe Ellen's portrait has been painted nine times, it is hardly surprising to hear of Newland thinking of her in such terms. Before he approaches Ellen in the film's impressionist-like portrait of her overlooking the lime-rock lighthouse, the narration tells of his tendency to use comparisons with inanimate objects to invoke her image. With the mention of her name,

> . . . the past had come into the present, as in those newly discovered caverns in Tuscany, where children had lit bunches of straw and seen old images staring from the wall.

Throughout the film we observe Newland's fetishisation of objects associated with Ellen in order to evoke something of her. Nothing suggests his longing as much as his mistaking Katie Blenker's Cameroons parasol for Ellen's, and his almost perverse sniffing of it. Backed by Elmer Bernstein's yearning oboe/harp duo at this moment, Newland might be delicately making his way through her underwear drawer. It is via such objects that Newland and the tribe regulate the threat and danger of desire, giving it material form through symbols. Objects, in this society, yield to reading and control by the symbolic order.

One of the dominant factors in the power of this 'hieroglyphic world' to enforce and regulate lies in the arbitrary shifting and changing of the meaning of its signs and symbols. Stern discusses the significance of the signs in the film:

> The flowers, like the red shoes and the boxing gloves, are totemic objects—they signify investment and conversion, and function somewhat differently for the characters within the film and for us. As components of a complex and shifting system of signs their meaning is in their relationship, not in some intrinsic value. So we should be alert to the fact that the meaning of the lilies of the valley, for instance, varies over time and according to place.[29]

Subjugation to, and arbitration over, the vagaries of signification is central to the system of authority in totemic societies. This is the central point at issue in the film—who is subject and who is arbiter over Ellen as the changing sign? Who has the authority to say what she means? It is the tribe that claims this authority. It must have the final co-operation of the melancholic, however, and accordingly will work hard to shift around the signs and their meaning to keep him under control. Its power to achieve this, or rather the power of its highest authorities, is demonstrated in the sequence of scenes around Catherine Mingott's aborted formal dinner 'to meet the Countess Olenska'.

The backing of Ellen by way of Catherine's formal dinner stands as an unthinkable gesture in New York society. Consequently it is a potent one. It reads as a bold assertion signifying, at almost the highest level, the end to the growing speculation and scandal surrounding Ellen. The general refusal of New York society to accept this invitation suggests the general refusal to accept the sign, resulting in a challenge to Catherine Mingott's not insignificant authority. Led by Larry Lefferts, the minor tribesmen have resisted this attempt at arbitration over the sign by offering the seemingly potent counter-sign of the refusals. Just like Newland's later attempt at deviance, this represents a significant challenge to authority and must not be allowed to set an example for other potential deviants. The intervention of the van der Luydens ensures that the example it sets to all is that—despite the intrinsic merits of a challenge to authority and its signs—those merits have no meaning other than the pleasure invested in reinscribing the totem authority. Ellen may incite the possibility of taboo transgression, but the meaning of that threat is signified only in so far as it does not conflict with the highest authority. The final ejection of Ellen by that same authority (Louisa dragging Ellen away from Newland at their final meeting—'We're taking dear Ellen home') underscores the point.

In many ways this negotiation over the sign matches Newland's own—with both centring on the body of Ellen. As in Newland's general challenge to his own tribe and its sense of order, Ellen is offered by Catherine and tribal order is briefly threatened but finally restored under the superior arbitration of the van der Luydens. Catherine, like Newland, asserts her opinion against prevailing prejudice. Both fail, although in different circumstances; however, in both cases the van der Luydens mop up, not for the protection of Ellen, but to secure the authority of their kin, Catherine and Newland.

The visual style and presentation of objects by Scorsese in this scene echo the struggle. Visually the sequence moves from a smooth, fluid tracking and editing style—in the presentation of invitations, foods, preparations and dining ware—through to a rupturing of the style as the busy kitchen dissolves into the image of an empty kitchen. The invitation refusals, 'cannot', 'regret', 'will be away', flip past as still and mortified poses as Newland and Ellen are blasted with bursts of colour. Fullness has receded into emptiness. The panic expressed by Mrs Archer requires the immediate attention of the van der Luydens, whose white-walled room, high above Madison Avenue, works as a calming antidote to the explosions of colour which mark the passion of the situation. Finally, the restoration of order and authority is made by the reassertion of signs and the fluidity of their presentation. For the social snubbing and invalidation of Catherine Mingott's 'appropriate plate. . . three extra footmen . . . and a Roman punch', the van der Luydens restore order by wheeling out 'The Travenna George II plate. . . the van der Luyden Lowestoft. . . and the Dagonet Crown Derby'. Bernstein's score swells with triumph as Scorsese tracks and dissolves smoothly around the dining room presenting the dishes, flowers and 'awfully assembled', somewhat ancient dignitaries. 'When the van der Luydens chose, they knew how to give a lesson.' This pattern of fullness/emptiness/restoration, complete with social and tribal overtones, is repeated when, at the final dinner party, May celebrates her triumph over Ellen and Newland.

As flâneur, Newland prizes his ability to read signs. As the narration points out, when the invitation refusals arrive, he knows the signs and exactly what they mean. Despite having superior reading skills, the melancholic such as Newland, subject to the sway of passion, can find himself in difficulty when interpreting the signs. The proliferation and variation in meaning of the signs of this world are great and complex. For Sillerton Jackson and Larry Lefferts, who keep themselves to the letter of the law, correct interpretation of the social milieu is their stock-in-trade. For those like Newland, whose moral concerns extend beyond family scandals and patent leather Oxfords, attention to such detail is hard to maintain. On the other hand, the melancholic's fetishisation of signs can lead to an ignorance of their meaning, as described by Benjamin in his discussion of the flâneur and the 'intoxication of the commodity'.[30] Too much attention to detail, surface over substance, part over whole, can lead to confusion and a temporary breakdown in a proper understanding of the sign system within which the part is a mere distraction—as it does with Julius Beaufort. 'Certain nuances escape Beaufort', says Sillerton Jackson. The narrative of melancholic angst relies on this breakdown in understanding in order to check and relocate the maverick melancholic. The maverick's misreadings are a sure sign that he is beginning to read the signs for himself, and is at odds with official interpretation. Checking Newland in this way is, of course, May—it is her designated role.

Newland's crucial failure lies in his inability to read May; her apparent lack of depth fools him into thinking she is totally transparent. Believing himself to be successful in convincing her of his earnestness in wanting to bring forward their marriage, he attributes his success to May's simplicity. As the narrator points out:

> He could feel her dropping back to inexpressive girlishness. Her conscience had been cleared of its burden. It was wonderful, he thought, how such depths of feeling could co-exist with such an absence of imagination.

Similarly, we discover that Newland thinks her innocent of social intrigue and ignorant of her lack of 'emancipation'. As he fears, he never manages to lift the curtain of her 'niceness', 'dropped in front of an emptiness'. When May dies his feelings are expressed by the narrator:

> The world of her youth had fallen into pieces and rebuilt itself without her ever noticing. This hard bright blindness,

her incapacity to recognize change, made her children conceal their views from her, just as Archer concealed his. She died thinking the world a good place, full of loving and harmonious households like her own.

Newland's inability to see beyond the curtain marks the limits of his imagination. He cannot see the manipulations she stages, both in their Florida discussions, and in the way she mobilises the tribe against Ellen in order to save Newland and her marriage. Deducing that May had pushed Ellen out by telling Ellen of her coming pregnancy, he is surprised at the extent of her tactics. Twenty years later he is again astounded to learn from his son Ted that May had 'guessed' his guilty secret. Although Newland is constantly made aware of her subtle influence, he does not understand it. It is Newland who remains in a 'hard, bright blindness' as the narrator says of May.

May's Rochée-modelled hands, which mark her presence after her death, signify Newland's inadequacies. White, soft and delicate, they appear harmless and suggest innocence. The work they have done, however, was swift, ruthless and permanent, while leaving only the traces of charm. For Newland, however, their work has gone undetected; he cannot see beyond the surface of their mystifying appearance, cannot make the connections. At the height of his confusion he meets Ellen in the 'art museum in the park' a place where he is expected to be able to read the signs in order to fathom the meaning of displayed objects. What he discovers is that obscurity may lie encapsulated behind glass without giving up its secrets, even to the connoisseur. Under a bizarre implement in the Art Museum a card is inscribed 'Use Unknown'. Brian Mc Farlane observes:

> Newland Archer lives in a world so crowded with things that it takes more than usual sensitivity and detachment to see beyond them and their way of muffling deeper chords of delight and pain—of living, that is.[31]

The restoration of signs at the final dinner party—the hired chef, the borrowed footmen, roses, Roman punch and gilt-edged menu cards— all presented by Scorsese using the familiar smooth tracking along the dinner table, marks the restoration of Newland and his fluency in reading signs:

From the seamless performance of this ritual, Archer knew that New York believed him to be Madame Olenska's lover. And he understood, for the first time, that his wife shared the belief.

As at the Patroon house, when his own stupidity suddenly dawns upon him, Newland finally sees the play. He sees the play because, as a privileged member, he is part owner of the game in which, as Henry van der Luyden tells him, 'grace is not always required. As long as one knows the steps.'

'The real things of life'

Following the news of May's pregnancy and her victory over Ellen, the fact of Newland's sacrifice, marked by his melancholy gaze, is swiftly eradicated by the narrator: 'It was the room in which most of the real things of his life had happened'. Thus the scene dissolves into a cavalcade of his life, cataloguing the births, death and rites of passage of his family. Contrary to Ellen's promise to stay a part of his life, there is no mention of her. 'The madness with Madame Olenska' has not only been consigned to the obscure past, but to the unreal, the fantasy of a single imagination. The mean and melancholy history has become a long-forgotten minor indiscretion in the mythology of a past generation. The birth of the male child marks the spot of its eradication and the assertion of tribal will.

In so far as Newland's obsession with Ellen has been read as representing the fantasy space of the melancholic crypt, it is for May and the tribe around her to test this fantasy and to relocate it within the safe confines of the social order. As his melancholia threatens that order it must be repressed or overturned. The relocation of this fantasy is brought about, being largely dependent on the agency of the melancholic, in a number of ways. The social world in which Newland exists provides his narrative with various agents of persuasion, reality testing and surveillance designed to bombard the crypt and check its delusions. The tribe puts forward examples to the melancholic, such as that of Julius Beaufort, which remind him of the consequences of his potential action. Finally, through the work of May, the authority of the tribe to name the signs is reasserted and the melancholic is brought under its sway by the power to name even the terms of his fantasy. In this way the arbitrary order of the tribal group, working in secret collaboration with the melancholic himself, enforces the totem law by enforcing the taboo on Ellen.

THE AGE OF INNOCENCE 41

The introductory narration over the Beaufort ball largely defines the day-to-day working limits of the tribal organisation.[32] Catherine Mingott and the van der Luydens, who possess higher and final authority in this world, are introduced later, when their presence is required. Reflecting Scorsese's interest in the gangster world, the scene of the ball introductions concentrates on the foot soldiers of New York society who, in tribal terms, do all the work. Apart from Newland, Sillerton Jackson, Larry Lefferts, Mr Letterblair and Julius Beaufort represent different types, embodying various aspects of the tribal machine. These characters symbolise the tribe from which Newland attempts to divorce himself. Their activities operate in relation to Newland's—to keep him in line.

Supposedly innocent of intrigues, May is the last to be introduced at the Beaufort ball—'May represented for Archer all that was best in their world, all that he honoured. And she anchored him to it.' It is her role, more than any other, to break up Newland's fantasy and to ground him within the safe confines of their group. She achieves this with subtle and discreet force, asserting her power over Newland through persuasion and reality testing. Her skills are demonstrated early in the film. Walking with her in an aviary, Newland—half guilty, half triumphant—tells May that he sent Ellen some roses. Without blinking, May casually dismisses Newland's confession, like the automatic reminder-slap of a mother cheerfully admonishing an infant child against a predisposition towards self-gratification. As if Newland had said nothing of consequence, May replies:

> She didn't mention it at lunch today, though. She said she'd gotten wonderful orchids from Mr Beaufort and a whole hamper of carnations from Cousin Henry van der Luyden. She was so very delighted. Don't people send flowers in Europe?

Newland's annoyance at this put-down is underlined by Scorsese's visual quote from *Citizen Kane*, when a brightly coloured parrot fills the screen with flapping wings and a shriek, mocking the melancholic and obliterating his gesture. In this way May takes on the ability to determine the sign and its meaning. It is by such methods that she works to achieve her role in anchoring Newland to the tribe by asserting the taboo over Ellen, and by determining Ellen's meaning.

The restoration of the social order marked by the final dinner party celebrates the victory of 'the harmless looking people', the 'quiet conspirators', over Newland and Ellen. As he sits at the head of the table, hemmed in by Scorsese's mise-en-scène—'a prisoner in the centre of an armed camp'—he 'understood that, somehow, the separation between himself and the partner of his guilt had been achieved'. The series of dissolves that take the scene through Newland's pocket, two envelopes and a piece of vellum to 'the key to his release' (the returned key to his rendezvous location with Ellen) is overwhelmed by a final dissolve into a medium close-up of a smiling May. Similarly, later in the scene, as the narrator speaks of Newland's realisation of May's knowledge about himself and Ellen, May suddenly enters the shot again, smiling with triumph. Like everything else in this world, this dinner is filled with suggestion. Beyond marking May's victory, it clearly spells out its terms, exiling Ellen and trapping Newland into its reality which is no longer prepared to sustain his scheme of fantasy.

Newland Archer as 'a prisoner in the centre of an armed camp'. Daniel Day-Lewis, Michelle Pfeiffer and others in *The Age of Innocence*.

May achieves the break-up of his fantasy not so much by stressing the un-touchability of Ellen as by asserting to Newland that she is 'touched', which is what he hates the most. His fantasy relies upon the public perception that Ellen represents his escape to a higher moral ground and away from the corruption of the tribe and its invisible tentacles of control. Central to this is the separation of his passion from a grubby, Beaufortesque backstairs affair. Newland's desire is to separate his fantasy from such a mundane event for two reasons. On one hand, such affairs are well grounded within the lazy corruption of the tribe. On the other, the implication of an affair suggests the carnal satisfaction of desire, which is always repellent to the melancholic so far as it suggests distance from that ultimate and unnamable desire for which he longs.

The 'mistress' motif has plagued Newland throughout the narrative. In conversations with Sillerton Jackson he is greatly affronted by gossip suggesting that Ellen was 'living together' with Rivière, who aided her escape from the Count. Later Newland anticipates Sillerton's suspicions that she has been Beaufort's mistress in one of his frequent outbursts— 'If everyone would rather she be Beaufort's mistress than some decent fellow's wife, you've all gone about it perfectly'. Finally Ellen herself appears to fall in with the wishes of the tribe when she speaks of practicalities in their relationship—'I think we should look at reality, not dreams'. In the carriage scene Ellen stresses the impossibility of a world beyond where words like 'mistress' do not exist—at least for them. All that is left them, she asserts, is the furtive affair, at which point Newland stops the carriage and gets out—rejecting her lack of faith. Later in the Art Museum, however, he agrees to it—'Come to me once then'.

The Art Museum agreement has forced Newland to see that his fantasy has been destroyed by its representation as a grubby one night stand. Despite the fact that the one night stand never happened, the fact that it has been percieved as happening revolts Newland. Having at last willed the encounter, he is revolted by his own loss of faith in the pleasures of desire-denial. The acceptance of the tribe's designation of his fantasy as 'affair' and its designation of Ellen as 'whore/mistress' is repellent to him for the use the tribe has made of its assumption that the taboo had been violated. May is overjoyed at the idea, as she demonstrates at the dinner. Her own hypocrisy and that of the tribe has achieved the designation of Ellen and her involvement with Newland as an 'excusable affair'. This, in the mind of May's beloved melancholic, is an eradication. Just as Beaufort's secret was in the 'way he carried things off', May taunts Newland after the party, 'It did go off beautifully, didn't it?', to which Newland replies with a defeated irony 'Oh, yes'.

'And when yellow roses were next available'

The narrative of the film's coda, which moves through the dizzy montage of 'the real things of his [Newland's] life' to his last refusal to see Ellen, contains nothing new to add to our understanding of Newland or his story. It may be a surprise to see Newland take this course, but it is really more of a summary of his pattern of desire and a poignant reminder of its cyclical nature. The last takes of the film remind the viewer of previous patterns by replaying images of Ellen by the lime-rock lighthouse, twenty years before at Newport. The aim of the sequence is to restage, yet again, the trauma of separation and loss which is both the end and the beginning of the melancholic's cycle of desire. It does not, or should not, surprise us that Newland elects not to see Ellen. The fact that he takes this course adds to our narrative pleasure and, therefore, should not be seen as repetition for its own sake. Beyond this, however, the sequence works to confirm the essential love of loss in the melancholic. Certainly, as Pam Cook points out, it portrays a bleak portrait of masculinity, and at the same time suggests a structure of desire that can never settle, that can never be at an end.

Cook's review of the film points out an aspect of Scorsese's picture of male desire found in the alterations the director has made to Edith Wharton's emphasis in the original novel. Observing that Scorsese's film posits Newland as 'pure victim', the resultant de-emphasising of the 'victimisation of Ellen' reinforces her role—the subject of desire in the narrative. She is merely image, an *objet d'art* to his connoisseur's eye which prefers to look rather than act. His inability to see beyond the curtain of May's niceness and his fetishisation in which he fixes his desire for Ellen in inanimate objects both point to the dead, immobile picture that directs his longing. His fixation on her as an unreal figure, 'safely locked away as a memory', reveals:

> . . . that the emptiness or lack he so despises in May is actually at the heart of masculinity. Once again, Scorsese creates a dark, pessimistic vision of male desire in which woman is never more than alibi.[33]

As Newland stands in the Rubens room of the Louvre gazing at one of the works on the wall, the narrator confirms the sense in which his memories of Ellen operate as images which both mark his loss and compensate for it:

> Whenever he thought of Ellen Olenska, it had been ab-stractly, serenely, like an imaginary loved one in a book or picture. She had become the complete vision of all that he had missed.

In his discussion with Ted there is a suggestion that—in Ted's active encouragement of his father's reunion with Ellen—May and the tribe are now giving Ellen to him. As in Julius Beaufort's marriage to Annie Ring, time has covered over the scandal and all that is left is the 'lovely daughter' of the marriage, set to marry Ted, who says 'As if anyone remembers any more. Or cares.' Any suggestion that Newland might act in a similar way to Beaufort and that the taboo on Ellen has been lifted by the tribe are sure to dissuade Newland from having anything to do with Ellen. The sense that Ellen had been designated as 'whore' by the tribe, and therefore has now become acceptable, is repellent to him. He still desires that which the tribe has forbidden him. Accordingly he maintains his cycle of desire by walking off, rejecting Ellen, who is now part of the symbolic culture.

This is no moment of triumph for Newland, however. Ellen may be Newland's aestheticisation, as Cook points out, but she is far from disposable. Cook proposes this reading:

> For Scorsese, as for Wharton, Archer's final decision to walk away from love is the last nail in the coffin of the past in which he is entombed.[34]

Nevertheless, such an entombment satisfies the melancholic's ultimate project. Any idea of the tribe now giving Ellen to Newland can only be sustained in his melancholic fantasy. His refusal to meet her is an extravagant and highly self-conscious gesture designed to reconfirm his sacrifice. It represents the point at which the desires of the tribe and the melancholic finally and inevitably become one. May's deathbed revelations to Ted, that Newland had given up Ellen, play a vital role. As already discussed, Newland is inexpressibly moved by his assumption that May had 'guessed and pitied' him. The effect on Newland of this perhaps dubious assumption is to play directly into his pattern of desire. May's pity confirms the reality of both his fantasy and his sacrifice. For Newland to see Ellen would be to renounce that sacrifice. It would threaten to disturb the solidity of the melancholic's crypt, his most precious possession, in which both he and his lost object lie buried in the ecstasy of stasis. This is the full and extravagant compensation payable to the male melancholic who gives up the forbidden object.

CHAPTER THREE

Raging Bull:

'Kiss the Boo Boo'

I done a lotta bad things, Joey.

Jake La Motta

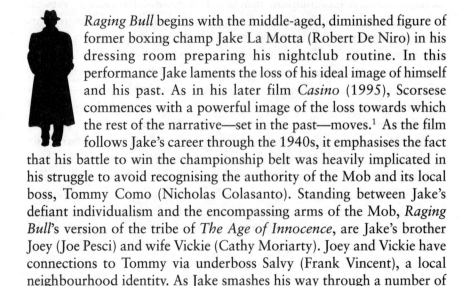*Raging Bull* begins with the middle-aged, diminished figure of former boxing champ Jake La Motta (Robert De Niro) in his dressing room preparing his nightclub routine. In this performance Jake laments the loss of his ideal image of himself and his past. As in his later film *Casino* (1995), Scorsese commences with a powerful image of the loss towards which the rest of the narrative—set in the past—moves.[1] As the film follows Jake's career through the 1940s, it emphasises the fact that his battle to win the championship belt was heavily implicated in his struggle to avoid recognising the authority of the Mob and its local boss, Tommy Como (Nicholas Colasanto). Standing between Jake's defiant individualism and the encompassing arms of the Mob, *Raging Bull*'s version of the tribe of *The Age of Innocence*, are Jake's brother Joey (Joe Pesci) and wife Vickie (Cathy Moriarty). Joey and Vickie have connections to Tommy via underboss Salvy (Frank Vincent), a local neighbourhood identity. As Jake smashes his way through a number of

challenges—including losing to arch-rival Sugar Ray Robinson (Johnny Barnes)—Joey negotiates with the 'family', knowing that obedience to the Mob's wishes will be Jake's only chance at a title fight. Jake's violence in the ring frequently spills over into his domestic life, where he beats and victimises both his wife and brother. The extent to which Jake confuses sexuality with violent expressions of desire—as well as expressions of homosexual and heterosexual desire—is made clear in his comment about an approaching bout with Janiro: 'I don't know whether to fuck him or fight him'.

Finally Jake agrees to Tommy's terms in order to gain entry to a title bout. Jake achieves this despite the fact that he refuses to (fully) obey the Mob and go down in the fixed fight. Winning the title marks the onset of Jake's decline. His violent jealousy and paranoid suspicion that Joey and Vickie are having an affair causes him to batter his wife and brother, with great savagery. This violence brings about a tragic rift with his beloved wife and beloved brother who make up his ideal family or 'primal horde'. In his final fight, against his old foe Sugar Ray, Jake stands against the ropes allowing Robinson to beat him savagely. The fight and Jake's career end in a technical knock-out, but not a knock-down. Jake's bloody defeat is compounded in a scene of howling rage inside the Dade County Stockade—where he has been sent for offences against minors—when he batters his head against the stone wall of his cell screaming 'I'm not an animal'. Returning then to its beginning, the narrative depicts Jake sitting in his dressing room reciting Marlon Brando's final speech to his brother from *On the Waterfront*. This is a supremely melancholic gesture filled with longing for an idealised past. His loss is symbolised by the destruction of his beautiful body, the failure of his relationship with his wife and his brother, and the dissipation of the primal horde over which he once ruled supreme.

Totem and taboo

Raging Bull explores two notions central to Scorsesean melancholia—the workings of the male group and the ritual workings of sacrifice. Jake is the quintessential loner, an outsider whose refusal to bow to the dictates of the Mob-dominated boxing fraternity leads to a fantasy cycle of horde posturing, sacrifice, punishment and atonement. In *Raging Bull*, Scorsese explores the group specifically in relation to the ancient themes of totemism, taboo and transgression. Jake not only fights against inclusion into this repressively conservative male group, with its strict rules and codes governing behaviour, but is also tormented by his repressed love for his beloved brother—a love which he scarcely understands. Jake's rejection of this male 'clan', and its rules, is closely connected to his desire to be free, to stand apart from the Mob and to express his unconscious feelings for his brother. The taboo against incest and homosexuality is a double taboo; the taboo, however, is not as important as the cycle of longing and repression, transgression and atonement which it sets off. Responding to the loss of his brother (and the loss of his horde), Jake descends into a state of obsession marked finally by despair and an outpouring of melancholia.

Taking into account key aspects of Freud's theory of tribal culture from *Totem and Taboo*, I will concentrate on Jake's passage through the Oedipus complex into the symbolic order.[2] Like Newland Archer, Jake also finally accepts his Oedipal destiny and assumes his proper role within the symbolic order. His acceptance, however, is similarly an equivocal one. Jake, also, can only enter the symbolic after fetishising his loss and continuing to mourn that loss as a sad and lonely figure. The difference is that Newland Archer's journey is more conventional. The forbidden object Newland relinquished is a woman. Jake's journey is more complicated. He must relinquish an impossible desire to become the primal father of the horde as well as an incestuous desire for possession of his brother. As in many narratives of male melancholia, *Raging Bull*'s protagonist plays out his drama within an all-male group in a context in which questions of male bonding and homoerotic desire become central.

Part One: The Horde
'Put my robe on right'

The male melancholic sees the tribal group, the Mob in *Raging Bull*, as a bulwark for the enhancement and projection of his own ego—his fantasy scenario. As I have observed in *The Age of Innocence*, however, the Scorsesean tribe is frequently represented more like an institution tottering on the brink of self-destruction, far less glamorous and powerful than the melancholic will recognise or accept. Such a representation is consistent with Freud's picture of tribal instability in *Totem and Taboo*.[3] The Mob's requirement for Jake to 'take them dives for the short-end money' is a good example. While Jake sees this gesture in quasi-sacrificial terms—he refuses to go down and weeps bitterly following the bout—it reads in fact as a pathetic and desperate attempt by the decaying organisation to ensure Jake's nominal conformity. As Carol Siri Johnson points out, despite the fact that the fight was under investigation by the District Attorney as an obvious fix and that Jake was suspended from competing, 'his nominal acceptance of the Mob's rules results in Jake's acceptance into Tommy's "family", and he is allowed to fight for, and win, the huge, jewelled championship belt'.[4]

Just as Newland Archer constructs his melancholia in a world of his own making, Jake constructs his own fantasy of a totemic scenario to fuel his masochism and, ultimately, his melancholia. Jake's picture of his struggle can be observed in terms of the film's structured opposition of the Mob, a fraternal clan, on the one hand, and his own primal horde on the other. Central to Jake's sense of his own dignified leadership of his primal horde is the possession of his brother Joey, bound up with the possession of Vickie. Jake's horde-posturing—in its incestuous dimensions—represents a double challenge to the totemic scenario outlined by Freud in *Totem and Taboo*. Not only does Jake take for himself the authority of the original patriarch of the archaic horde, but he also violates the fundamental taboo on incest. In Freud's mythic scenario these offences constitute the very crimes that the fraternity, or band of brothers, was established to prevent. Jake's own horde presumptions place his fantasy scenario back at a point before the band of brothers committed the 'primal murder' of their horde patriarch father (later to be memorialised in the ritual of the 'totem meal')—a point or place which he longs to occupy.[5] The reality of his world, however, grants him no right to such power or dignified office. The post-Oedipal Mob merely requires him to 'fall into line' and facilitate their money-making operations.[6] To Jake the idea of being a mere 'earner' amounts to nothing more than being an animal. The dynamics of sacrifice implied in the dive he is required to take thus direct his paranoia towards a perhaps unconscious fear: that the group requires him to undergo a sacrifice, not as the god/primal father himself, but as merely his surrogate—the totem animal. In short, as is evident in his horde posturing and struggle with the fraternal clan, Jake sees himself as the embodiment of the primal father, the father himself, and not his mortal representative or animal proxy. Taking a dive 'for the short-end money' thus stands as a horrendous gesture of collaboration with a corrupt process and with the fraternal clan he despises.

Given Freud's observation of the common ancestry of all clan members to their totem animal, this mundane act would make Jake merely one of the fraternity, a brother, easily sacrificed, as a stand-in or proxy for the real authority, the primal father.[7] The animal, Freud suggests, played the role of substitute for the dead Oedipal father in order to bring about continued identification with him through ritual renewal.[8] Jake's animal anxieties express themselves frequently throughout the film and, in his yearning to be set apart from the animalistic, we see the type of sacrifice he longs to enact—the more noble destiny he seeks for himself. In the Dade County Stockade scene Jake wants to shake off the animal robe he wore in the boxing ring at the beginning, to relinquish the role of being just another member of the fraternal clan, a surrogate for the martyred primal father, for whom every subsequent animal sacrifice is a substitute secondary gesture.

Jake's fantasy scenario is a hopeless one. Acknowledging the existence of the Mob (by struggling against it), Jake can only place himself in the double-edged position of assuming the garb of the totem, a role of limited kingship, as discussed by Freud. According to Freud, the 'mana' or 'mysterious power'[9] of such a leader was such that he was heavily guarded and his taboo was immense:

> We know already why it is that rulers must be guarded against. It is because they are vehicles of the mysterious and dangerous magical power which is transmitted by contact like an electric charge and which brings death and ruin to anyone who is not protected by a similar charge.[10]

Similarly the ruler arouses considerable hostility with his demand for kingly veneration and can easily and arbitrarily be put to death when the perceived protection of his people falls away.[11] Jake discovers that his sacrifice can only be of this type. He cannot be the primal father— the mythic figure who signifies the symbolic order. Rather the social state in which Jake exists springs from that symbolic death. Any attempt on his behalf to assume the role of paternal authority is doomed—he is both the son and the totem 'animal' destined to enact one of the regular symbolic sacrifices of fraternal atonement. Like the sovereign discussed by Freud, he is 'worshipped as a god' in the boxing ring one day and sacrificed as a totem animal, a 'raging bull', the next. It is this fate against which Jake rages but to which he ultimately submits. Melancholy rather than martyrdom will be his reward. Any real pursuit of the primal position can only lead to madness or psychosis. Like Hamlet, who desired to be the father and possess the mother, Jake risks full madness in his more archaic desire to possess the horde, which signifies a desire to possess everything and everyone.

The band of brothers

For all Scorsese's interest in providing a small portrait of the authority of neighbourhood 'dons', such as Paulie in *GoodFellas* and Tommy in *Raging Bull*, his main interest is at the level of the wiseguys hanging out on the street and in bars, with the dons held off at a distance. Scorsese has commented on the differentiation between the two levels by comparing his own approach in representing the Mob to that of Coppola's in *The Godfather* (1972). Coppola's approach, he suggests in an interview with Gavin Smith, 'is like epic poetry, like *Morte d'Arthur*. My stuff is like some guy on the street corner talking.'[12] Les Keyser draws on the Smith interview and observes that Scorsese's characterisation of *GoodFellas*' Henry Hill is not so much concerned with Henry's humanity but with Henry as a central point of access to the wider operations and lifestyle of the Mob around him.[13] This is a central tension for the male melancholic, that is, the dialectic which arises in relations between the role of the individual in contrast to that of the tribe. In *Raging Bull* this tribe is the Mafia 'crew' comprising Tommy, as the local don, and his men Salvy and Charlie. Jake and Joey are 'street guys', but, as I have argued, Jake also has pretensions to becoming patriarch of his own horde. Scorsese's films demonstrate the extent to which characters such as Jake and Joey are needed by the Mob, although they are not 'made men' or members of a crew. The often volatile interaction between the two levels points to the undermining of the hierarchies that such divisions attempt to enforce. In effect this erosion of hierarchical differentiation confirms the comparison with the fraternal clan as outlined by Freud in *Totem and Taboo*.

The fraternal clan is dependent upon and largely defined, in *Totem and Taboo*, by the drama of the totem meal. The original murder and devouring of the patriarch of the primal horde is repeated again and again by way of the ceremonial slaughter of the surrogate totem animal (man, prisoner, enemy or traitor). This ritual operates to renew the contract of guilt which exists at the heart of fraternal law and its social organisation. The eating of the original totem meal and its symbolic repetition exorcises the hatred and jealousy aroused by the primal father, or any would-be successor, and in this slaughter establishes a stronger covenant with his ghost, a powerful 'deferred obedience'. The repetition serves to remind the clan of the reasons for the institution of its totem organisation and its central taboos, not to kill the totem (or any member of it) and not to attempt to possess any women (or man) of the same totem.[14]

The breaking of the incest taboo stands as the essential form of transgression open to the Scorsesean melancholic in his pursuit of separateness and limited social rebellion. The forbidden love of Newland for Ellen, and Jake for Joey, encompasses the dimensions of their rebellion. Despite his higher ambitions, the melancholic is one of these brothers, or at least a member of the fraternal regime established by these original murderous brothers. Like all the brothers, he longs for the power once possessed by the primal father. This was the power for which the brothers killed in the first instance. The melancholic's narrative may be read as the private drama of transgression which each brother enacts internally, stimulated by the ambivalence of taboo prohibition. His longing to transgress is not as strong, however, as his eventual affirmation of the fraternal group in its deferred obedience to its primal father.

The male melancholic, thus, can only begin to covet the power of the primal father in an act of sacrifice. Furthermore, he can only enact *a* small sacrifice (the giving up of transgression), as opposed to *the* larger sacrifice (of the primal father) which represents a socially regulatory and affirming act. As such his sacrifice is never a glorious and guiltless primal death. It is only a loss, a deprivation, like the acts of renunciation enacted by Freud's murderous sons. Unlike his brothers, who accept their place within the tribal group or fraternity, the melancholic periodically struggles against his destiny. It is an implicit, but repressed, recognition of his sacrifice as *merely* a small personal loss that provides the impetus for his melancholic display. Resisting such a lesser destiny, the melancholic enshrines and glorifies his loss in order to mark his position above the group, to keep alive his desire—the desire for the forbidden other—in the potent but impossible guise of the primal father. Melancholy, and its status of cultural validation, is his reward for exemplifying a fundamental tenet of fraternal authority—the impossibility of desire outside the group's authority. This is to demonstrate the impossibility of assuming the place of the dead primal father, the impossibility of possessing what Lacanian psychoanalysis describes as the phallus:

> The phallus is the very mark of human desire; it is the expression of the wish for what is absent, for reunion (initially with the mother).[15]

As a boxer, Jake conflates his desire to be the primal father with the desire to be the phallus—an impossibility, for the phallus is merely a signifier.[16] The associations he draws between his fist and his penis, and between his violence against men in the ring and notions of sexuality ('I don't know whether to fuck him or fight him') align his fist and his ferocity with the phallus. The boxer's ability to assert himself physically and wield his fist against other men leads him to assume, mistakenly, that he can be the phallus. Jake is a fighter who defeats all opponents and only ever loses 'on points', never on questions of pure physical prowess. In his 'castration' of the 'young, good-looking, popular' Janiro, Jake attempts to assume the role of the primal father, but it is a move destined to fail.

Jake's desire for phallic power marks his attempt to assert his difference and separateness from the fraternal group. Desiring to be that which the other desires places Jake in an antagonistic position with the band of brothers. The band exists within the symbolic and derives its status from the law of the father (the power of the phallus). Unlike the brothers, Jake dismisses the law's hold over him, seeing himself as the primal father and possessor of the phallus (the law). The very impossibility of maintaining such a position suggests the structure of unsatisfied desire central to Jake's melancholic trajectory. As Jake invokes the phallus as the sign of his desire, he similarly, and by definition, invokes an implied narrative of punishment and loss which are central to the struggle of the male melancholic. Accordingly Jake's battle to assert possession of his own horde against the power of the fraternal band and his recourse to notions of sacrifice reflect the oscillation of his desire. That is the oscillation between his rebellious attempt to be the phallus (the law) and the fact of his own castration (the obedient and conformist son).

The struggle between horde and clan

The portrait of Jesus in Scorsese's *The Last Temptation of Christ* (1989) is of a man who is lured (temporarily) away from the brotherhood and, as Mortimer puts it, 'hangs around with women and children'. In this 'period of soft, gushy remission from his vocation, Jesus is swamped in *femaleness*—he grows old in it'. Mortimer assesses this situation, not as representative of the Scorsesean hero's transcendence but of his distraction from his role as redeemer of the brotherhood.[17] Similarly, although certainly not soft and gushy, Jake La Motta is marked as being such a man. He defines his dignity by association not with the Mob brotherhood but with his *own* family—an aesthetic (of sorts) of femininity. Having beaten Vickie savagely, he begs her not to leave him;

'I'm a bum without you and the kids', he confesses. Jake's excessive jealousy and possessive paranoia over Vickie and Joey point to the way he clings to his horde as if to distinguish his power and identity from the oppressive tribal regime of Tommy, Salvy and the band of brothers.

Unlike Tommy and Salvy, the former being paired with the diminutive Charlie,[18] Jake is always associated with a wife. The film begins with a scene of Jake abusing his first wife, Irma, and ends soon after Jake is shown abusing Vickie. Unlike any of the Mob figures, he both allows for and relies upon the presence of a woman in his group. Apart from the important presence of Vickie early in the film, neither Tommy nor Salvy make any such concessions. As in Juliet Flower MacCannell's 'totemic paradigm', in which the brothers—not the father—constitute the new collective of modernity, the sister is excluded.[19] Indeed, in the scene at the Chester Palace dance, Salvy collects Vickie from a table with a number of women. As they leave, however, Scorsese places the central focus on Vickie, largely excluding the other women. Such scenes of the restricted fraternal clan contrast with a notable scene prior to the Janiro fight. Having argued with Vickie and then kicked her out of the kitchen, Jake rejoins her in the living room to make up. Moving around on hands and knees, among his own brood, together with Joey's wife, Lenore, and their brood, kissing the babies and Vickie, Jake constructs a perfect picture of the horde with himself as animal-patriarch. Joey's absence from the scene suggests both the exclusion of the younger males and the possession of many wives by the head of the family that Darwin saw in the primitive horde.[20] Such hordes were dominated by the 'gorilla', the very thing Salvy calls Jake in the following scene.

Jake's assumption of the role of the primal father, ruling over his own extended horde, introduces a strong point of tension in relation to the image of the ineffectual and apparently decaying fraternal regime of Tommy Como. Given his physical placement as 'one of the boys' in many scenes of the film, and given the decay of his authority (his inability to deliver Jake), Tommy can in no way be confused with the primal father. His authority, rather, resembles that of the first among equals, with no authority other than of boss or top dog. Jake's superior physical strength, his denial of Tommy's authority and his paternal pretensions threaten the fraternal structure with the return—in Freudian terms—of a primal father. The juxtaposition of these two structures or groups— Jake's horde and Tommy's clan—is manifest in the way they eye each other in scenes at both the tenement pool and the Copacabana. The antagonism between them is expressed around the question of which group will possess Vickie and in the intermediacy of Joey, who initially moves between the two.

The battle for Vickie and Joey

Prior to Jake's championship win, much of *Raging Bull* stages itself around the exchange of looks between Jake's horde and the fraternal clan led by Tommy but dominated by Salvy. The film's representation of Jake's gaze towards Salvy is consistent, in its slow motion, with the sexually aroused gaze he directs towards Vickie. The politics of this antagonism revolve around the importance of Vickie as a commodity object exchanged between the two groups, signifying an exchange of eroticism and violence. This exchange indicates the terms of desire and envy which each regime plays out and arouses in the other. Jake's horde-posturing suggests Vickie has a vital, if subservient, sexual role to play in the horde. In the clan, however, Vickie serves merely to signify the collegiate nature of the group. She is present, but only to signify that no one may possess her. Her association with Salvy's group (at the pool and the dance) prevents the possibility of Jake's patriarchal horde threatening, or even taking over, the authority of the fraternal regime. Vickie thus stands as a vital go-between for these antagonistic tribal orders.

Just as Vickie acts as a threat to the make-up of Jake's horde by her interaction with Salvy's crew, so too does Joey. Jake's constant questioning of Vickie about her relations with Salvy and Tommy is matched by his condemnation of Joey's social exchanges with them. In his anger with Joey for inviting Salvy and his friend to the training session, Jake pounds Joey violently. Later, prior to his title fight, he abuses Vickie for kissing Tommy, who has come to wish him luck. Joey becomes involved in the argument, feeding Jake's paranoia as to Joey and Vickie's possible involvement with Tommy and Salvy. 'I'm disgusted with the two of yous', Jake says. Jake's obsession not only with Joey's possible sexual involvement with Vickie, but also with the involvement of these two with Tommy's clan, is further sparked by Vickie's mock confession to Jake:

> I fucked all of them, what do you want me to say? I fucked all of them, Tommy, Salvy, your brother, all. I sucked your brother's cock. What do you want me to say? . . . Yeah, I sucked his cock and everybody else on the fuckin' street too. What do you want? You're nothing but a fat pig selfish fool . . . His fuckin' cock's bigger than yours too!

Joey and Vickie's refusal to act as if they were Jake's possessions represents a threat to Jake's desire to control the horde as if he were a patriarch with total power.

In *Totem and Taboo* Freud points to the rebellion surrounding the sons of the horde as the key to the fraternal organisation. Jake here looks very much like Darwin's higher ape controlling the horde and regulating sexual promiscuity within it by the force of his jealousy. Darwin's following conclusion paints a clear picture:

> . . . primæval man aboriginally lived in small communities, each with as many wives as he could support and obtain, whom he would have jealousy guarded against all other men.[21]

Joey's role in Jake's horde is positioned ambivalently between that of an object of possession and rebellious son who deserves to be purged.

Jake's paranoia revolves around the equivocal position of Joey in relation to Jake, and Joey's conception of his own authority. Finally, as is consistent with the structure of the horde—that there is only one dominant male—Joey is violently attacked by Jake and driven out of Jake's horde. This occurs when Jake stupidly believes Vickie's sarcastic comment that she has 'fucked all of them'. Joey has become sexually threatening to the point of infringing upon Jake's sole possession of Vickie. Prior to this, however, Joey's position in the horde has been secured by his subservience. As Siri Johnson points out, Joey assumes a 'feminised' self, and does not feel it necessary to enter the tribal Oedipal battle.[22]

Joey's assumption of a feminised position in relation to Jake is emphasised throughout the film in its countless suggestions of homoerotic desire between Jake and Joey. This is evident, most notably, in their first scene together. In the scene, Jake has banished his first wife, Irma, to the bedroom while he complains to Joey that he will never fight heavyweight champion Joe Lewis. Jake laments the fact that both he and Joey have small 'girls' hands. Jake tells Joey to hit him in the face, which Joey is reluctant to do; Jake becomes aggressive, insists and calls Joey a 'faggot' for refusing. Joey responds hitting Jake over and over again; Jake taunts him sexually; 'You throw a punch like you take it up the arse'. Finally, having pounded Jake's face repeatedly, Joey stops, telling Jake that his cuts are starting to open up. Jake gives a cheeky smile and twinks Joey's cheek in a patronising but amorous way. Joey's diminutive physical presence and his role as agent/punching-bag (Jake's training requires him to beat Joey frequently) for his bigger brother visually places him in the subservient role in Jake's horde in which he is essentially a possession to be counted along with the women. By allowing/forcing Joey to beat him, Jake adopts the masochistic position—apparently enjoying his symbolic rape by his younger brother. Because of the film's association of Jake's fist with the phallus there is no doubt that the encounter is symbolically a sexual one. Joey's sexual subservience confirms, on one level, Jake's horde authority.

Jake's consideration of his power is, at the same time, further complicated by the way in which the scene emphasises castration. As with Jake's appearances in the ring—his own self-staged sacrifices—this brotherly encounter revisits the castration scenario with its shocking emphasis on the pounding of Jake's face, particularly the opening up of his cuts. The scene demonstrates how the melancholic constructs his authority not in spite of his castration but in collaboration with it. Just as the melancholic has entered the symbolic, it is essential that he form an alliance with the fact of castration. Hence he goes to extreme lengths to bring castration about, constantly restaging it and displaying it. This performance bears comparison with Julia Kristeva's 'denying or manic position' in *Black Sun*. It demonstrates Jake's identification with the symbolic 'father, form, schema' vital to the pathology of Kristeva's melancholic. Like the mania of the melancholic, Jake's performance says, 'no, I haven't lost; I evoke, I signify . . .'.[23]

Apart from Joey's assumed sexual contact with Vickie, Jake's ability to deal with the Mob threatens him at the core of his fantasy. Jake's separateness from the group is undermined by Joey's cooperation with it and by Joey's inability to understand Jake's reluctance to do likewise.[24] In his amiable interaction with Salvy and Tommy, Joey displays the kind of cooperation Jake resists but must adopt in dealings with the group in order to obtain his desire—the championship belt. Cooperation promotes in Jake a fear of accepting the 'feminised' position taken up by Joey and Vickie, and subjection to the desires and authority of Salvy and Tommy and their decaying, but still potent, fraternal regime.

As I have suggested, in so far as the feminine 'other' is an outsider in relation to the symbolic order, the melancholic covets that position. It is this utopian prospect that inspires the male melancholic, who, like the subject of Freud's 1911 case history on paranoia, Dr Daniel Paul Schreber, appears to regard a degree of feminisation or transformation— particularly identification with the other—as a way of marking his difference from the conformist tribal group.[25] It sets him apart from the brothers. However, the feminine also operates as a metaphor for the general subservience of any individual brother within the fraternal regime. In the general giving up of power, on behalf of the fraternal ideal, each brother has accepted a feminised position in that he is not patriarch, in that he has endured a loss or deprivation. The male melancholic parades that loss by assuming a feminised position in order to overcome that loss and re-empower himself. He seems to say to the brothers (in the end): 'Like women, we have all been stripped of power and, therefore, we have all endured loss. But as I might have been primal father/patriarch, my loss is greater that yours, and my feminisation sets me further apart from the fraternity than yours. I am greater than all of you and your compromise with a regime of impotence.' For Jake, feminisation is part of his desire to sacrifice himself in order to redeem the world.

The first Copacabana scene demonstrates the fraught interaction between the groups in the way Joey and Vickie mediate between the two factions, leading eventually to the arousal of Jake's violent hostility. Following on from the living room episode, in which Jake cavorts with his horde, the scene cuts away from the Copacabana sign to establish a camera position on the stage, suggesting the point of view of the comedian. Panning across the room, the camera comes to rest on Jake's table just as he is singled out by the comedian, who refers to him as a well-known local celebrity. Jake's pre-eminence is diminished somewhat by the arrival of Salvy, who kisses Vickie en route to the bathroom, much to Jake's aggravation. Salvy approaches Jake's table; they shake hands circumspectly as Salvy points out, to Joey, Tommy's presence at a table across the room, made evident by a cutaway. As Salvy leaves the table, Joey exclaims 'Minghia!' (Dick!) and comments on how good-looking Salvy is in 'that suit'. A slow-motion shot, from Jake's point of view, reveals Vickie kissing Tommy and Charlie before she returns to face an interrogation by Jake. 'Are you interested in them?' he demands. The waiter interrupts in order to serve drinks sent to Jake's table by Tommy. This activity perpetuates the visual dialectic between two groups. As is consistent with the deliberately casual logic of the editing pattern which intersperses the scene with cuts to the comedian delivering one-liners, Joey is next seen approaching Tommy's table to pay his respects. Tommy indicates that Jake should come to him, which he does, reluctantly leaving the women behind.[26]

With the exception of one woman, seen briefly with her back to the camera, Tommy's group is emphasised in the scene as a male band. The guys talk about men beating men and men fucking men. The fraternal clan is marked by its aggressive playing out of the sexual tensions between its two dominant members, in this case Jake and Salvy. Salvy's (Tommy's) group, however, contrasts with Jake's own smaller group in which women-as-possessions play a more predominant role under his paternal authority. The Copacabana scene visually places the two regimes in a confrontation highlighting Jake's outsider status. Resisting inclusion within the group, Jake jealously guards that precious thing which keeps him apart—his horde, in which Vickie and Joey play a vital role.

Homoeroticism and the horde

The basic requirement of Tommy and the fraternal clan in *Raging Bull* is for Jake to fall in and accept Tommy's help in throwing the fight. For Joey and Vickie it is an act of practical compromise for Jake to make in order to win the championship belt. For Jake, however, this act of compromise takes on the importance of an existential melodrama of struggle against the dictates of a dehumanising (animalistic) tribal conformism. In so far as Jake's horde stands as a symbol of his struggle against such conformity—and a symbol of his personal authority—Joey is a vital component of that horde. Similarly in *The Age of Innocence*, Ellen also represents an alternative to the conformity of the group for Newland and offers him the possibility of personal salvation. When, towards the end of the film, Joey rejects Jake, refusing to see him, not only is Jake's horde in final and total disintegration but Jake is emotionally distraught. Jake's loss of Joey is as devastating to him as is Newland's loss of Ellen. Nevertheless both melancholics have played an active part in bringing about that loss.

In his analysis of Jake's love for Joey, Robin Wood demonstrates the way Jake's desire portrays 'the disastrous consequences, for men and women alike, of the repression of constituent bisexuality within our culture'.[27] Wood argues that Jake embodies the repression and release of homoerotic desire within the fraternal clan built around Vickie, Salvy and Joey. Of the three, Salvy is the only one Jake does not hit, suggesting the extent of his repression of erotic desire for Salvy, which he is used to expressing by way of violence. When he says of Janiro, 'I don't know whether to fuck him or fight him', the twin desires become one and the same; violence is at the heart of his sexual expression. As already mentioned, Jake equates his penis with his fist. After making love to

Vickie he pours ice on his erection, just as he plunges his fist into a bucket of ice after a fight. It is the arousal of violence in relation to men that allows him to engage sexually with Vickie, who exists primarily in the context of his desire for men. The few sexual or emotional encounters they have are juxtaposed with scenes or evocations of violent encounters with men, particularly with Joey. Vicki and Jake make love for the first time in front of a picture of the two brothers in the pose of a boxing shape up. Later, on her return to the house, they make up after he has savagely beaten his brother. Vickie functions as a heterosexual alibi standing between Jake and his sexual desire for his brother and others within the brotherhood. In this way, as Wood points out, Scorsese echoes the Schreber case, in which Freud concluded that 'Schreber's original love-objects (for whom all later men were stand ins) must have been his own father and brother'.[28]

The significant factor is how the relationship between the two brothers inflects upon and produces Jake's paranoid fantasy that he is caught up in a war of tribal conflict. Although it has been convincingly demonstrated by Wood and others that the fraternal relationship is central to Jake's repressed desire for men, I believe that it is also central to the wider framework of his desire to become the primal father, his later descent into melancholia and subsequent fetishisation of his loss. Jake's impossible desire to be the phallus is the desire to possess other men in all ways, sexually and in terms of leadership and authority. Jake's desire seems to be without boundaries—hence his coveting of both Vickie and Joey. In this context Jake's pre-Oedipal pleasures are homosocial in the widest possible sense.[29] Jake's repression of his love for Joey constitutes a self-inflicted wound which is the result of the tribal struggles and questions of taboo which emerge from his paranoid delusions. This conflict places Jake's love for Joey in the context of his desire to maintain control of the horde. The loss of Joey is thus directly related to Jake's loss of his horde, both losses driving the general narrative movement towards melancholia. As in the example of the Newland-Ellen relationship in *The Age of Innocence*, the relationship with Joey is not an end in itself, but part of the wider project of fantasy leading to the fetishisation of loss and the ensuing pleasures enjoyed by the melancholic: a sense of uniqueness, of being above the crowd, of moral superiority derived from the act of sacrifice—an experience of painful pleasure in re-enacting the loss in fantasy.

Jake's confused expression of his repressed love for Joey can be read in terms of the ambivalence over the central taboo of incest. The paranoia that Wood and Freud have seen in the Schreber case, which is the result of a repressed homosexual wish and desire for the father and brother, manifests itself in a tribal scenario.[30] The desire in the Scorsesean melancholic to create his own world, which both Wood and Lesley Stern have observed, enacts itself here around the primitive taboo against incest, as discussed earlier. The driving force behind Jake's fantasy scenario, like the delusions of Dr Schreber, is the idea that he is a superior being and that, like a god, he is not subject to the petty taboos and prohibitions laid down by decaying regimes. It is worth pointing out that Freud quotes Schreber's court judgement delivered on his release from Sonnenstein Asylum in July 1902:

> He believed that he had a mission to redeem the world and restore it to its lost state of bliss. This, however, he could only bring about if he were first transformed from a man to a woman.[31]

Jake's desire to assert himself as primal father rather than as tribal brother lies in his ability to deny the import and influence of taboo on his actions. In that an incestuous relationship with Joey stands as a violation of one of the two primary taboos, Jake's ongoing possession of Joey marks his desire to violate taboos. His homosexual desire for his brother signifies the extent of Jake's horde aspirations and is to be contrasted with any notions of general homosexual identification that Freud and Carole Pateman have considered in the fraternal regime.[32] Given the dynamics of taboo and the ambivalence towards it, it is clear that the violator of taboo is that person who, perceiving the decline of tribal authority, refutes its waning power and its arbitrary attempts to regulate sexual and general freedom. The violator of taboo, if he can get away with it, sets himself up in opposition to the primacy of the tribe and its power to make laws.

Just as he took sole possession of Vickie, Jake allows himself such freedoms because he refuses to accept that he is one of Tommy's clan. In other words, Jake refuses to see himself as symbolically occupying the place of one of the rebellious sons in *Totem and Taboo* who grew jealous of the father's possessions and horde pre-eminence and took part in his murder. Accordingly, for Jake, whose melancholic delusions involve becoming that superior authority, such prohibitions do not apply. The ambitious son or potential patriarch thus claims the right to determine sexual freedoms within his horde according to his own will. In this context Joey, like Ellen Olenska, becomes taboo because he arouses a desire in Jake which is outside a notion of desire sanctioned by the Mob fraternity. Jake's love for Joey does not fall within that general homosexual identification existing among the band of brothers that Freud speculates upon.[33] This love exists as an expression of rebellion against that entire social system. Jake's desire for Joey is the central element of his horde fantasy. As Newland's identification with Ellen operates to set him apart from his tribe, Jake's allegiance to his own horde and Joey as its central defining member marks his separateness. His difference is also marked by his desire—at times—to adopt a feminine position in relation to Joey, as demonstrated when he forces Joey to punch him.

In winning the championship belt, Jake experiences confirmation of his belief that he is a man apart from the group. What in fact it confirms is the melancholic's essential conformism, the fact that Jake has fallen in with Tommy and that only from Tommy and the clan could such a prize be won. The closer Jake comes to the belt, the more he loses control of his horde and hence his fantasy-aspirations towards becoming the

Jake doing it their way. Robert De Niro, Joe Pesci and others in *Raging Bull*.

patriarch. On realising this, Jake is forced to redeem and empower himself in the only way left—by deliberately throwing his final fight with Robinson. In the end, Jake can only prove he is the patriarch—now shown to be an impossible metaphor for his melancholia—by staging his own self-sacrifice, by literally 'making a meal of himself'.

Part Two: The Sacrifice
'You never got me down, Ray'

Following his pounding of Jake in their final bout of the film and Jake's pursuit of him after the bell—'You never got me down, Ray'—Sugar Ray Robinson looks at Jake with amazement and incredulity. While Ray's trainers accept the bloodbath merely as an inevitable part of the world championship fight, the moment of mute communication between the two men suggests something else. Ray seems to be asking the question in the mind of the spectator, 'Why on earth did Jake subject himself to such punishment?' Unlike Newland Archer, Jake is under no obligation from the tribal organisation to stage such a self-sacrifice. The realities of Mob involvement in Jake's career—those requiring him to succumb to such debasement—ended when he took the 'dive'. Winning the championship belt, however, implies a painful extension of that involvement—he could not have done it without Tommy and the fraternity. In this sense the championship belt, which Jake later smashes with a hammer, signifies the primacy of the Mob fraternity over Jake's horde in two ways. It demonstrates the social efficacy of the dive, which is so abhorrent to Jake, and also marks the advent of the loss of his horde and, in particular, his loss of Joey.

Having won the belt, but lost Joey, Jake is once again threatened by his own fears of being cast as an animal and having his sacrifice—the dive—and his championship win downgraded. This animal anxiety pursues Jake throughout the film, culminating in the fear Jake expresses in the Florida stockade, 'I am not an animal'. His career as a boxer, his continual experience of being in the ring, exhibited before a crowd, the necessity of keeping his body muscular and fit, the practice of wearing an animal skin before and after the fight—all these experiences locate Jake in a liminal space between human and animal.

In terms of the negative connotations held in his community about being an 'animal', Jake is understandably concerned about the social significance of being viewed in this way.[34] His paranoia thus casts him not as primal father but as that passive animal surrogate-victim sacrificed for the token gains of the decaying fraternal regime.[35] Furthermore, such a scenario works to confirm his status as merely one of the brothers via a common ancestry through the totem,[36] a status which is so odious to him. What Jake was hoping to achieve was to stage a self-sacrifice which would override all of these concerns. Despite the loss of his horde and the realisation that the championship belt affords him no primal authority, the self-sacrificial gesture works to confirm—at least in his own mind—his fantasy picture that he is the primal father. In this fantasy Jake is an animal, the blood-shedding raging bull which Freud and Joseph Campbell have seen variously as a mythic symbol of fecundity, rebirth and brotherhood-affirming sacrifice and redemption.[37]

The bout follows Jake's aborted attempt to apologise to Joey on the telephone. In refusing to speak to him, Jake demonstrates the melancholic's inability to climb down and articulate his guilt in simple, everyday terms. He prefers to atone for sins in dramatic gestures such as the self-sacrifice that follows immediately after their encounter. Joey's assumption that it is Salvy calling him partly explains Jake's reluctance to speak to Joey. Having driven Joey out of his horde there is, perhaps, fear in Jake that Joey has now given his allegiance to Salvy and the fraternal clan. The obscenity Joey hurls down the phone links all three of them, and Jake's mother, in the very terms which echo Jake's original outburst against Vickie and Joey: 'Your mother sucks fuckin' big fuckin' elephant dicks. You got that?' The threat of becoming an animal and the threat of the original desire to possess the mother is emphasised here as dominating relationships within the horde and among the fraternal clan.

The sacrificial bout which follows opens with Jake's trainer bathing his back and chest with a blood-soaked sponge. With animal noises screaming on the sound track, Jake, seemingly defeated, proceeds to fight back strongly in the next round, punching Robinson repeatedly and without fear of retaliation. Once again Jake is relying on a knock-out to win against Robinson, who is winning on points. The ringside commentator makes it clear that, even after his comeback barrage of punching, it is too late for Jake to win on points. Joey, watching on television, remarks, 'that was his last shot'. The confidence Joey has held in Jake's ability to stage a final round knock-out has left him effectively stamping the kiss of death on his brother. The thirteenth 'hard luck' round sees Jake offering no retaliation or opposition to the three assaults of vicious punching he sustains. After the first, he urges a reluctant Robinson to continue. After the second, Robinson pauses momentarily, raises his hand high and brings down the *coup de grace* which begins the final bloody attack. The fight is stopped; Jake, still standing, is covered in blood, his flesh torn and battered. Scorsese cuts to Joey before the television and the shot takes in Joey's long look at the events taking place. Cutting back to the ring, the moment of Ray's triumph is ignored by the camera, which focuses on the drops of blood falling from the ropes.

By staging his own sacrifice, Jake publicly demonstrates his pretensions towards offering himself as if part of a noble religious rite. Although he offers no resistance to Robinson in the thirteenth round and lays no punches, there is no suggestion that he is taking another dive. On the contrary, Jake's gesture of resignation is made for Jake's own benefit and in order to nullify the effect of the earlier dive taken on behalf of the Mob. The dive, later validated by the winning of the belt, is thus overshadowed by Jake's wildly extravagant gesture of bringing on his own defeat, punishment and loss of the championship belt. In line with Jake's desire, his deliberate act of self-sacrifice eradicates that scenario which would cast him as totem-animal sacrificed at the whim of the fraternity. Jake thus stages a scene of self-sacrifice, dramatically denying his subservience by trying to assume the role of the god, the primal father, who died to usher in a new social order.[38] Jake's vision of sacrifice is thus similar to Julia Kristeva's in her *Revolution in Poetic Language*. As Kristeva scholar John Lechte has observed, for Kristeva sacrifice is not an 'unleashing of animal violence' and social chaos, as in René Girard's formulation, but a 'regulatory' gesture made at the threshold of the symbolic, a 'symbol of the social order'.[39]

Guilt

As with the primal murder, Jake's self-sacrificial fantasy anticipates the guilt of Freud's cannibalistic sons—the basis upon which the social order is founded through the prohibition against incest and murder. Following his second loss against Robinson (the first loss represented in the film) Jake explains to his outraged brother, 'I've done a lotta bad things, Joey. Maybe it's coming back to me.' In this vein, the self-sacrifice demonstrates Jake's assumption of a high level of guilt, which is appropriate to his fantasy of being the paternal redeemer. Clearly, in his treatment of Vickie and Joey, Jake has much to make him feel guilty, but perhaps not so much as to destabilise his personal sense of ultimate authority. The guilt he assumes, as demonstrated by his acceptance of punishment, goes beyond his personal sense of guilt to incorporate the guilt of others.

Throughout the film Jake asserts the culpability of those around him: the oppression and injustice of Tommy and the Mob for forcing him to fight for their gain and the weakness and infidelity he suspects in Vickie and Joey. These accusations or complaints are demonstrated in the final scene when Jake sits rehearsing his Brando speech in the mirror. Like the redeemer, Jake assumes the guilt and iniquities of those around him, of all humanity. Even the guilt of the fraternity is assuaged in Jake's scenario by his self-sacrificial gesture; he has enabled them to say 'It is not we who destroyed the bull/father; he destroyed himself'. Hence Jake does not apologise to Joey on the telephone but makes a more spectacular gesture of atonement in his act of self-sacrifice in the ring.

For all the scene's connotations of sacrifice there is no death, as Jake's taunt to Ray ('You never got me down') shows. Totem-animals and scapegoats die in religious sacrifice in order to offset the violence or primal guilt threatening the heart of a fragile social order. In his fantasy, Jake refuses to cast himself as such a victim. He sees his gesture in more grandiose terms.

The concept of the primal father of the horde is central to my interpretation of Jake's actions and thus central to any speculation on the nature of his sacrifice. Jake's picture of his sacrifice is, however, totally his own. At the end of the bout, Ray is amazed at Jake's feat of endurance but totally ignorant of the grandiose sacrificial terms in which Jake sees it. Vickie and Joey, watching the fight, empathise with Jake's physical punishment. Only their personal experience of Jake's confused behaviour, however, gives them any greater understanding of the reasons behind it. The ringside commentators tritely reduce his actions to a gesture of retirement—'He wanted to go'. None of the fraternity is there to witness the rite, nor to be bathed in Jake's sacrificial blood. Jake's melancholy vision is entirely his own. Just as he cannot be the primal father, nor can his own sacrifice bestow upon him any sense of godhead or the desired role of redeemer. It stands, to all but Jake, as merely another night at the 'fights'—at most, another rite of animal sacrifice. As Richard Librarch's (1992) review of the film suggests, the journey has been in vain:

> Jake La Motta's imitation of alienation from himself cannot overcome his highly externalized locus of control, and he thus abrogates any privilege of martyrdom: seeing himself as a victimized object of circumstance and subcultural disadvantage, Jake can never shed his blood as a subject of grace,

and he must ultimately resign himself to being bathed in the blood of others more worthy. Even though his enemies do in fact exist, he cannot behave like the sacrifice who denies his enemies' existence despite all imminent evidence to the contrary.[40]

Some conflict has emerged between Paul Schrader, one of *Raging Bull*'s writers, and Scorsese as to the question of Jake's redemption or salvation. Scorsese indicated his position with the concluding quotation from John 9:24: 'All I know is this: once I was blind and now I can see'. Schrader commented, 'I don't think it's true of La Motta either in real life or the movie'.[41] In such an exchange, the nature of sacrifice, salvation and redemption is subject to different interpretations. In my view the nature of Jake's sacrifice has not been fully understood. The scene in which he allows Ray to beat his once magnificent body into a bleeding pulp represents Jake's final attempt to become the patriarch. His previous attempts to assume this role have failed. The horde has been destroyed (by Jake's own actions) and the rift between himself and his beloved brother cannot be healed. The only way he can demonstrate that he is different from his brothers, that he is above the fraternal clan, is by staging his own self-sacrifice in the boxing ring before a crowd of adoring fans. He is beaten but not humbled. He is, in a sense, feminised. In so far as Jake sees the fist as a phallus, he has submitted himself to it, just as he once forced Janiro and his other opponents to submit. Jake's feminisation also recalls the Schreber case in which Schreber believed that in order to 'redeem the world' he must first be 'transformed from a man to a woman'.[42] In Jake's case, feminisation relates to his experience of loss and his subsequent fetishisation of loss. Like other melancholics before him, Jake asserts himself very strongly as a masculine figure while taking on the 'feminine' tropes (loss, impairment) of melancholia. Positioned as an outsider, he nurses his pain like a wound—a lonely figure locked into a cycle of pain and the outpourings of grief.

Castration

If, as I argue above, Jake's desire to be the primal father signifies an impossible desire to be the phallus, then the trajectory of the phallic narrative cannot be complete without reference to castration. In bringing on his own sacrifice, Jake embraces his castration, and in effect embraces the totem authority of the fraternity. As we have noted briefly in considering sacrifice from the positions of Freud and Kristeva, the boon

Jake provides in his sacrifice merely serves the fraternal band. This brings about Jake's identification with the group not as primal father but as fellow brother. Jake's propensity towards sacrifice demonstrates the oscillation in his desires. On one hand he wants to be the primal father, the figure who lays down the law. On the other hand Jake desires the status of obedient son who undergoes castration in order to shore up his status and power in the world. As in Kristeva's vision of sacrifice, the melancholic hovers between the symbolic and the imaginary. It is the longing for imaginary unity, totality and non-differentiation which underpins his melancholia. Jake, as melancholic, seems to say, 'If I cannot display the phallus, I display my loss of it through the wound of castration. See, here, my bleeding heart.'

Jake's sacrifice in the public arena is, therefore, his castration. Allowing his body to be beaten and bruised, his cuts to be opened up, he becomes a walking wound, a patent symbol of castration. His fighting tactic of 'playing possum'—wearing down his opponent by enduring rounds of blows before violently fighting back and defeating him—makes clear the role of punishment in Jake's desires. It might be argued that the very act of boxing is structured by such an economy. A number of associated motifs of castration that predominate throughout the narrative, providing Jake with the opportunity to display his melancholic's wound. One of the most telling of these motifs relates to the 'boo boo' scene between Jake and Vickie.

'Kiss the boo boo'

During their final exchange in the car park, as Jake tries to kiss and be kissed by Joey, Joey says to him, 'Let me call my wife and kids. Don't you want them to see the kiss?' Whether it is Jake kissing Joey or the reverse, Joey understands how his brother's fantasy operates. The kiss Jake expects demonstrates his desire to perform publicly and to be celebrated as the sensitive and complex male. Joey's wife and kids saw Jake's shocking act of aggression in his attack on Joey. Now Joey mockingly suggests they should witness Jake's so-called remorse. Joey's resistance to his brother's bombastic affection is understandable. Having been so badly abused, why should Joey allow Jake the opportunity of demonstrating openly his capacity for sorrow, pain and atonement? From Joey's perspective these are insincere emotions. For Joey to reciprocate Jake's affections, in front of his own family, would only serve to validate further the melancholic's desire to wear his grief publicly.

The earlier sequence moving from Jake's defeat of Robinson to the scene following his next fight with and defeat by Robinson—a cycle of fullness and loss—demonstrates how Jake sees his wounds as a source of social legitimacy and validation. In the bedroom following the first of these two fights, Jake elicits his own sexual arousal from Vickie. Lying on the bed, Jake beckons Vickie to his side—despite his own interdiction against 'foolin' around before a fight'. As she sits before him, he tells her to kiss his bruises and cuts in the infantile expression he might have used as a child talking to his mother, 'Kiss the boo boo. Make'em better.' This moment of foreplay replicates the melancholic's fantasy scenario over his emotional loss, which is marked by his wounds. In making this demand of Vickie, Jake seems to want the world to acknowledge and worship his wounds, his loss, and to validate that loss as an act of selfless giving—an act of redemption. As he demonstrates through his expressions of pleasure, Jake is aroused by such. His desire is such that the superiority and respect he gains in his display of the phallus is only balanced by the cultural legitimacy and empowerment desired from his display of castration.

Arousal through wound worship, however, stimulates again Jake's desire to become the phallus. At a crucial point in their foreplay, just before Vickie is about to fellate him, Jake realises the danger and rushes into the en suite bathroom where, before the mirror, he pours a pre-prepared jug of ice cold water into his pants and douses his swollen cock. As much as he desires to be the phallus, he equally desires to be diminished, to be castrated; he must prevent an over-determination of the phallus in order to bring about the masochistic side of his desire, his eventual melancholia and loss. The logic of this episode is found in sporting lore which warns sportsmen about the dangers of losing their hunger and killer instincts by indulging sexually before an event. The melancholic's hunger is more complex. His desires are not limited to the killing because he also desires, in part, to be killed, castrated.

Having defeated Robinson in their previous encounter, Jake's potency will be deflated in their next bout. Unlike Joey, who reacts violently to the defeat by smashing a chair in the dressing room, Jake is unmoved. His calmness in defeat contrasts with Joey's outrage at the judge's decision and Jake's own tearful response in a similar scene later following his dive. Glibly announcing a personal reason for his defeats—'I've done a lotta bad things, Joey'—he seems more preoccupied by staring at his own wounds again, displayed in a mirror. The effect of his technical defeat by Robinson is augmented by Jake's own agency. As he sits and stares into the mirror he douses his inflamed hand in a bucket of cold water. Scorsese's repetition of the ice water motif brings together an unmistakable association between penis and fist. Jake's desire is constructed in the alternating images of a display of power followed by deflation. The pattern of desire representation in *Raging Bull* is not dissimilar to that played out in Newland Archer's game of hide-and-seek with Ellen in *The Age of Innocence*.

The mise-en-scenè of the bedroom scene emphasises this alternation. As Jake pours water on his cock, Vickie leaves the bathroom and lies on the bed dangling her legs over the side and kicking them in the air just as she kicked them in the water when Jake first caught sight of her at the tenement pool. This image of original desire is re-invoked and played out before Jake who, still dousing himself, closes the bathroom door on the scene of Vickie in the bedroom. On either side of the door hang portraits that echo the pattern of Jake's desire. Mary and Jesus face Vickie on the bed; the madonna and child display their sorrows and their loss in the wound of the bleeding and sacred heart—an image designed to elicit the adoration of their followers. The scene stages itself as a 'stand-off' between potency and castration—it emphasises the interplay of Jake's desire to signify both positions. Standing/sitting before the mirror dousing his cock and fist in ice cold water, Jake takes pleasure in the new image of himself as that martyred god, pulling back his mortal shell and pointing to his own sacred wound for all believers to see.

The loss of the brother

Jake's night club performances represent a pathetic display of personal loss. In no other context could Jake more dramatically parade his melancholia than in these bars and clubs, low-life dives, where he performs his rise and fall as a boxer. What little we see of his routine is dry, repetitive, cliched and cribbed; it continually rehearses and restages his career, intermingling this sad tale with melancholic allusions to a catholic selection of authors including Shakespeare, Rod Serling[43] and Tennessee Williams. Consistent with that Kristevan state of 'intolerance for object loss' and 'the signifier's failure',[44] Jake's location in the symbolic is unstable. As we see in the stockade scene, Jake easily slips into asymbolia and madness as he oscillates between imaginary and symbolic utterances. Lacking in expression and sophistication, his nightclub routine is not far removed from the animal cries and wall-beating of the stockade scene. Thus melancholy, like sacrifice, demonstrates the 'maintaining of the community between men and animals' that Kristeva sees on 'the other side' of the boundary.[45] Twice we see Jake perform before an audience, both times rehashing old chestnuts about wives cheating on their husbands. In the final scene, also the opening scene, we gain a more substantial insight into Jake's complete story.

In the solitude of the dressing room the melancholic's fantasy is emphasised as a solitary one. It may even exist for no one but himself. The stockade scene emphasises the extent to which Jake is fighting with himself. The drab isolation of the dressing room conveys a sense of hopelessness but shows that Jake is somehow satisfied in his fantasy world—'I'm the boss' he repeats as easily as he asserted the fact before his championship win. Jake's loneliness, matched with his optimism, imbues the scene with a sense of pathos. His struggle against the fraternal band to assert what he considers to be his primal right to a horde and supreme authority has been thoroughly defeated and yet Jake still believes in the truth of his own vision. To the spectator Jake is a figure of pity, perhaps even a sympathetic figure believing in himself when all those around have forsaken him. To this extent the lone melancholic, seemingly repentant, attracts our indulgence. As Pam Cook has rightly indicated, the spectator gives Jake's fantasy an extra vote of credence by becoming easily enfolded in it.[46]

In neither the stockade scene nor the dressing room scene is the spectator privy to Jake's private state of mind. His actions in both scenes merely replicate and rehearse the performances he has made all his life, before huge audiences. The Barbizon Plaza may not be Radio City Hall but, despite some of the seedy bars Jake has performed in, the Barbizon suggests that in the late 1950s people were still coming to hear his melancholy history. When the Barbizon stagehand (played by Scorsese) tells Jake that the house is 'crowded', we know that we are not the only ones who have come to hear and see Jake's performance. Jake's isolation, his struggle to maintain his inner vision, is opened out by a wider public willingness to hear his story. Jake's fantasy scenario, the creation of his own world, thus gains wider cultural legitimacy and validation.

By placing his own story among those of other boxers and great men of film and literature, Jake sees his tale as part of a wider cultural tradition—perhaps even of mythic significance. In this way his nightclub performances play a significant part in his melancholic display. Like the stories he draws upon, his performance represents a continuation of his struggle against what he perceives as injustice. It also continues his fight with the fraternity to be the primal father and to possess the horde. But, as we know, this struggle has been long since lost. What the nightclub performances achieve is the mastering and validation of that loss. There is also a clear element of theatre to Jake's shows. Just as Jake continually played possum in his boxing career, just as he allowed himself to be sacrificed in the ring, Jake's nightclub routine restages his loss for the pleasure and applause of others. These performances effect a permanent and public state of sacrifice and castration.

As with Newland Archer, the melancholic Jake manages to invoke the ghost of on object in his performance of his loss. As Newland looks back to his vision of Ellen in earlier times at the lime-rock lighthouse and from the distance of his fifty-seventh year, she finally turns and smiles. In this vision Newland maintains his fantasy-crypt of loss and melancholy, ignoring the reality of Ellen, who has grown old with him, waiting for him in the apartment above. From a similar solitude and in the decrepitude of age, Jake sees Joey emerging from a store and walking to his car. With his thin moustache, shorter hair and warm coat, Joey has clearly changed. Unlike Newland's vision of Ellen, however, Joey refuses to turn around. Instead Jake follows him and compels him to turn around, forcing himself and his embraces on an obviously unwilling brother. Following this awkward exchange, Joey reluctantly agrees to call Jake 'in a few days'—but it is clear that he will never call. In the following scene (six years later) in which Jake rehearses his tale of loss before the mirror, it is clear that Joey has been lost to Jake forever.

Jake is oblivious to the change in his brother. Like Newland, he has no eyes for anything that might disturb his fantasy picture. His final recitation of Brando's speech, with its heavy emphasis on the blaming of the brother, indicates his failure to deal with reality, particularly of his own violence towards Joey. Jake quotes Brando's character, Terry, addressing his brother:

> It wasn't him, Charlie, it was you. You remember that night at the garden you came down in my dressing room and you said, 'Kid, this ain't your night; we're goin' for the price on Wilson'? Remember that? 'This ain't your night'? My night. I could've taken Wilson apart that night. So what happens? He gets a title shot outdoors in the ballpark, and what do I get? A one-way ticket to Palookaville. I was never no good after that night, Charlie. You was my brother. You should've looked out for me a little bit. You should've looked out for me just a little bit. You should've taken care of me just a little

bit insteada'makin me take them dives for the short-end money. You don't understand. I coulda had class. I coulda been a contender. I coulda been somebody instead of a bum, which is what I am. Let's face it. It was you, Charlie. It was you, Charlie.

Despite the reality of the situation, Jake uses Joey as an alibi[47] for the memorialisation of his own personal loss. He ignores change as an indicator of reality and conjures a fantasy picture of Joey as a signifier of the loss of his horde and a focus for his nostalgia and hostility. Jake's loss has been largely created by his inability to read signs correctly. Like Ellen Olenska, Joey represents for Jake 'the symbol of everything he had missed'. The loss of Joey represents the loss of the horde and the defeat of his desire to be the primal father, to be a man apart from the rest of the fraternity. In reciting the Brando speech, Jake is invoking memories of his brother—the object of invocation and the arousal of the melancholic fantasy—just as Newland achieves in his mind's eye view of Ellen standing by the lighthouse.

In such an evocation the brotherly hostility expressed in the Brando speech is not inconsistent with the ambivalence which is attributed to the lost object by the melancholic, as we have seen in Freud's discussion and in the example of Newland Archer. As is consistent with the self-reproach and castigation of others we have observed in the melancholic, Jake's sense of self-reproach is similarly ambivalent. His masochistic tendencies exemplified so violently in the ring and stockade have, in a sense, been turned on the object of desire. Joey, once the adored brother, is now treated with that hostility reserved, as Freud points out in *Totem and Taboo*, in tribal cultures for the recent dead initially feared as demons. Jake's ambivalence towards Joey positions Jake in the melancholic's favoured nexus between critique of others as a reproach aimed at the 'patient's own ego'[48] and a critique of others as a call for adoration, that is, as a 'moralist critic of society'.[49]

Joey's hostility at seeing his brother is consistent with a key aspect of the melancholic scenario. The melancholic's narrative, his achievement and demonstration of melancholia, is always maintained at the expense of a lesser other—usually the object of his desire. The melancholic's wider narrative incorporates the melodrama of punishment and victimisation endured by this other. Joey's hostile response to his brother is largely explained by the punishment he received at Jake's hands. It is also this fraternal drama which has created the context in which Jake's melancholy has been achieved and displayed. Thus it is the response of the melancholic's object of desire that largely drives his narrative. The loss of that object provides the essential matter of the melancholic narrative. The object's castigation of the melancholic evokes that sadistic victimisation he once dealt out and which continually renews and gives strength to his fantasy.

CHAPTER FOUR

Taxi Driver:
the melancholic as flâneur

He's a prophet and a pusher, partly truth, partly fiction
—a walking contradiction.

Betsy quoting a Kris Kristofferson lyric

 Travis Bickle (Robert De Niro), a Vietnam veteran, takes a job as a taxi driver working at night because he cannot sleep. As he cruises around New York City he fetishises its most frightening elements. Travis reflects in his diary, 'I believe that one should become a person like other people'. The series of mirror-identifications with people that he makes on his nightly round reflect his limited capacity to make sense of the urban environment and its crowd, and his inability to construct a stable subjectivity.

Hovering above the prostitution, street violence, drug abuse and pornography—and drawing Travis's gaze—is Betsy (Cybill Shepherd). Dressed in white, Betsy appears to him as an angel floating above this 'filthy mess' and he attempts to make a connection with her but without success. On their first date he takes her to a 'Swedish marriage manual' cum soft porn movie, hopelessly confused as to how to relate to her.

Following the failure of his desire to win Betsy—his failure to build a unified self—his outlook becomes darker. A customer, played by Scorsese himself, draws Travis a full description of the way he intents to shoot his wife's 'pussy' with a .44 magnum pistol. This psychotic killer represents everything about the city that Travis loathes, but neither presidential candidate Palantine (Leonard Harris) nor his fellow cabbie 'The Wiz' (Peter Boyle) can give him any answers (beyond hopeless clichés) to assay his loneliness or moral indignation.

In rescuing a child prostitute, Iris (Jodie Foster), from the clutches of her pimp, Sport (Harvey Keitel), and effecting that rescue via the attempted assassination of Palantine, Travis sees his mission, his raison d'être, and his chance to clean up the city. Easy Andy (Steven Prince), gun salesman and pedlar of all the commodities that underwrite urban violence, provides him with a stockade of weapons. His planned assassination of Palantine, like all Travis's intentions, is frustrated and his bloody shoot-out with Sport and various other low life takes its place as the outlet for the 'bad ideas' Travis has confessed to The Wiz. Rather than being punished for his violence, Travis is made 'urban hero'. Iris is 'restored' to the suburban horror of life with her parents, and Betsy, impressed by Travis's unintentional heroic act, seeks him out. Their final meeting is played out as an exchange of looks in Travis's rear-view mirror. In this reflection Betsy remains an alluring image of desire, but as she alights from the taxi to pay the fare Travis can hardly look at her. Just as Newland Archer refuses to see Ellen (except in his ideal image of her) at the end of *The Age of Innocence*, Betsy has become redundant to Travis. He drives off, leaving her on the sidewalk behind him, in what is perhaps the most traumatic moment of the film. Gazing into his mirror he does a 'double take' as if catching a glimpse of a horrific sight—himself, a melancholic with a real sense of loss.

Look but don't touch

Travis represents a telling example of the Scorsesean male melancholic as flâneur. In *The Paris of the Second Empire in Baudelaire*, Walter Benjamin considers the flâneur as a nineteenth-century Parisian urban stroller, voyeur and street critic who sought to mediate and understand the dilemmas of the onset of modernity, and his own place within modernity, in the urban crowd. Emerging from the urban maelstrom, Travis embodies the flâneur's dialectical relationship with the urban crowd around him. He seeks to rise above it, as its hero and redeemer, while at the same time attempting to construct a stable self-identity in the images it presents to him. As with the flâneur's project of urban heroism and mastery—which I will consider in critical works on the flâneur by Keith Tester (1994), Graeme Gilloch (1992) and Rob Shields (1994)—Travis's attempts to construct for himself such a rebellious identity are doomed to failure.[1]

The flâneur is, from the beginning of his journey to its end, a bourgeois.[2] Like the Scorsesean male melancholic, his journey begins through his association with his tribal group, which dictates the dominant culture and his place within it. Steeped in post-Enlightenment liberalism, the flâneur selects the crowd of urban modernity as the mise-en-scène of his existential journey into the underworld. As Benjamin observes, the crowd offers up an erotic image of desire (a woman or stranger) from its bag of forbidden objects, further tempting the flâneur towards an identification with it. In this identification the flâneur perceives transgression—a flirtation with the idea of escape from the oppressive confines of what Benjamin calls a 'satiated reactionary regime'.[3] This appears to be the flâneur's project, although as an escape his journey is always limited and ultimately unsuccessful. In reality the flâneur is bound up with the loss and failure he requires for the success of his true project. The flâneur pretends to himself that he 'wants out'. His project provides a 'brief encounter' with a sign or system of signs constructed by the dominant ideology to suggest transgression. The flâneur is almost always a fetishist and can only orient himself in this strange world by interpreting its signs according to his familiar paradigm. Inevitably he fails and returns to the bosom of his tribal group. There he mourns the loss of that time during which, he had convinced himself, he stood as an individual—outside the oppressive demands of tribal conformity. Here he exposes the true object of his flânerie—melancholia. Prior to his journey (Newland Archer in *The Age of Innocence* offers a perfect example) the 'melancholic flâneur' has everything he requires except the knowledge of the loss of everything. His social pre-eminence has brought him the gifts of the dominant culture; his flânerie is an attempt to take possession of the subdominant culture, to experience and control the alien condition. The flâneur aestheticises loss and converts it into a melancholia with which he returns to his tribe, placing it among the Victorian clutter of his mantelpiece as a souvenir of a holiday in a distant country.

Benjamin's discussion of the flâneur is only one of a variety of similar discussions on a topic about which there is little critical uniformity.[4] In her chapter 'The flâneur: The city and its discontents', Priscilla

Ferguson has detailed the various roles and guises assumed by the flâneur throughout the nineteenth century, from Balzac, as 'true' flâneur-artiste of the pre-1848 period, via Baudelaire to the flânerie of failure and urban bombardment in Flaubert's embodiment of the vanquished 'baudad' (gaper) and 'dupe' (sucker) of the Second Empire.[5] Beyond flânerie's association with specific historical personages, it has taken on a general importance for those attempting 'to get some grip on the nature and implications of the conditions of modernity and post-modernity'.[6] The Janet Wolff/Elizabeth Wilson (1992) debate over the existence of a 'flâneuse' suggests something of the critical dilemma raised by the concept of the flâneur—that any assertion made about this nineteenth-century Parisian stroller/observer is immediately somehow inverted.[7] This range of critical positions surrounding the flâneur appears largely sympathetic (although logistically challenging) to the picture of the male melancholic, whose nature is also contradictory and ambivalent.

Despite these differences, the notion of the flâneur helps us understand the Scorsesean melancholic. This is particularly so with a figure like Travis Bickle, whose whole existence is bound up with that of the crowd. Although Travis is not a member of the middle classes, he is a kind of flâneur who observes and critiques the urban crowd from which he has emerged and from which he feels himself to be apart. Again we can see how important the group is to our discussion of the male melancholic. Whereas Newland Archer cultivated his melancholia from within the sheltered walls of the tribe, and Jake La Motta constructed his loss from his failure to negotiate between his fantasy horde and the fraternal Mob, Travis is part of a crowd, an anonymous mob which is both the source of his livelihood and the cause of his melancholia.

'This filthy mess'

On their 'coffee and pie' date, Betsy tells Travis that he reminds her of a song by Kris Kristofferson: 'He's a prophet and a pusher, partly truth, partly fiction—a walking contradiction'. By invoking this lyric in relation to Travis, Betsy provides a valuable insight about the melancholic flâneur of late modernity. As 'prophet', Travis, like the flâneur, stands as the 'hero' of modernity. Both enter the market place, on one hand, to critique its shortcomings and 'right its wrongs'. Travis spends much of the film indoors composing a diary of his reflections and observations like the flâneur-artiste of Benjamin's reading who retires at the end of the day to record his rapidly gained and insightful impressions.[8] This is the flâneur's self-image as the philosopher of the

Travis as 'philosopher of the crowd'. Robert De Niro in *Taxi Driver*.

crowd—the role which nourishes his dignity by placing him above the crowd through the power of his insight. On the other hand, the flâneur always risks becoming implicated in the immorality he tries to rise above, not least due to his delusions of self-importance. As critic of the urban malaise, he easily becomes 'pusher' and conductor of those commodities which increase the 'evil' within the crowd. Entering the marketplace to find a buyer for his insights and observations, he becomes aligned to the criminal world—seeking the exploitative materialism of modernity. Travis, misunderstanding Betsy, defends his position by saying 'I'm no pusher. I never have pushed.' The pusher, who stands as the antithesis of his moralistic self-image, is later exemplified in the figure of Sport. Travis's denial, and the subsequent violence that we associate with him, outlines the prophet/pusher dialectic which structures the series of contradictions common to the Scorsesean melancholic, and his counterpart the flâneur. Both strive to be the 'man apart' and yet end up as the 'conformist'.

Benjamin's flâneur is faced with an organisation of authority which is marked by a tedium of life endured under a regime of reactionary despotism. In contrast to the tribal organisations of *The Age of Innocence* and *Raging Bull*, *Taxi Driver*'s regime of authority stands as a subtle, more obscure entity matching the 'background' and 'secret' nature of authority in Benjamin's nineteenth-century description.[9] In the absence of a clearly defined power structure in his world, submerged within the popular rule of the urban crowd—'We *are* the people' is Palantine's pathetic attempt to sloganise it—Travis points his melancholic flâneur's desire to transgress in two directions: firstly towards the city and the crowd itself, as in his diary/voice-over narrative ('All the animals come out at night . . .'), and secondly towards random and diverse representatives of that authority, from Palantine and the secret service agent to Sport and his Mafia connections. Neither are, in themselves, entirely satisfactory targets for Travis's rebellion because neither holds any significant authority over the decaying body politic against which Travis hopes to define his sense of being. Oedipus has become a pale metaphor.

Against such a background of decay and depravity the male melancholic assumes the role of representative of 'change'—Freud's licensed and critically qualified melancholic rebel.[10] Newland Archer glibly embraces 'modern views' in relation to the archaic and highly restrictive rights and freedoms of women in the nineteenth century. Travis, on the other hand, bombarded by liberal decay, represents the forces of change according to his 'coffee and pie' conservatism.[11] It is through the twelve-year-old prostitute Iris that Travis expresses his crusade for change. Meeting her for breakfast he exhorts her to change her life, telling her 'You should be at home now, goin' to school and goin' out with boys your own age'. Her pimp, Sport, calls Travis a 'cowboy' and tells him of his horse that was killed on Coney Island when hit by a car. Their brief exchange over the nature of 'hip' emphasises the extent to which Travis, described initially as a cowboy, jars with modern sensibilities as representative of the old-fashioned morality of the western.[12] Such a moral code, represented as hopelessly inadequate by the oppressive suburbanism of the letter from Bert and Ivy Steensma (Iris's parents) at the film's end, marks Travis's 'difference' from the corruption around him and his conservative yearning for the typical Scorsesean 'more perfect' commitment to an erstwhile authority.[13] It places him in a position like that of the melancholic flâneur, often found wandering through the arcades of nineteenth-century Paris walking his turtle, mourning the loss of gaslight and automobile-free streets.

A piece of Errol Flynn's bathtub

An essential part of the melancholic's transgressive energy is his struggle to avoid conformity with the group's networks of control. The bombardment of taboos, laws, customs, manners and objects work to contain the melancholic, as Benjamin has emphasised for the flâneur, in the absence or failure of the various 'repressive' arms of authority. As Travis tells Iris, 'Cops don't do nothing', and his own escapes from the law on two occasions bear this out. Travis's assassination attempt on Palantine and final massacre of Sport and his associates demonstrate how the crowd first hides him (in the assassination attempt), and then makes a hero of him (after the shoot-out). In giving the secret service agent a false address, Travis reveals he has some understanding of operations of this level of control. He understands the platitudes of Palantine and the self-satisfied bumbling of the police and secret service, and he despises both. What he does not understand are the more subtle signs of control and authority which lie deep within the caverns of the crowd. In this, Travis demonstrates an (in)ability in the reading of signs which is similar to that of Newland Archer.

In late modernity these signs of oppression have moved away from what Freud refers to as 'the etiquette of taboo' to that which Benjamin sees as the 'intoxication of the commodity'.[14] Flânerie, as a guide to modernity, has taken the melancholic and his taboo-like, object-fetish oppression into the marketplace and towards commodities. The melancholic's object fetishisation, when read in relation to the flâneur's commodity intoxication, renders both characters as subservient to the object or 'thing'. His inability to understand the more complex signs, and his intoxication with these very signs, renders him vulnerable, like the collector/courtier, to 'share the situation of the commodity'. This is to lose himself in the crowd—his worst fear.[15] For Travis the threat of commodity intoxication emerges from the street—the drugs, prostitution, and even the piece of Errol Flynn's bathtub offered to him by fellow cabbie Dough Boy (Harry Northrup). These stand as the debased objects of his environment which signify the system of oppression he strikes out against in his final killing spree.

Just prior to Travis's first sighting of Betsy—'She appeared like an angel out of this filthy mess'—Scorsese shoots a crowd filing past and away from the camera and from Travis's imaginary point of view. He repeats this visual motif in *The Age of Innocence*. There an extreme long shot of old Broadway is filled with men walking either to or from work, all wearing the same type of derby clutched to their heads in the wind. Both scenes, and Scorsese's representation of the crowd/group in general, echo what Frederick Engels saw in the Manchester crowd: '[T]he brutal indifference, the unfeeling isolation of each in his private interest'.[16] It is this dehumanising uniformity that Scorsese's melancholic rebels against most strongly, particularly the threat of becoming lost in the ordinary unreflecting mass of conformity—witnessed in Jake La Motta's struggle against the fraternal band. In Benjaminian terms, this constitutes both salesman and commodity in one—to be reduced to the plaything of a distant and corrupt regime. Newland Archer 'may give up the law' to travel abroad at the drop of his derby, but Travis Bickle cannot divorce himself from the bazaar and thus is beset by the greater fear of becoming Sport, the pimp, or Easy Andy, the gun salesman who can supply the full range of delights available in the marketplace of late modernity.[17]

The hero of modernity

In the melancholic's drive to transcend the group, he inevitably seeks to become, to some extent, its hero. In defending Ellen, Newland tries to redeem his tribe from their petty prejudices, thus validating his own higher and more liberal morality. As primal father and primal sacrifice, Jake sees himself as smashing the despotism of the corrupt and decaying fraternity and redeeming society.[18] The melancholic sees the fallen and the alien/undesirable as especially worthy of that state of grace which his revolution will provide. As redeemer/hero the melancholic can legitimise his connection to the group, corrupt as it is, and at the same time stand aside from the tedium and banality of its everyday concerns. As discussed in relation to *Raging Bull*, this is the nature of his sacrifice—'to redeem the world and restore it to its lost state of bliss'.[19]

Travis designs his role as hero in a number of ways common to the flâneur, his Parisian ancestor. Possibly the dominating factor in this is the extent to which his heroism is, on one level, self-delusory. Like Jake, Travis constructs a scenario of his own heroism in which he can rectify the evils of the city—unlike the equivocating popularist liberal, Palantine—by assassinating a culpable criminal (Palantine/Sport) and rescuing a suffering victim (Iris). He pursues this 'mission' by assuming various covert identities, alternating between extremes of legal authority and criminality. He validates his assumption of duty via his solitary pursuit of it and by the delusion that he has a vocation—'Loneliness has followed me all my life . . . I'm God's lonely man'. As diarist he assumes a certain 'calling' by his pretensions to a critical-artistic-philosophical insight over the city and its crowd. This is a practice which also gives his imagination material form, like any other 13-year-old, as Scorsese sees him.[20] Like the flâneur, Travis places a possibly unconscious emphasis on his power to make his own meaning out of the city, its spaces and crowds—to create a world rather than merely finding it.[21] Susan Buck-Morss emphasises this in the way she sees the flâneur's 'fields of action'—like those of the prostitute and the gambler—as 'wish images'.[22] Such activity has great scope for undermining the very insight the flâneur claims; however, as Keith Tester points out, the lack of acknowledgment of his mission by those around him often plays a central role in his self-delusion, as can be observed in Jake. For Tester the 'nobility' of the urban poet-flâneur (Baudelaire) comes from his knowledge that he is mediocre in the eyes of others. The very danger of being 'just a face in the crowd' is essential to the poet's creativity and inspiration. Knowledge of that danger proves that 'the poet is a man apart even though he might well appear to be a man like any other.'[23]

In discussing the paradoxical nature of Benjamin's reading of Baudelaire's 'heroism of modern life', Graeme Gilloch stresses the importance of the apparent ambiguity. On one level, Gilloch suggests, Benjamin rejects any sense of heroism in modernity. On another level, heroism provides Benjamin with key insights about modernity by extending and recasting the notion. Thus Gilloch sees three characteristics of heorism in the Benjamin view of modernity: 'the attempt to shape the modern, the antagonism towards it and its phantasmagorical character or 'irreality".[24]

Gilloch suggests that by coding his deliberations on modernity in terms of the interpenetration of the old and the new, Benjamin exposes himself to the thin line between exposing the urban illusion and contributing to it. The uncertainty of Benjamin's flâneur/hero—expressed in moments when he is heroic and when 'sham'—appears matched by his own dubious heroism, 'raging against modernity while unwittingly and unavoidably reasserting it'.[25] The reflected neo-classicism in Benjamin's Paris—a 'mirror city'—finds its heroic expression in the reaction of its ordinary 'sober bourgeois citizens' to the hazards of the urban wilderness as outlined by Poe, Dumas and Sue. These figures, defying fate, risk the modern metropolis alone. Shunning the tempataions of the commodity, they maintain their identity in the midle of the crowd. And yet, although they see themselves at odds with modernity, they are addicted to it.[26]

For Travis, such heroism is reflected in his willingness to 'go anywhere any time' and to engage with the 'scum' of the city without fear. It emerges from a basic belief/delusion in the constancy of his soul and of his vision—the belief that he can enter the marketplace but not give in to its soulless temptations to buy—exercising the flâneur's true code of 'look but don't touch'.[27] As Tester points out, such a distanced interaction is, in Baudelaire's vision, 'an intrinsically modern existence since it represents a synthesis of the permanence of the soul of the poet with the unexpected changes of public meetings'.[28]

In his letter to his parents and in his bragging to Iris, Travis describes his fantasy existence as a government secret service operative on important duty. In one of his series of mirror identifications in the film, he stands beside a security officer mimicking his stance watching the crowd gathering to hear Palantine speak. In their subsequent discussion, Travis tells the officer that he thinks he would be suited to the secret service because he is, like the flâneur, very observant and good with crowds. In putting on the imaginary and uneasy garb of the detective, the Scorsesean melancholic begins to codify the essential powers of his heroism and particularly those pertaining to his powers of insight. Like the flâneur Benjamin identifies in the so-called 'physiologies' of Parisian life,[29] his pretension calls upon a certain 'empiricism' which allows him a high degree of understanding of the urban scene. Extending from this flâneur's boast over his ability 'to make out the profession, the character, the background, and the lifestyle of passers by',[30] he casts himself as urban philosopher, reader of signs and objects, mixing his effortless insights with the observations of the penetrative, creative and quick eye—the dream of the artist.[31]

The key to the flâneur's 'heroism' is his ability to maintain an anonymity and to hide himself in the crowd. He desires to remain unseen, the better to make his observations out of the corner of his eye or from behind his newspaper as he sits in a Paris cafe. In this he is the secret spectator of the spectacle of the city.[32] Frequently he satisfies this anonymity by combining it with his habitual desire for difference by affecting a range of roles, poses and disguises. A paradoxical situation arises in which the flâneur's search for anonymity is made by pursuing the disguises of self-conscious display. In this he shares the apparent ambivalence of the melancholic, whose 'condition' balances a 'secret heart' with a patent and often manic display. What hides him is the difficulty of pinning him down due to the general fluidity of his identity created by his assumption of various roles. Tester quotes Baudelaire's *Paris Spleen* in a description of the poet's rights and capabilities in this:

> The poet enjoys the incomparable privilege of being able to
> be himself or someone, as he chooses. Like those wandering
> souls who go wandering for a body, he enters as he likes into
> each man's personality.[33]

The flâneur's association with the bohemian, affecting 'an attitude of protest against the vulgarised materialistic civilisation of the bourgeois century',[34] and indeed with the dandy, suggests both his assumption of roles and the extent of the paradox of display they provide.[35] Both roles are marked by an excessive theatricality of costume, deportment, habits, manners and speech. These roles draw attention to themselves and their difference from those of their own social class as much as they hide the flâneur behind the pose.[36]

Beyond his various occupational titles, such as journalist, print maker, poet, novelist, painter, musician, sculptor or general man of leisure, the flâneur may adopt the guise of the detective, as has been discussed. In his article 'Fancy footwork', Rob Shields discusses another role open to the flâneur which stands, potentially, as the detective's opposite or nemesis—the 'Savage Mohican'—a guise which Travis literally adopts for the shoot-out episode towards the end of the film.

Locating the non-Parisian/foreign element in Benjamin's portrait of the Paris crowd, Shields opens up the discourse of difference, placing the flâneur as Paris Mohican—the permanently wandering and displaced native.[37] In the flâneur's love of self-display, his being influenced by the various poses and roles of dandyism and his Anglomania he exemplifies Benjamin's conception of the modern metropolis, which, with its exchange with foreign others, renders both insiders and outsiders as 'displaced'.[38] Despite his love of difference, however, he is never a foreigner, but a 'stranger'. As we have considered, his place in the crowd is essential. The stranger tag allows him the exploration of difference, as it does for him as bohemian and dandy (to an extent), as it does for the melancholic who explores positions of alienation and feminisation, especially as Shields codes it under Simmel's conception of the stranger as 'a foreigner who becomes like a native, whereas the flâneur is the inverse, a native who becomes like a foreigner.'[39]

In this sense the stranger, with his 'double-edged identity', evokes what Shields calls 'the beautiful illusions of commodity form'. In this sense both commodities and people have to be interrogated as to their true identity. The act of concealing identity. 'the cloaking of use-value with exchange values—is the logic of the arcade.'[40] Like the Savage Mohican, the flâneur's displacement makes him unreadable and covert. This suggests some dangerous qualities of excessive individualism:

> . . . which bypasses social norms in favour of idiosyncratic behaviour and eschews transcendent moralities for relativistic situation-ethics elaborated 'on the fly' makes the *flâneur* a potentially treacherous friend and a dysfunctional social element who provokes the need for discipline.[41]

Similarly, there is a sense of the native struggle with his environment. The city of modernity has been 'made strange' and the flâneur's wanderings are an attempt to regain and retain 'his native's mastery of his environment'.[42]

'You ever try and look at your own eyeballs in the mirror?'

Of Scorsese's melancholics, all of whom desire to be the 'stranger' in their group, it is not surprising that Travis, who possesses the most infantile subjectivity, should match such infantilism with an extreme fluidity of identity. Examination thus far has observed him in the various roles of detective, secret service operative, soldier, cowboy, 'man on a mission', urban vigilante, urban critic-philosopher, moral crusader and self-sacrificer. These are roles furnished by his imagination and the flâneur's predilection for creative circumspection. In relation to Baudelaire's characteristic of the poet/flâneur's 'wandering souls who go looking for a body', we can see further disguises for Travis in the series of mirror identifications he makes throughout the film. As with Newland and Jake, Travis shares a propensity to stage identifications with objects of desire. Many characters of the city arrest his gaze (e. g. the funky dressing African-American's staring at him in the cafe) suggesting that the city itself, its physical and popular environment is in fact the overriding identification constructed in his mirror. Eight specific mirror identifications (six of which involve actual mirrors) highlight the point. The mirror shots are also central to Travis's sense of his own identity. His fear that—like those he observes—he is also lacking inside, without fixed identity.

Travis's fantasy scenario in relation to Betsy casts himself as the all-American 'boy next door' who can attract the popular, attractive and socially acceptable 'star-fucker', as Paul Schrader calls her.[43] He also derives an identification with those very characteristics. Among the many images caught in his taxi's rear-view mirror, that of Scorsese himself as urban psychotic-in-a-suit places a further coating over Travis's developing neurosis. The television, porn movie and rear-view-mirror screens carry visions of couples in various stages of intimacy, also providing images of Palantine to match the proliferation of his poster image throughout the city.[44] Beyond the iconic 'you talkin' to me' and Easy Andy scenes, the mirror identifications with The Wiz, the secret service agent and Sport are less literal, but still significant scenes of mimicry which contribute to the constitution of Travis's subjectivity.

Travis first sees Sport, one of his most significant encounters, in his rear-vision mirror. When later they meet, Sport stands in a doorway, the frame in which he remains for the rest of the narrative. Sport moves about restlessly, but almost always remaining within these confines. Occasionally he leans back against the door with his arms spread across it supporting him. It is the pose he assumes later following his final shooting by Travis. Travis stands against this narrow image frame three times, just as he has stood against that of his bedroom mirror. In the first instance he sidles up to the image, keeping his sunglasses on against the disturbance of Sport's vicious sales pitch regarding Iris. The second approach is more forthright. Without sunglasses and somewhat cleaner than before—with mohawk haircut and the look of the displaced stranger, camouflaged master of his jungle-like environment and potentially 'dysfunctional social element'—Travis carries out the shooting, promised and practised before the mirror. Their final encounter, minutes later, is a reverse reflection of the previous meeting; Travis now stands on the other side of the door in which Sport is finally shot dead.

The emphasis upon Travis's detestation of Sport suggests the strength of the identification. As he says to Iris, 'He's the scum of the earth. He's the worst sucking scum.' What strengthens the identification is the extent to which Travis mirrors Sport, who is designated as Comanche by his hair and by the so-called 'Scar scene'—in which he lovingly embraces a disturbed and frightened Iris as they dance to the Bernard Herrmann slow jazz tune. Their encounters play on Travis's identity first as detective, then as cowboy and finally as 'Indian'. As flâneur, Travis's 'heroism' allows him to assume this dangerous and potentially antisocial identity to achieve his aims. It is in this temporary assumption of a 'savage' difference that Travis thinks he can distinguish himself from the tribe, that is, the base mentality of the urban crowd represented by Sport.[45]

Such overt and numerous disguises are not common to Scorsese's melancholics, nor to male melancholics in general. The motifs of disguise and role-playing, however, predominate. The male melancholic almost always assumes at least two roles, ranging around the politics and expression/suppression of what I have referred to as his 'secret heart of woes'. This is particularly obvious with Newland Archer. The first of his poses, both of which are equally untenable, is the face displayed to the group or tribe, which is one of propriety and conformity. It hides, temporarily, the expression of another face which contains all his secret longings, yearnings and desires. This is the face in which Benjamin reveals that in the big city everyone carries a secret that, if known by others, might make him/her an object of fear and loathing.

As suggested, both roles are deceptive but perhaps the second one more so in that it is played so well that it nearly resembles the truth. For the stability of his tribe, the melancholic is required to hide his secret longings like a clandestine affair. But in order to exercise those longings he is equally obliged to disguise, before the object of his desire and perhaps to himself, his secret face of tribal conformity. His temporary transgression is dependent upon the maintenance of the fiction that he is a non-conformist—which is, for the male melancholic, a grand self-deception. Hence his manic/melancholic display. His narrative journey operates, in this sense, as a recurring cycle of the alternation of masks.

The anonymity which is the aim of this alternation is designed to hide his 'secret', which is the key to his existence.

Seeking to achieve transgression and heroism via identification with an alien or diminutive object of desire, the melancholic flâneur may choose a woman or man to be that object—as we have seen in relation to Ellen Olenska and Joey La Motta. Travis describes himself as a lonely man and, like Newland and Jake, this is a loneliness which is, in part, cultivated to serve his mission. The apparition of the object of desire for the melancholic not only distracts from this loneliness but defines it. It presents the lonely man with the 'shock of the new', fresh, extraordinary experience which he feels himself alone in admiring:

> I first saw her at Palantine headquarters at 63rd and Broadway, she was wearing a white dress. She appeared like an angel out of this filthy mess. She is alone. They . . . cannot . . . touch . . . her.

Based on physical appearance—which, according to his own terms, he later finds to be deceptive—Travis's reading of Betsy is perhaps no more superficial than the attributes Scorsese's other melancholics see in their various objects of desire. Ellen's uncluttered frankness and her example of 'free living' are virtues greatly desired by Newland. Similarly, when Jake first sees her at the tenement pool in *Raging Bull*, Vickie stands out like an angel (in slow motion) amongst Salvy's men. What Travis sees and desires in Betsy is an identification outside the 'filthy mess'. Both Newland and Jake employed such objects to distinguish them from the corruption of their social context. All three attempt to possess the image in order to assert their identity beyond that context. In Travis's case, Betsy represents the ideal combination of dream girl/girl next door, by association with whom he can be lifted out of his oppressive environment. Furthermore, identification with Betsy gives him a more conventional lifestyle, defined in Travis's ideal world by meeting a girl and taking her home to Mum and Dad. Following the disaster with Betsy, Travis sends a card home to his parents detailing his fantasy of a stable identity. This includes a job ('secret work for the government') and a girl ('I have been going with a girl for several months now and I know you would be proud').

Central to this identification in the Scorsesen male melancholic is its logical extension—a desire to *become* his object of desire. The melancholic carries the narrative of an 'other' around with him as a model scenario of his melancholic fantasy. This requires a temporary identification with an alien object of desire, be it a woman or otherwise. Through such an identification the melancholic makes use of that object's alien condition to best effect his rebellion, temporary separation, excess of sensitivity and experience of loss. The extent to which this involves the desire of the melancholic to assume the identity of the 'other' has been observed by Carol Siri Johnson in *Mean Street*'s Charlie (Harvey Keitel) and his relationship with the epileptic Teresa (Amy Robinson):

> Charlie wants to be a woman: if he were, he wouldn't have to close off his desire for love, intimacy, religion and security; he wouldn't be locked into this struggle with himself, his friends and his community.[46]

The image

Earlier I alluded to eight mirror identifications (six of which involved literal mirrors) which Travis makes in an almost hopeless quest for stability. The two most significant of these are his encounters with Sport, which I have already discussed, and with Betsy, which I shall discuss further in relation to the film's final scene. The pimp and the white goddess stand as the major extremes of identification in Travis's attempt to close the gap at the centre of subjectivity. Here I shall describe, briefly, how Travis's other mirror identifications contribute to that process, how they represent the various urban identities between the extremes of Sport and Betsy, and how they contribute to Travis's own image of self (as unified and complete), his descent into madness and his melancholia of incompletion. The six characters to which I am referring are: Iris, The Wiz, Charles Palantine, the Secret Service agent, Easy Andy, and the psychotic murderer in Travis's cab, played by Scorsese himself.

Like most of the significant characters that inflect upon Travis's narrative, Iris is first seen by Travis in his cab's rear-view mirror. Struggling to get away from Sport, Iris, and the captivity which Travis sees in her, are briefly encapsulated in the image of her reflection. Following his subsequent failure with Betsy, Travis seeks a new purpose in his commitment to rescue Iris, a child prostitute. In her evocation of innocence mixed with sexual desire, Iris holds a troubling fascination for Travis. As a child prostitute she is associated in his mind with the corruption of her trade. Travis sees her, nevertheless, as signifying the ideal image of childhood—a victim to be saved from the ravages of the urban malaise. Just as Travis sees his ideal self-image as that All-

American hero suitable even to chaperone Betsy, that self is also fit to protect 'sweet' suburban girls like Iris. In his response to Iris, however, we observe Travis's immaturity. In his desperation to preserve an idealised identity in the face of urban decay, Travis appears naïve and infantile. Thus the child prostitute is a perfect counterpart for him. Exhibiting all the impressionability of a child, Travis is constantly threatened with engulfment by the crowd. In such a way the flâneur fears equation with the prostitute. That is, he fears his role of crowd philopspher will be undermined to the point at which he becomes like Benjamin's prostitute, the commodity of late modernity.

The Wiz is a stereotype cab driver who prides himself on his experience of people and on his often unwanted opinions. It is this experience that Travis seeks in The Wiz when he approaches him with a confused expression of his 'bad ideas'. Barely has Travis begun his inarticulate questioning when The Wiz launches into a rambling and meaningless 'the world keeps turning' style story which he hopes will alleviate Travis's anxieties. This provides Travis with further evidence of the incoherence

Jodie Foster, Robert De Niro and Martin Scorsese on the set of *Taxi Driver*.

which already surrounds him. The Wiz even agrees when Travis calls his speech 'the dumbest shit I ever heard'. As a supposedly streetwise guy, The Wiz has nothing to contribute to Travis's state of being other than confusion.

Nor has Charles Palantine, the presidential candidate, any solutions or answers for Travis. Again a character introduced to Travis in his rear-view mirror, Palantine offers only glib political clichés in response to Travis's disturbed and disgusted rant about the state of New York City. 'Well Travis, it isn't going to be easy', is the beginning of his bumbling attempt. Throughout the film Palantine's image comes to Travis on the television and on posters plastered both in his room and throughout the city. Everywhere Travis is confronted with this image which contains the contradiction of responsibility, authority, respectability but also ineffectuality. Travis's choice of Palantine as the scapegoat for his anxieties is, I consider, a random choice, but one that is not surprising given the irreconcilability between Palantine's high office and his inability to act.

Like Travis, the Secret Service agent suggests the need for crowds and the creating of a subjectivity based on surveillance, of a protected individual (Palantine) and of hostile elements (such as Travis) which threaten both the individual and the community. In their encounter Travis struts his credentials as potential agent, just as he is perceived by the agent as a 'suspect'. Travis is proud and amused by both aspects and plays a game with the agent, first by mirroring his stance and actions, then by engaging with the agent's ruse to learn Travis's address. Their encounter speaks of the fluidity of identity—in the alternation of detective/criminal positions one should know that another would never give his address without risking detection. Travis's encounter with the agent both emphasises his image as law enforcer while also coming dangerously near to affirming Travis's criminal status.

Travis, Iris, Sport, Palantine and Betsy all have something to sell in the market place of late modernity. Easy Andy, who sells guns to Travis in a hotel room—just as Iris sells herself in a similarly rented room—is the ultimate pedlar of commodities of value in the urban chaos. His sales pitch is manic and intense. He lays his guns out on the bed and both men worship them. Travis looks at himself in the mirror wearing a gun and holster—'isn't that a little honey', says Easy Andy. As they conclude their business, Andy bombards Travis with the full range of his goods for sale: guns, uppers, downers, women, Cadillacs ('with the pink slip'). As pedlar of commodities, Andy is unscrupulous and panders to the corrupt and diseased elements of society. There is nothing he cannot provide, no desire he cannot gratify. In the encounter with Easy Andy (a name more likely for a prostitute), Travis is faced with the character who has not merely become the wares—like a prostitute—but has become all wares.

The character, played by Scorsese, who threatens to shoot his wife's 'pussy' with a .44 magnum pistol, seems to embody all the psychotic horrors of the city in one. And yet he wears a suit and sits in the cab where Palantine, another well-dressed, upper-middle-class man, sat. To Travis he represents the total degradation of urban, upper-middle-class respectability. The Wall Street lawyer/stockbroker gone crazy, the model of respectability damaged by life in the city, swamped and overtaken by its vice. Despite this façade, he is responsible for such vice, hovering somewhere between Palantine and Easy Andy.

These are the faces of the crowd, the objects of desire and identification that Travis follows—like the narrator/flâneur in Poe's *A Man in the Crowd*. These characters are the mirrors or imaginary projections in which Travis tries to, or is forced to, construct a sense of self. No single image sticks, but each contributes to his unstable and explosive identity, augmenting the melancholia that arises from his deeply felt sense of incompletion.

The concept of the flâneur provides Juliet MacCannell with an appropriate tool for a critique of the individual in modernity and the group modelled on it. We may apply such a critique to Travis's hopeless attempts to construct an identity through his mirror identifications. MacCannell quotes Benjamin to the effect that the flâneur only breaks his isolation 'by filling the hollow space created in him by such isolation with the borrowed and fictitious isolation of strangers'. The obscurity of the modern group, the band of brothers, is modelled on the paradox of the individual feeling himself to be the creator of the universe made in the image of his isolation, while similarly desiring full absorption in the crowd.[47]

The crowd in this sense is thus more imaginary than real. Benjamin's allusion to Baudelaire's expressed sense of 'crowd-pleasure' lying in the 'enjoyment in the multiplication of numbers' speaks of a group that 'can only be formed by an extension or expansion of the ego, multiplied and endlessly reflected'. The crowd therefore provides the flâneur Travis with a means to sort out his existential dilemmas. What he sees in the crowd assists him in the construction of his own identity. This is not about a recognition of otherness, but a mirror image through which he reads the crowd as an extension of his own ego. His own identity absorbs the isolated egos in the crowd to reinforce his ego's own construction of objectivity. Travis's heroism, relying so heavily on his ability to create his own world, is accordingly compromised as his original desire for separation from the crowd is exposed to reveal him as at one with it. His creation of himself as an individual leaves him the same as all others in the urban mess.

The image fades

Graeme Gilloch reflects on the failure of flânerie by exposing its pretensions towards heroism within an environment of loss—modernity as 'the enactment of sorrow'. Accordingly flânerie and its heroism stand as part of modernity's 'self-deception'. The hero/flâneur/poet and his hubris merely embody its paradoxes, 'blind to their own participation within that social order they reject.'[48] In such an environment of deception, the flâneur's capacity for transgression is thoroughly closed off by his capacity for 'self-deception rather than rage' and by the melancholia that comes with the realisation of this and his confinement to the conformist tedium of modernity. For Benjamin the heroes of modernity are those who endure it while all the time seeking to undermine it. Confined within a narrative of suffering and boredom the modern hero is both melancholic and stoic.[49]

Heroism, amid the urban tedium of modernity (from which there is no relief), becomes a role playing at heroism, not 'tragedy' as it is translated in the Zohn Benjamin edition,[50] but 'Trauerspiel' (sorrow-play). As Gilloch's vital footnote elaborates, the ancient hero is tragic but the modern hero is a melancholic figure of the sorrow-play. This hero is not a character of great deeds but one who endures the 'sorrowful futility' of modern life.[51] The many roles the flâneur/hero assumes have their significance and potency undermined by the flâneur's lack of conviction.[52] In relation to motifs demonstrated in *Taxi Driver*, flânerie 'is a theatrical presentation before a mirror, to an audience of one'.[53] Travis addresses his mirror:

> You talkin' to me? Well who the hell else are you talkin'. . .
> you talkin' to me? Well I'm the only one here.

Tester sees that in Baudelaire's interpretation of the poet/flâneur, there is a dialectic operating of 'control and incompletion'. On one hand he has control over the meaning of his world, on the other he is compelled to continually rejoin the crowd for fear of 'incompletion'. Thus completion 'requires an escape from the private sphere'.[54] In this sense the private sphere appears 'utterly barren' to the flâneur,[55] who shuns it but at the same time diminishes his potential to stand outside the crowd he seeks to read.[56] Bound up with this compulsion to join the crowd, as Gilloch points out, his 'disappearance into the crowd' becomes a possibility because 'the instant in which they become "one flesh", means the flâneur's extinction'.[57] The undermining of the flâneur's own trans-gressive desire brings us to the essence of his 'hollow protest' and the superficial failure of his project. It is part of the bourgeois fantasy of the 'crowd-as-safe-haven', 'the comforting assumption not that you were just like everyone else, but that everyone else was really like you.'[58]

The failure of transgression for the male melancholic is, of course, no failure at all. Bourgeois fantasy, as Carol J. Adams (1994) points out in relation to *Raging Bull*, stands as bourgeois reality:

> Susanne Kappeler argues that culture is patriarchy's self-image. Kaschak tells us that men and the patriarchal society in which they are part are culturally arrested at this engulfing stage of male entitlement, in which individual men mirror society, and society mirrors them. The looking glass world—Scorsese's extreme interest in mirrors in his movies might be noted here (recall the triple mirrors that reflect Vickie's image when she tells Joey at the Copa that she feels like a prisoner)—is the world in which Raging Bull circulates.[59]

"Well I'm the only one here"

It is to this 'looking glass world' that the male melancholic returns at the completion of his flânerie. In Scorsese, the failure of the melancholic's flânerie is commonly marked by an explosive situation late in his narrative. The 'third act' style sacrificial climax to *Taxi Driver* is followed by a denouement, common in Scorsese's work, which is more about the future of his melancholic than about tying up a sense of that past which lies in the preceding narrative.[60] Paradoxically the truth of that future is inevitably bound up with the cyclical structure of desire in Scorsese films which is constantly repeating the past in one form or another. The final three takes of the film, in which a sharp discordant note sounds, prompt Travis to 'double take' and look into some horror located in his rear-view mirror. This suggests an ever-threatening regression into what Julia Kristeva has called a pre-symbolic state, a site experienced by the child before the intervention of the 'father'. For Travis, despite his recent affirmation of stable identity, this is the very state in which he has been wandering for the entire narrative.

It is a disturbing, traumatic ending.[61] Rather than allowing us to relax into the final rendition of the jazz number, it jolts the spectator into some empathy with Travis as he jumps at some obscure disturbance that he sees in his mirror. What he sees is his own image, which is held for a second before dissolving into the image of the crowd and the passing scenes of street life. The traumatic 'double take' is the important issue here, and what it implies about Travis's recognition of his own image. This is not the first time he sees himself in reflection in the film, but it is, as Iris has already suggested ('Why don't you look at your own eyeballs in the mirror?'), perhaps the first time he reads his own image with some understanding.

The previous scenes of the blood-splattered shoot-out marks a definite break in the narrative and in Travis's subject formation. Just as it plots out a ritual of sacrifice and death for Travis, the predominance of blood in the scene suggests the concept of birth. The scenes which follow make a heavy insistence on the emergence or 'social birth' of Travis as the person he has always wanted to be—'like other people'. Scorsese has said that the film was 'about a guy who desperately needs to be recognised for something, but he has nothing he can do to gain himself the recognition'.[62] Having gained that recognition in the newspapers, in the gratitude of Iris's parents (the suburban American family) and finally from Betsy, Travis attains that subjectivity which relies on recognition and acknowledgment. The first time we see him after the shooting, he is marked as 'one of the guys'. Standing on the street outside the St Regis Hotel with The Wiz, Dough Boy and Charlie T, he looks much easier in their company than before. The Wiz, as usual, makes a sexually suggestive joke and Travis laughs with the rest of them. There is none of the dull incomprehension in him that has marked their meetings before. Similarly he is easy and smilingly polite in conversation with Betsy about Palantine's nomination and the shooting.

What emerges here, in Travis's reunion with Betsy, is a suspicion brought on by the play of looks which occurs in the rear-view mirror. Visual communication throughout the entire cab journey takes place in the mirror and Travis only looks at Betsy at the very end before he drives away. Scorsese cuts between a medium close-up of Travis driving as he glances up to his mirror to look at her and a shot of what he supposedly sees in the mirror—an unframed image of her looking windswept and seductive. The lack of frame definition is noticeable only when we first see Travis reflected in the mirror, which has its frame clearly defined (we see this again in the last shot when it seems to be the camera's point of view). This looks to be Betsy's point of view. The next time we see Travis in reflection, as Betsy is getting out of the cab, it is marked as a different perspective by the lack of frame definition. So we seem to have three points of view: firstly, Travis's view of Betsy in unframed reflection; secondly, Betsy's (later the camera's) view of Travis framed; and, finally, an unframed reflection of Travis from an unspecified point of view, perhaps looking at himself.

The third point of view is the last take we see of Travis and the one which he sees and is so traumatised by. The traumatic look—the melancholic stare—seems to suggest that what he sees is an image of himself that points to the darkness within, perhaps even the lack at the centre of his being. It also seems to suggest the flâneur's tragedy—when he looks at his own identity in reflection he sees it is merely a reflection of those identities in the crowd he seeks to transcend. Where he once saw the variety of city low-life, he now sees himself. He has ceased to be the detached observer/loiterer and has become Benjamin's 'sandwich man', that walking advertisement board we still see in our city streets today, 'diverting the audience from its tedium' by selling the attractions of mass culture in a fascist regime. In Travis's case, his glance back at himself reconfirms his melancholia, which is indicated on the soundtrack by the final return of Bernard Herrmann's jazz tune. In this sense, Travis's melancholia, as Keyser points out, is the sign of his social conformity:[63]

> The confluence of Schrader's Calvinism and Scorsese's Catholicism bathes Travis' slaughter in the holy waters of ritual without absolving him. Travis has confused sacrifice with slaughter, *Taxi Driver* shows, so he cannot achieve martyrdom and salvation. Instead his rewards will come from Caesar and Mammon; he will be celebrated in an evil land as the new hero.[64]

Like those final moments of looking back in *The Age of Innocence* and *Raging Bull*, this is a reflection of loss and denial—essential as a disavowal of the threat of a semiotic identification.

As flâneur, Travis achieves/confirms that failure which is central to male melancholia. His flânerie sets out, in existential terms, a dynamic between his own modern heroism and its engulfment by the crowd.

This dynamic matches the notion of melancholia I have established as a dynamic between the male melancholic as 'a man apart' and as 'conformist'. Both dynamics are established upon a trajectory leading to failure. In this way, while the melancholic may not always be a flâneur, the flâneur is always a melancholic. Like the turtle-strolling arcade walker of nineteenth-century Paris, he was born at a moment of anxiety at the loss of a 'time before' brought on by the advent of modernity— the beginning of the flâneur's engulfment by the crowd.

CHAPTER FIVE

GoodFellas:

among the Italians

Ever since I was a kid I always wanted to be a gangster.

Henry Hill

The narrative of *GoodFellas* traces what Henry Hill (Ray Liotta) refers to as 'the life' he experiences on the fringe of the Italian American Mob from the 1950s to the late 1980s. Based on the true story of Henry Hill, the film opens with Henry, his friends Tommy De Vito (Joe Pesci) and Jimmy Conway (Robert De Niro) driving along a highway at night. They hear a noise coming from the car boot and pull over. Sheepishly, Henry opens the boot and reveals a bloody, half-dead character, Billy Batts (Frank Vincent), who begs Tommy for clemency. Tommy responds by repeatedly thrusting his knife into Billy's chest, before Jimmy finishes him off with a gun. Henry slams the bootshut and stares into the camera as his voice-over remarks, 'Ever since I was a kid I always wanted to be a gangster'. This macabre prologue is followed by an extended sequence of Henry's adolescence and teenage years as small time criminal selling stolen cigarettes and parking Cadillacs for the local Cicero family. Henry's adult career is charted through his organisation of the highly lucrative Air France theft, his prison experience and his drug trafficking escapades. Henry's married life with Jewish wife Karen (Lorraine Bracco) is set up against his 'family' life of involvement with Tommy and Jimmy on the fringe of the Cicero Mob.

Through Henry's eyes we gain a detailed portrait of the workings and organisation of the Italian American crime Mob—its rules and conditions of membership. The murder of Billy Batts, a 'made man', brings down the wrath of the organisation. Attending the secret ceremony in which he expects to be 'made' himself, Tommy is shot in retribution for his unauthorised murder of Batts. Throughout the narrative, Henry is reminded of one vital aspect of the Mafia code of omertà—the importance of keeping silent. Henry's own violation, prefigured by dealing drugs against the orders of his boss Paulie (Paul Sorvino), comes about when he is arrested and makes his confession to the F.B.I. Unlike Tommy, however, Henry does not receive a glorious execution at the hands of the Mob. At his trial, Henry identifies Paulie and Jimmy as the subjects of his confessions before walking out of the courtroom. Finally we see Henry's real punishment. He is destined to go on living like a 'schnook' in the mundane, suburban realities of the witness protection program. The film ends with an image of Tommy dressed in the style of the 1930s gangster and firing his gun at the audience—a symbol of the romance and excitement which Henry has lost forever.

'When you belong to a crew'

From the moment he walks into his local Mob-controlled cab-stand for an after-school job, Henry Hill is accepted into the group. Despite the fact that his voice-over has explained the fantasy nature of belonging to a crew, Henry becomes part of this world with ease. When a letter from the school truant officer threatens to upset Henry's work for the Cicero Mob, they affirm Henry's importance and sense of belonging by roughing up the mailman. When Henry is 'pinched' for selling stolen cigarettes, the all-powerful Mob embraces this twelve-year-old as a hero. It is a pattern of acceptance that is maintained throughout the narrative. Even when Henry has clearly contravened Paulie's orders against drug-trafficking and expects assassination, the Mob is reluctant to let him go. Not only does Henry walk free, but a hurt and disappointed Paulie hands him a thirty-two-hundred-dollar wad before pushing him out of the nest. On one level, it seems that Henry easily achieves a secure place within this host organisation, which requires very little of him in return.

Henry is not 'one hundred per cent Italian', so he can never be a 'made man', but beyond this, membership, to all practical purposes, is within his grasp. Wandering in and out of tribal groups, the Scorsesean male melancholic encounters very little resistance. Indeed, Henry demonstrates that, for the male melancholic, becoming a member of a tribal group is rarely a difficult thing—as long as he shows a willingness to conform to a small number of vital criteria.

Despite the apparent ease with which Henry lives in the Cicero world, I suggest that Scorsese's film emphasises the fact that Henry is a stranger to this world and that, as the film's co-author Nicholas Pileggi has said, Henry is represented as essentially a visitor and outsider.[1] One casual expression of Henry's voice-over demonstrates his awareness of his own stranger status. When Tommy is supposed to be 'made' and is in fact 'whacked', Henry's voice-over explains the situation and concludes:

> there was nothing that we could do about. Batts was a made
> man and Tommy wasn't and we had to sit still and take it
> because among the Italians it was real grease-ball shit.

Henry's mother is Sicilian and his life is spent working and in friendship with Italians, and yet, at this moment of Tommy's denial of membership, Henry designates 'the Italians' as something other than himself.

In this chapter I consider the way the male melancholics in Scorsese's films embrace the status of the stranger. *GoodFellas* provides an unusual example of the melancholic's self-estrangement. In each of the films considered so far, the Scorsesean melancholic is represented as embracing estrangement within the confines of his own tribal group. In Newland's 'madness with Madame Olenska', Jake's hoard posturing and Travis's fantasy mission, we see the melancholic affecting a scenario of difference as a means of escaping the corrupt and oppressive community immediately surrounding him. The majority of Henry Hill's story takes place outside what we might call his home community. Henry's mundane reality is indicated throughout the film and he will inevitably return to it, but the essence of the narrative captures his full enjoyment of the fantasy gangster life. It is within this expression of difference, as a gangster, that Henry's melancholic penchant for estrangement is emphasised. Even within the community of his fantasy, the melancholic will seek to be 'a man apart'.

In *Strangers To Ourselves* Julia Kristeva presents a useful profile of the stranger, an outsider, exile and foreigner, which will help to demonstrate estrangement as a key characteristic of the Scorsesean melancholic.[2] I will address Kristeva's model before concluding with a reading of the male melancholic as 'tourist', that is, one who embraces foreignness only to the point where it enhances his status within his home community. As a prelude to this discussion, however, I will consider the way in which *GoodFellas* represents Henry as a stranger to the Italian American Mob. Henry's stranger status will be discussed in four categories: the essential facts of his ethnicity, his inability to speak the Mafia language of violence, the ambivalence of his linguistic silence in relation to the Mafia code of *omertà* (the code of manliness and manly behaviour), and finally his status as stranger as emphasised by Scorsese's use of a stylistic strategy of exclusion.

Sei un mio Paesano?[3]

I have outlined the conservative nature of the tribal organisations surrounding Newland Archer and Jake La Motta. The Italian American Mob of *GoodFellas* is no less conservative and displays its totem rigidity clearly in its anxiety over ethnicity. As the 'one hundred per cent Italian' rule for Mafia membership suggests, ethnic purity is of great concern to this superstitious and backward-looking organisation. Ethnic others, such as Jimmy and Karen, as well as racial others, such as the African American, Stacks Edwards (Samuel L. Jackson), are easily condoned but never fully accepted, never trusted to be one of 'us'. Accordingly, this notion of compromised ethnicity marks the central exclusion of Henry and denies his claims for an ultimate sense of belonging. As he explains in his voice-over at the time of Tommy's 'making'/execution, it is of little significance that his mother is Sicilian—Henry's Irish blood through his father means everything.[4]

Henry's marriage to a Jew, Karen, further dilutes his Italian purity and increases his status as outsider. Tommy outlines the Mob's anti-Semitic prejudice when he tells Henry that he has encountered anti-Italian prejudice in a 'Jew broad'. Tommy is incredulous that a Jew would discriminate against an Italian. Nevertheless he enlists Henry's support in 'trying to bang this broad' and Henry agrees to go along on a 'double-date'. It is on the date when Henry is paired with Karen, following some initial indifference, that their courtship and marriage begin. As an outsider, Henry has the freedom to flout Mob ethnic prejudices that Tommy never has. Tommy's girlfriends include at least two Jewish women—one of which, in her expressed admiration of a Nat King Cole type crooner, espouses dangerous, inter-racial desires

An Irishman, two Italians and Henry Hill. Robert De Niro, Joe Pesci, Paul Sorvino and Ray Liotta in a publicity still for *GoodFellas*.

which clearly threaten him. The fact that—despite the pleas of his mother (Catherine Scorsese)—Tommy never settles down thus looks less like Don Juanism than an inability to accept an ethnically compromised woman in his mother's place. Henry, however, has no such concerns. By marrying Karen and demonstrating that freedom, Henry confirms that he never could be considered a 'real Italian' in the first place. Were he pure, like Tommy, he could never consider mating with a Jew because she would be considered as 'of the wrong tribe'.

In an excellent review of *GoodFellas*, Raffaele Caputo outlines a number of points which emphasise the displacement and exclusion of Henry as the film's central character. Commenting on a small scene which occurs at Henry's bar, 'The Suite', Caputo raises an interesting dilemma concerning ethnicity in the film. The recently paroled Billy Batts is celebrating his release and offers to buy the next round of drinks for 'those two Irish hoodlums', Henry and Jimmy.[5] Jimmy replies, 'There's only one Irish hoodlum here'—an odd comment—which, in support of his argument, Caputo reads as referring to Henry. In Caputo's reading, Jimmy's comment further emphasises the exclusion of Henry on ethnic grounds. That is to say, Jimmy designates Henry as not an Italian, not one of them, but as an Irish outsider.[6]

In contradiction, however, I suggest that Jimmy is not referring to Henry as the Irishman but to himself. The film tells us that Jimmy, whose surname is Conway, has Irish blood and it thus seems incomprehensible that he should refer to Henry as the only 'Irish hoodlum here'. For Jimmy to thus exclude Henry from an Irish heritage better supports Caputo's point about the film's strategy of excluding Henry. Ethnically Henry floats from not quite belonging to one ethnic community, to not quite belonging to another. He is neither Italian, nor Irish, nor Jewish. Henry belongs to no 'us', he is the complete foreigner.

Language Barrier i: Violence
In *Strangers To Ourselves* Kristeva considers the silence of the foreigner. Weighed down by the mother tongue, the foreigner's illusion of 'resurrection' in the new language is soon 'burst':

> when you hear, upon listening to a recording, for instance, that the melody of your voice comes back to you as a particular sound, out of nowhere, closer to the old spluttering than to today's code.[7]

Like the foreigner, upon passing into the host environment of the Italian-American Mob, Henry Hill encounters a highly elaborate code of behaviour and communication. This code is Henry's language barrier and it is in his inability to master the dialect that his estrangement is represented. Two aspects of this code will serve here to demonstrate the fact that Henry is really a stranger to this world: his reaction to the carrying out of violence, and his ambivalence over the Mafia code of omertà. In the face of these signs and the fluency of those around him, Henry's response is not only 'spluttering' but bears all the marks of what Kristeva describes as, 'the anesthesia of the person that is snatched up by a foreign language'.[8] Unable to fully articulate in the code, Henry is reduced to the silence of the foreigner.

Despite Scorsese's protestations to the contrary, violence is presented in *GoodFellas* (as in many other of Scorsese's films) as a central and regulating fact of Mob life.⁹ The murder of Billy Batts, the pay-back murder of Tommy, and Jimmy's serial assassination of the Lufthansa heist gang members (including Morrie (Chuck Low)) are central events in the film. The bloody execution of Stacks Edwards, the noisy gun-shot wounding, and later killing, of Spider (Michael Imperioli) are similarly traumatic punctuations of the text. Murder and summary violence is a language spoken in this film with fluency. None of these acts of violence, however, has anything to do with Henry and he plays no central role in carrying them out. There are three incidents in the film in which we see Henry partake in violence—the 'pistol-whipping' of Karen's neighbour, Bruce, the stand-over threats to Karen's boss and the car-seat punching of the Florida hood which leads to Henry's imprisonment. Vicious as they are, these are the sole examples of Henry engaging in any type of violent activity in the film. Furthermore, when compared with the brutal excesses of Tommy and Jimmy, Henry's flirtation with strong-arm tactics is relatively restrained. Thus I would argue that *GoodFellas* largely excludes Henry from its language of violence, representing him as neither committing acts of violence nor having such acts committed upon him.

Rather than being the instigator of acts of violence in the film, Henry is given the role of the 'straight-man', acting as a foil to the excessive and spectacular performances of Tommy (in particular) and Jimmy. In various scenes of potential physical outburst, it is Henry who plays the 'good cop' role, acting as conciliator and intermediary between Tommy or Jimmy and those who have incurred their wrath. Following Tommy's initial hostile exchange with Billy Batts at The Suite, it is Henry who apologises to Batts and diffuses the situation. When Tommy smashes a bottle over the head of Bamboo Lounge owner, Nick, and refuses to pay the bill, Henry arranges the meeting with Paulie to ensure Nick's protection against further violence. At the first of a number of important mediations between Morrie and Jimmy, Henry coos to a reluctant Morrie to pay Jimmy the money owed to him. When Jimmy bursts into the room and ropes the telephone cord around Morrie's neck, Henry tries to normalise the situation by putting on a fake laugh—as if Jimmy's violent gesture were merely a joke between friends. Accordingly we see that not only is Henry excluded from violence, but that he is an active agent in stopping or regulating violence.¹⁰

Another aspect of Henry's role as straight-man is in the way he registers a response to acts of violence and images of the macabre. Caputo has considered Henry's look of incredulity, shot by Scorsese in freeze-frame, at the shooting and knifing of Billy Batts in the film's prologue.[11] We observe similar responses of shock and horror on Henry's face (in medium close-up) after Jimmy and Tommy have kicked Batts half-dead in Henry's club, and again when Henry finds Spider shot dead, following another of Tommy's explosions. This pattern is established by Scorsese in the scenes of Henry's boyhood. When a shot and bleeding man runs into a Cicero family pizzeria, Henry responds not by locking the door, as Underboss, Tuddy (Frank Dileo), would have it, but by binding his wounds with eight aprons. Tuddy berates Henry for his lack of toughness and emphasises Henry's relative response to the violence by accusing him of wasting 'eight fuckin aprons'.

Henry's general exclusion from the notion of violence in *GoodFellas* is given sharp emphasis in his final meeting with Jimmy. Henry knows Jimmy is planning to have him murdered when Jimmy asks him to go to Florida to 'do a hit with Anthony'. In his voice-over, Henry comments that he knows Jimmy's scheme because 'Jimmy had never asked me to whack somebody before'. The two freeze-frames Scorsese employs stress the poignancy of the moment between the two long-time friends and Henry's second guessing of Jimmy's plan. A vital issue is, in the tension of the scene, however, somewhat obscured. Throughout the course of the film, *nobody* has asked Henry to 'whack' anybody before. We know that Jimmy has been doing 'hits' for the Mob since he was sixteen. Given Tommy's penchant for killing and the fact that achieving membership of the Mafia is popularly understood to be dependent upon killing, or 'making your bones', for a Mob family, we also assume that Tommy has a number of hits under his belt. Despite the fact that 'Murder for Hire' plays a demonstrative part in the world of *GoodFellas*, we neither see, hear nor assume Henry taking any role in it. His factual counterpart aside, Scorsese makes no attempt to show Henry in this role and even seems to be ridiculing him for it in this final confrontation with Jimmy.

In addition, this final encounter with Jimmy emphasises the fact that Henry is never subject to violence. Obviously, he escapes Jimmy's (and all further) attempts to murder him for his anticipated 'ratting out' of his friends and associates. Although Henry raises the ire of Paulie by abandoning Karen, peddling drugs and arousing suspicion that he will become a 'rat', Paulie never punishes him. In fact, as mentioned above, Paulie passes up a golden opportunity to punish (murder) Henry, and protect himself, in the scene in which he gives him the thirty-two-hundred dollars. Despite the fact that Henry suspects assassination as soon as he is given parole, he is never 'hit'. I will discuss the full implications of this below but here I want to comment on the effect of Henry's escape from punishment and the way it enlarges on his general exclusion from violence.

There are a number of contextual reasons as to why Henry (and Jimmy for that matter) is not punished for his involvement in the Billy Batts murder. It is clearly Tommy's argument with Batts that led to the murder and, for their part, Jimmy and Henry were merely carrying out Tommy's action. Nevertheless, Tommy's sole punishment for the murder, at the time when he expects to become a 'made man', is noteworthy for the way in which it excludes the other two, and Henry in particular. The Batts murder scenes clearly demonstrate the non-violent role of Henry in the killing. However, Henry collaborates (after the fact) with Tommy in the murder by concealing information about the killing from Paulie. Despite his (albeit minimal) involvement, Henry again escapes censure. Later when Jimmy is killing the various members of the Lufthansa robbery gang, Henry is again excluded. Jimmy's wrath had been ignited by those gang members who had threatened to betray Jimmy with their conspicuous spending of the loot. Johnny Roast Beef (John Williams) arrives at the post-heist celebration with a new wife and a new car. Carbone (Frank Sivero) arrives with his old wife, but a new mink coat. In the very next scene, Henry arrives home at Christmas, brandishing expensive presents and saying 'I got the biggest tree they had'. For his sin Johnny and his new wife end up dead, shot in the front seat of their new car. It takes the authorities two days to thaw out Carbone when they find him hooked up in a meat refrigeration truck. Despite flatly contradicting Jimmy's warning, however, Henry incurs none of Jimmy's anger. Henry is able to say that these murders 'had nothing to do with me'.

What *GoodFellas* stresses is that anything to do with its code of violence has nothing to do with Henry Hill. Not being subjected to punishment by either the Mob per se or by Jimmy, as an element outside the Mob, points to Henry's lack of presence and importance in this world. Henry's inactivity towards the violence of this world thus emphasises his estrangement. While others speak this language with fluency, Henry neither speaks nor is spoken to in a language he fails to master.

Language Barrier ii: Omertà
Henry's last memory of childhood, in the film's extended sequence of his adolescence, is the moment following his first 'pinch'. I have already

mentioned this as a moment in which Henry is embraced and popularly approved by his new Mob family. It is also the moment when he learns the most important lesson of his life with the Mob, when Jimmy tells him 'never rat on your friends and always keep your mouth shut'. Keeping silent is the cornerstone of popular representations of the Mafia code of honour and, although only one aspect of that code, it is usually considered to be its sole element.[12] In essence, *GoodFellas* is concerned with the story of a man who 'talked' and broke silence by 'ratting out' his friends in order to save himself. Given that, in popular mythology, nothing denotes a sense of belonging in Mafia circles more than the observance of omertà, nothing indicates the sense of exclusion more than the lack of its observance. Henry Hill is a stranger to the Mob because he is the ultimate non-observer of omertà. His final act of ratting confirms that which the spectator has suspected all along. Keyser quotes the comments of Scorsese's co-scriptwriter, Nicholas Pileggi, as to the real Henry Hill's ambivalence towards the whole notion of omertà:

> The honour code is a myth. These guys betray each other constantly. Once Henry's life is threatened, he has no qualms about testifying. He does no soul searching because he has no soul. The F.B.I., the marshals, were all astounded at the quickness with which he turned. I mentioned this once to Henry, and he didn't know what I was talking about.[13]

In a sense, Scorsese's film has captured the essence of the real Henry Hill's ignorance of the myth and has placed Henry as an 'innocent' within his highly complex representation of that myth. Accordingly Henry looks out of place.

Silence is the major aspect of omertà as it is considered in *GoodFellas*. It is consistently asserted throughout the narrative. The impetus for Tommy's infamous Bamboo Lounge scene, a horrific bluff/joke at Henry's expense, 'you think I'm funny?', is a gag about the interrogation of Tommy by a cop, Bing, in which Tommy refused to tell Bing anything but 'go fuck your mother'. Under the subsequent 'you think I'm funny' interrogation by Tommy, Henry flounders. This prompts Tommy to prophesy 'I wonder about you sometimes Henry, you may fold under questioning', as indeed he does at the end of the film. The anxiety about silence is further stressed in the scene when Tommy, Jimmy and Henry try to sneak undetected into Tommy's mother's house to borrow a shovel to bury Billy Batts. Tommy's mother awakens and insists on cooking for them. As they eat, Tommy's mother comments on Henry, obviously shell-shocked from the Batts incident, sitting at the dinner table in silence. This prompts her to tell a joke about her friend Campari, who, like Henry, used to sit around with friends and say nothing. When asked about it Campari replies, 'What should I say, that my wife two-times me?', to which his wife barks, 'Shut-up you're always talking'. Three times the film alludes to the dangers of mobsters who 'talk on the phone'. The third time is in the scene discussed above, when Jimmy meets with Henry for the last time. Their conversation is, in fact, another interrogation of Henry 'to see if I was going to rat them out'. As Henry observes, it is clear that Jimmy has no confidence in Henry's ability to keep silent, when he asks him to make the hit with Anthony in Florida. The victim of the putative mission is, as Jimmy says, a rat who talked.

Paradoxically, in relation to Kristeva's reading of the silence of the foreigner, in the community of the Mob it is the person (Henry in this case) who speaks and articulates who is the outsider. The natives, the hosts, demonstrate their belonging by remaining silent. Silence is a language, nevertheless, a complex code of communication which the foreigner must learn in order to have any claims on belonging. Therefore if *GoodFellas* is the story of someone who talked, it is the story of a stranger. By ratting out his friends, Henry graphically demonstrates his non-observance of omertà, essential to the wider code of membership. By talking, Henry is speaking another language and communicating with the powers of WASP authority, attracting attention to his difference and suggesting his ultimate allegiance.

Strategies of exclusion
Matching his meditations on ethnicity, violence and omertà in *GoodFellas*, Scorsese further emphasises Henry's exclusion by formal and stylistic means. A sequence early in the film demonstrates the way Scorsese and his cinematographer, Michael Ballhaus, use camera movement and the placement of Henry in the mise-en-scène to disturb our perceptions of his centrality in the narrative. Following an establishing shot of the Bamboo Lounge, the scene cuts to its interior and the camera moves through the restaurant as Henry's voice-over introduces us to the extended cast of assembled characters. Each character greets the camera—'Howyadoin buddy?', 'What's up, guy?', 'I took care of that dame for ya!'—combining with the voice-over to give the impression that they are addressing Henry. Furthermore, beyond

the effect of demonstrating Henry's 'connections', the brief context of selected greetings suggests Henry's importance through his involvement in various forms of gangster business. Having established the idea that the camera is in the place of Henry, Scorsese has Ray Liotta move into frame, not from behind the camera or over its shoulder as we expect, but from the extreme left and top of frame. Furthermore, from the fact that Henry is wheeling a trolley of fur coats into the kitchen, he is hardly in the position of the mobile character, walking the room, who was the implied subject of the camera's gaze. That gaze which the spectator took for Henry's—the gaze of an important and popular member of the group—is thus revealed as the gaze of someone else.

I have mentioned how Henry's exclusion is emphasised by the way the camera registers his response to acts of violence, particularly in close-ups of his shocked expressions. Scorsese also creates this effect by using techniques of narration, film speed, editing and sound to represent Henry's disturbed point of view and his ill-adaptation to this community so dependent upon violence. The murder of Billy Batts, for example, is represented more than once in the narrative. Like the return of the repressed, the issue of Batts' death keeps coming up to suggest its—perhaps overlooked—importance. The film opens with the shooting of Batts' bloody body in the car boot. Fifty minutes later we see the events leading up to that shooting. Then, following the Campari anecdote scene, we witness what reads like a sequence taken from Henry's distracted point of view. The scene is supported by his voice-over and its events are presented in a highly edited, temporally illogical cross-cutting montage. Minutes later Paulie asks Henry what he knows about the killing. Finally the three friends must return to the site of burial to dig up the body and relocate it for fear of its being discovered during the building of 'condos'. In the next scene, Henry, like Macbeth, cannot seem to wash away the reminders of Billy Batts from his car boot. The murder refuses to disappear and is re-presented, like a repetitive trauma across the text. Thus through the constant punctuation of the text by the Batts murder and the representation of the event from Henry's point of view, we can establish his discomfort with that act.

Another example highlights the contrast between Henry's perceptions of violence and those which the film codes as belonging to Tommy, Jimmy and the Mob insiders—the murder of Stacks Edwards. The Christmas scene preceding the murder, 'I got the most expensive tree they had', employs Henry's voice-over to suggest his own point of view. In the next scene as Tommy and Carbone enter, Henry's narration has ceased and the soundtrack playing 'Bells of St Mary's' soon fades. Tommy follows Stacks into the bedroom and, while Stacks is tying his shoelace, fires a bullet into the back of his head. Without ceremony, but with a little comic banter between Tommy and Carbone as they exit, the scene ends. The first version of the event is followed by the return of the soundtrack playing 'Bells of St Mary's' and Henry's voice-over. This second version of the same event, however, is significantly different. This, I suggest, is Henry's perception of the event, showing the way in which his anxieties about violence are magnified and his exclusion is emphasised.

This second version is stripped of the presence of Carbone, his comical routine with Tommy and the incidental chit-chat between Tommy and Stacks. The second rendition is pared down until it contains nothing but Henry's perception of its essential violence. In the first version, constructed in two takes, we see Tommy fire the first bullet, followed by a cut to Carbone coming to the door with the coffee pot. We hear Tommy fire three further shots before he enters the frame and the camera holds to watch the men as they banter and leave the apartment. By contrast, the second version highlights Henry's disturbed perception of the event. We see, in slow-motion, the firing of the gun by Tommy which, in the first version, only Carbone could see. Now Carbone is noticeably absent from his expected place in the shot. The slow-motion serves to highlight the light from the spark of the firing gun which assists this new point of view in heightening the effect of the scene's violence. This heightening of violence is nowhere more apparent than in Henry's exaggeration of the number of shots fired by Tommy following the original gunshot. Carbone saw, and the spectator heard, Tommy fire three shots. In Henry's version, however, we see Tommy fire five times. The variation of recollection continues into the second take. An alteration of mise-en-scène in Henry's version has moved Stacks's chair out of frame and his guitar into frame. Henry, it must be remembered, has previously made the association between Stacks and his guitar. In the first version the guitar was located on the other side of the bed. I suggest its placement here is not merely to indicate a character who 'used to hang around the lounge and play guitar', but to designate this as Henry's version of events. Above all, the variation suggests that perspective of the outsider, to whom killing is more than the 'no big deal' Henry once called it in his voice-over.

The most violent formal rupture of the text occurs in the trial scene when Henry directly addresses the camera and walks from the courtroom. Although the technique of direct-address is not unknown in American narrative cinema, it continues to have a startling effect on the narrative film spectator. This effect is emphasised by the fact that, although a filmmaker deeply influenced by the French New Wave (which popularised such ruptures), Scorsese had never before used this form of direct-to-camera address in a narrative fiction feature. Its use in the court-room scene, however, has a significance beyond special effects and New Wave homage. The final trial scene stands as the culmination of the sequence, beginning with the 1980s section of the film, which increasingly distances Henry from his Mob friends. This sequence, dominated by Henry's domestic affairs, his arrest and arousal of suspicion in his remaining friends, finds its ultimate destination in Henry turning to the audience and away from those (Jimmy, Paulie) who have represented his 'walk on the wild side'. When Henry addresses us, stands up and walks from the court, nobody notices. Nobody turns to stop him, nobody even watches him go. Henry says that it was easy for 'them' to disappear and this scene demonstrates the fact that he never really belonged there in the first place. Just as Henry escapes punishment by the Mob, he is allowed to walk free, confined by nothing but the suburban existence of the witness protection program where he belongs. It is as if he was never really there at all.

The melancholic as exile

> We all know the foreigner who survives with a tearful face turned towards the lost homeland. Melancholy lover of a vanished space, he cannot, in fact, get over his having abandoned a period of time. The lost paradise is a mirage of the past that he will never be able to recover.[14]

Thus far we have considered Henry as a stranger, with mention and implication of his being also an outsider, visitor and foreigner. To these categories we must also add the category of 'exile'. Just as the Scorsesean melancholic embraces loss, sacrifice and disempowerment, he also embraces the status of the stranger, which is to experience a voluntary (if temporary) exile. As flâneur we have observed the melancholic Travis's love of disguise, his embracing of estrangement and his fluidity of movement between casting himself as native and foreigner. Kristeva has observed the melancholy properties of the stranger as part of her ultimate conclusions concerning estrangement as an outward sign of the

foreignness within.[15] As John Lechte has highlighted, exile and estrangement in Kristeva's theoretical formulations and personal experience has
'had an extremely positive side to it'.[16] In this spirit, I want to make
some brief comparisons between male melancholia and some of
Kristeva's observations as to the identity of the stranger. We have seen
how the Scorsesean melancholic has cast himself as sacrificial victim and
flâneur. My emphasis here is that the male melancholic employs such a
notion of exile and estrangement as another identity position (like the
sacrificial victim or flâneur) and strategy to gain personal empowerment.

Like the male melancholic, the stranger also strives to be the man
apart. On the foreigner's face Kristeva sees 'the non-existence of
banality'.[17] The foreigner has a perspective that the hosts have not. For
Kristeva, the foreigner thinks they are the only one to possess a
biography—a life of ordeals, perhaps even catastrophes and adventures.
But less than this, at least:

> . . . simply a life in which acts constitute events because they
> imply choice, surprises, breaks, adaptations, or cunning, but
> neither routine nor rest. In the eyes of the foreigner those
> who are not foreign have no life at all: barely do they exist,
> haughty or mediocre, but out of the running and thus almost
> cadaverized.[18]

Just as the male melancholic achieves a separation from the crowd by
his affectation of insight and creative, tortured genius, the foreigner
evokes a separation from those around by an impression of living
beyond the humdrum of ordinary life.

The foreigner's particular loss is, of course, a loss of country—a
homesickness. This homesickness is the sign of a 'secret wound' which
has driven the foreigner to 'wandering' in the first place. For Kristeva,
the foreigner's most distant memory is 'delightfully bruised', and they
are misunderstood by, and a stranger to, their mother. It is this lack or
absence that the foreigner displays with pride as they wander towards
the inaccessible territory beyond.[19] Having lost their mother, this display
requires an aloofness on the part of the foreigner in the new host
community, 'the resistance with which he succeeds in fighting his
matricidal anguish'.[20] For it is part of the foreigner's wound that they
are an orphan, of no account, because, in the eyes of the host community,
they are of no origins and are guilty of parent murder:

> I erect my new life like a fragile mausoleum where their
> shadowy figure is integrated, like a corpse at the source of
> my wandering.[21]

The ambivalence the stranger holds for parents and origins is not merely
translated into pure admiration and adoration for their new host. The
lack of biography the stranger perceives in the host indicates the
humdrum and mediocre lives of the host. This is like the humdrum
existence that the stranger has left behind. As we have observed, the
male melancholic seeks the role of a man apart—recognising both
the corruption and tedium of the world or social group around him—
and thus seeks a new and unusual community to assert that status. The
male melancholic as stranger also perceives this tedium in his new
community:

> He readily bears a kind of admiration for those who have
> welcomed him, for he rates them more often than not above
> himself, be it financially, politically, or socially. At the same
> time he is quite ready to consider them somewhat narrow
> minded, blind. For his scornful hosts lack the perspective he
> himself has in order to see himself and to see them.[22]

Just as the male melancholic presents a potential danger to his friends—
an argumentativeness, rebelliousness, a disloyalty—when he becomes
the stranger his aloofness also presents the possibilities of confronting
'everyone with an asymbolia that rejects civility and returns to a violence
laid bare'.[23]

Like the flâneur, that cross-dressing hero of modernity, the foreigner
is an actor playing a variety of roles and wearing multiple masks. Had
they stayed home, Kristeva argues, the foreigner might have become a
'dropout, an invalid, an outlaw'. The male melancholic as foreigner,
like Kristeva's foreigner, boasts a fluidity of identity, a luxurious
instability of self, a settled self and no self—all to combat the politics of
being a stranger.[24]

Kristeva divides foreigners into two categories—ironists and
believers. The ironists are those who 'struggle between what is no longer
and what will never be'. The believers, however, are the true
melancholics, and they share the love of loss with the eternal optimism
of unsatisfied desire:

... there are those who transcend: living neither before nor now but beyond, they are bent with a passion that, although tenacious, will remain forever unsatisfied. It is a passion for another land, always a promised one, that of an occupation, a love, a child, a glory.[25]

The male melancholic belongs everywhere; he is at home anywhere he chooses. Globalisation is his colonialism and anywhere within it he can claim, as did John F. Kennedy in 1962, 'ich bin ein Berliner'. When he leaves home he is sorely missed and the call of duty is never far away from him. When he is away he can speak the language, when at home he can move easily among the indigenous others. Where else can he find himself a stranger but within? Kristeva's model suggests that 'one becomes a foreigner in another country because one is already a foreigner from within'.[26] The male melancholic visit is so short that, although a frequent flier, his real sense of foreignness is just as well articulated by his old maxim, 'stay at home and see the world'.

The flight from the banal
Far from placing Henry Hill as a man apart from the humdrum of everyday life, *GoodFellas* employs Henry in a lively critique of working- and middle-class American life—the life of the 'average nobody' which Henry is forced to take up at the end of the film. Henry's critique of both his own working-class origins and the middle-class malaise surrounding Karen and her family represents the essence of their flight from likeness into strangeness and the exotic attractions of their new Mob family.

Scorsese introduces us to the non-life (Henry calls his Mob existence 'the life') of Henry's working-class family in the sequence of his youth. Later in the film Henry compares his Mob life with 'those goody-good people who worked shitty jobs for bum pay cheques, who took the subway to work everyday, worried about their bills.' For Henry they 'were dead, they were suckers, they had no balls'. We know the lives of these people, because we have seen their origins in Henry's origins. Henry describes his childhood as consisting of regular beatings by his father, who was always 'pissed off' at his low income, small house and large family, and by the fact that he had a son in a wheelchair. This is the world where people have 'to wait on-line at the bakery', go to school to try to pull themselves out of the working-class lot, 'swear allegiance to the flag and sit through good government bullshit'.

Later, when Henry and Karen are living a life of excess, Karen's voice-over proudly compares Henry and his friends to those who live in this world:

> It was more like Henry was enterprising and that he and the guys were making a few bucks hustling, while the other guys were sitting on their asses waiting for hand-outs.

While Henry's escape from working-class banality may resemble a flight to a tacky middle-class lifestyle, it is not without criticism for that middle-class establishment of Karen's neighbourhood. Soon after their marriage, when Henry is out all night with his friends, we see a snapshot of that from which Henry and Karen fly. This is the life of a gilt-framed, dark wooden furniture in a soft-carpeted Jewish middle-class home, dominated by a noisy and theatrical blonde-rinse mother and diminutive, silent father—'Leave your father out of this. The man hasn't been able to digest a decent meal in six weeks.' During their courting at a respectable holiday resort, an uncomfortable Henry pulls out a wad of cash to pay a drinks bill, only to be told by Karen that 'you have to sign for it here'. It is here that they encounter Bruce—the boy next door—a well-dressed, respectable youth who drives a red sports-car and later date-rapes Karen. In contrast to their life of prosperity and camaraderie within the Mob, this picture of respectable middle-class suburban life is presented as just as stifling and tedious as life on the other side of the tracks.

If Henry and Karen's critique of working-class America is articulated verbally in their voice-overs, Henry demonstrates, physically, his loathing for suburban middle-class propriety. I have already considered the way violence estranges Henry from the Mob. When in the few brief occasions that Henry resorts to violence, it is always in establishing his connection to the world outside the Italian American Mob. When Henry assists Jimmy in beating up a Florida gangster and dangling him in the lions' cage at the zoo, they are soon successfully prosecuted and sent to gaol. Henry and Jimmy are thus made to account to the world of law and justice outside their own because the Florida gangster has a 'civilian' sister who reacted to her brother's situation by going to the police. In a brief courtroom scene, we see the sister's hysterical reaction to her brother's occupation and the friends he keeps. This is not the reaction of a Mob insider, but of one who lives in a world which finds the excesses of organised crime to be shocking and deplorable. This is the world of those who have no code of silence, the world of those who 'talk'. She is a citizen of straight society, grounded in the middle-American belief in the rule of law. Her connection to this world is no better emphasised than by the fact that she was 'working as a typist for the F.B.I'.

Another example of Henry indulging in rough-house tactics is when he enlists Jimmy and Tommy to help 'straighten out' Janice's (Henry's mistress) boss. This action is part of the lead-up to Karen discovering Henry's infidelity, her attempt to threaten him with a gun and Henry departing the marital home to live with Janice. It is a sequence which marks the high-point of Henry's excess as a gangster and his indifference to the dictates of traditional behaviour. The separation brings on a visit from Paulie and Jimmy and a stern warning to Henry that he must 'go back to the family'. The essential point is that they are not concerned with business or any core aspect of *cosa nostra*, but with Henry's obligations to his family and his own world outside the Mob's sphere of interest. A recent example from Mafia annals demonstrates this separation of business and family matters in Mob circles. In the biography *Underboss*, the story of Sammy Gravano (underboss to famous New York Mob leader John Gotti) Peter Mass relates how Gravano's wife Debbie was not harmed when Gravano 'informed' and broke omertà. It was assumed that, as part of his marital family, she had nothing to do with his life and his Mob family. Her denouncement of him by divorce was considered satisfactory.[27] In a similar way, the emphasis given to Henry's domestic obligations stresses the extent to which the film mires him in the world of middle America, outside that of the Mafia.

Nothing establishes Henry's connection to normal society more than his most violent act—the pistol-whipping of Bruce. This act is completely out of the sphere of Henry's Mob connections and reads as a violent assertion of loathing for the middle-class ties that bind Henry and Karen to normal society. Clearly the scene demonstrates Henry's ability to use violence. The fact that it is such a rare event in the film suggests that Henry uses it when he considers it is most needed. Thus he resorts to violence, not in the process of Mob business to further establish Mob ties, but to break the tie to the suburban middle-class life which is to be his destiny. The pistol-whipping thus looks like a violent and desperate assertion of his estrangement from the world Bruce inhabits. In this it is a highly successful gesture. The confidence with which Bruce greets Henry—'What do you want, Fucko'—suggests the pistol-whipping is contextually unexpected. In Bruce's suburban world of sports cars and college sweaters, people do not pistol-whip each other on the front lawn. When Henry gives Karen the bloody gun to hide, her voice-over stresses the fact that this is not seen as 'the done thing' in her neighbourhood. Nevertheless, as Karen says, 'it turned me on'. Henry's action looks very much like that of the dangerous and exciting outsider to middle-class propriety.

Significantly, however, although pistol-whipping Bruce makes Henry look like a gangster, it has no effect on further establishing his ties with the gangster world. Violence is not mobilised here by Henry on behalf of *cosa nostra*, but on behalf of Karen. The shot of Karen hiding the gun is immediately followed by their wedding. Like all Henry's acts of violence, the incident with Bruce draws Henry away from the world of Paulie and highlights the existence of the world outside the Mob and Henry's connections to it. This is the world of marriage, family, law and decency— the banal existence to which Henry returns at the end of the film.

Henry's wound

There is an amusing moment in *Raging Bull* when Jake takes Vickie to his parents apartment, clearly intending to seduce her. As they enter the apartment Jake calls out 'Daddy' but there is no reply. Jake tells Vickie that his parents are 'probably shopping'. There is a strong sense that Jake knew his parents would be out and that he has used the apparent security of their house to seduce Vickie. It is an old tactic. Whether or not Vickie is taken in by the ruse is unimportant. The joke is, not only are Jake's parents absent from *Raging Bull*, but parents are largely absent from the narratives of Scorsese's male melancholics. Newland Archer has no father and Travis's parents exist only as recipients of a card he sends to further construct his fantasy sense of self. In *Mean Streets* Charlie's parents are similarly absent—a fact which is only exaggerated by the ironed and monographed shirt left out for him by the mother we never see. Like Jesus in *The Last Temptation of Christ* and the Dalai Lama in *Kundun*, the Scorsesean melancholic renounces his mother for a new affiliation with a new father and a different family.

Henry's biological family play an unusually large role in this instalment of Scorsese's melancholic narrative—a role which emphasises his status as stranger. Their presence in the young Henry sequence and the return of the notion of biological family—Henry's brother and Karen's mother—in the final 1980s sequence indicate the role of biological family and origins in the melancholic stranger's narrative. This is what Kristeva reads as the integration of parents into the stranger's 'fragile mausoleum'. We might consider the fragile mausoleum as part of the secret heart of woes, the crypt the melancholic builds to his loss and displays as a monumental wound. Kristeva writes of the foreigner as evoking a sense of being misunderstood by his parents and thus possessing a 'delightfully bruised' memory.

Three short scenes demonstrate the origins of Henry's sense of being misunderstood, the bruising he carries into life with the new host. Henry is sent off to school by his mother standing at the front door. As we discover, he is not going to school, but she reminds him to 'bring back milk' and 'watch how you cross'. Later, when his truancy is discovered, Henry is savagely beaten by his father. Finally, Henry arrives at the front door dressed in a suit and leather shoes. It is as if he is playing the role of coming home a success, to greet his disapproving mother, who says 'you look like a gangster'. Henry is thus beaten as a kid and berated in his suit phase for being his ideal self. When his father beats him, Henry accepts this calmly as an inevitability of life, a necessary bruising he must accept in order to realise his ambitions. Furthermore, these encounters with his mother at the front door foreshadow the exile's fantasy future. Henry will 'bring back milk' in the form of success and money. The exile's real ambition is to return home in triumph— 'one day there'll be a knock at the door and it will be me'—as Travis writes home to his parents. At the beginning of his journey, however, the stranger is the subject of the disapproval which frees him from his family bonds.

The only time we see Henry's parents again is at his wedding when, following the breaking of the glass, the scene cuts to Karen's parents, looking concerned, and then pans to Henry's parents, looking out of their depth. They remain so much out of their depth that we will not see them at the dream-like wedding breakfast which follows, nor for the rest of the film. Significantly, we do see Karen's family again. Henry's return from 'the life' will not be to the working-class drudgery of his parents, but to the relative ethnic and class difference of an existence similar to Karen's origins. The wedding scene thus demonstrates Henry's display and 'execution' of his parents. At the wedding breakfast, Henry's parents are presumably stuck in a corner, forced to watch him being fêted by his new family with money and glitz. Henry's parents are uncomfortable because they are unable to compete. Henry wears their embarrassment and discomfort like a wound, just as at the same time he 'executes' them—perhaps his most violent gesture—and proclaims himself 'orphan'.

I have already noted that it is odd that such an Italian American Mob 'wannabe' as Henry should marry a Jew. An Italian marriage, if allowed, would clearly enhance his alliance with Paulie's family. What is more, Tommy's expression of the ethnic inferiority of a 'Jew broad' would appear to stigmatise marriage with Karen, to wound Henry all over again with the tag of stranger. But stranger is just what Henry wants to be. His marriage to Karen is clearly based on her arousal of desire, but, conscious or not, this marriage clearly provides Henry with a separating factor which he may wear like a fresh wound to sign his ambivalence for his new host culture.

Henry's ambivalence

When Karen goes to a hostess party, the ambivalence she and Henry maintain for their host environment is indicated by her view of the Mob wives, their 'bad skin, too much make-up . . . double-knits and pant-suits', as vulgar and cheap.[28] As Kristeva points out, the stranger exercises an ambivalence for the new community when its own humdrum and mediocre nature becomes clear. Just as Henry saw Paulie and Jimmy as omnipotent, he soon sees them as vulnerable and weak. It

Scorsese and 'the most feared guy in the city' (Robert De Niro) on the set of *GoodFellas*.

is not a long journey from the young Henry's vision of Paulie in the 1950s as a distant deity to the broken and sad figure of the 1980s, destined to die a lonely death in prison. One of the last images we see of Jimmy—'the most feared guy in the city'—is of him as a somewhat comical suburban figure answering the door in a blue terry-towelling bath robe. The penultimate image we have of Tommy is of him lying dead in his own blood. Just as Henry has full knowledge of the fascination and attraction of the Mob, like the foreigner he clearly sees the oppression, narrow-mindedness, fear and lack of perspective that goes with it. While demonstrating a willingness to collaborate with this regime, Henry quickly draws on a sense of rebellion and disloyalty. He has no qualms about flying in the face of Paulie's dictates against peddling drugs and, as stated, his only concern about 'ratting out his friends' is that he should go 'no place cold' when he enters the witness protection program.

Henry as *Inglesi Italianato*

As someone who tries to eradicate his origins by immersing himself in a new culture, Henry plays many roles. The exile is an actor playing the role of one who does not belong to their culture of origin. Similarly, any attempt by the exile to fit into the new culture is purely theatrical. Thus in Henry's attempts to become one with the Italian American Mob, he plays at not belonging to the banal world of his parents. What Paulie and Jimmy do not see in Henry is that, as an actor pretending to be one thing rather than another, Henry is the *Inglesi Italianato*, which Dante—himself an exile—called 'the Devil incarnate'. Just as Henry betrays his own origins, he will betray his new family.

Like the flâneur, the matricidal exile wears masks to cover over his wound, his complete lack of identity. As a character that Scorsese uses to guide us through this other world, Henry has been considered by a number of critics as little more than a cipher.[29] No matter how much screen time Henry occupies, the casting of Liotta always ensured that Henry's centrality in the narrative would be continually challenged by the iconic presence of De Niro and Pesci. As in the case of Charlie in *Mean Streets* and Newland in *The Age of Innocence*, the male melancholic's subjectivity is frequently undermined by the way the spectator's attention is diverted by the melancholic's more attractive and excessive other. Johnny Boy's anarchism in *Mean Streets* and Ellen Olenska's rebelliousness are, indeed, the very qualities that attracted the melancholic to them in the first place. It is little wonder that they should occlude the presence of the melancholic himself. Keyser points out that, as the F. B. I. used Henry Hill as a means to read the Mafia, so too Scorsese guides us to look at the more interesting details of Mob life through Henry.[30] Thus *GoodFellas* provides an interesting example of the way in which the Hollywood star system, and casting habits, can assist in decentring a character such as Henry. Looking through Henry at the performances of Scorsese regulars such as De Niro and Pesci, we inevitably question the extent to which Henry exists with a full subjectivity within the text. Walking from the witness stand at the end of the film, unopposed, uncontested and unnoticed, Henry hardly seems to exist in their world at all.

Henry as tourist

The final image of Tommy, firing his gun at the audience, is not a flash-back to any event which happened in the film. Just as Newland sees a sunny vision of Ellen Olenska at the lime-rock lighthouse turning to smile at him, this image of Tommy is Henry's fantasy of desire. Perhaps Jake's final vision, that of himself in the mirror, is the more honest of Scorsese's melancholics. Henry and Newland are conjuring images of the other merely in order to relive the ideal image of self. For located now back in the realm of the audience, Henry, as Kathleen Murphy says,[31] constructs this image as travel souvenir, a reminder of his desired self, the bounty of loss he sought from his voyage. That was the point of the entire journey. Henry's ambivalence masks an important element of his true desire. He does not want to be a full member of either the Italian American Mob or the mundane world of his working-class origins. As a melancholic, he is not so much a foreigner to the Mob or a stranger to his family, but a stranger to himself. As what Kristeva calls a 'believer', Henry memorialises the image of Tommy as the perfect gangster as that which he has lost and that which remains forever just out of reach.

Henry begins his journey peeping through the blinds at his local cab-stand longing for the fascinating world of the Mob which operates from there. That journey finishes some thirty years later with Henry stranded deep within a Levit Town suburbia, day-dreaming of the Mobster life he has lost. I have considered the extent to which this loss is prefigured in the narrative, both as a voluntary and involuntary process for Henry. Henry is seen in the film as an ethnic foreigner, a stranger to Mafia code and custom as well as being generally decentred from pride of place in the narrative and excluded from a position of knowledge and control.

Indulging in the status of the stranger, however, Henry plays an active role in his estrangement from Mob culture. If the Italian American Mob and the life of a 'wiseguy' is Henry's desire, it is only to be enjoyed temporarily before being jettisoned and reconfigured as Henry's beautiful memory and object of loss. Considering Henry's gangster past as a 'foreign country', we might conclude that whichever role the Scorsesean melancholic may play—foreigner, stranger or exile—he is undoubtedly, above all, a tourist. Just as the nineteenth-century flâneur seemed a world away from the New York cabbie life of Travis Bickle, so too it is difficult to conceive Henry Hill as the guide-book-waving, Pentax-snapping tourist. Nevertheless, the profile of the tourist provides us with a useful description of the melancholic's brief journey beyond the confines of his home base, and back again.

In *The Tourist Gaze: Leisure and Travel in Contemporary Society*, John Urry details a number of criteria concerning the practice of tourism that we should apply to Henry and the Scorsesean male melancholic in general. 'Tourism', Urry argues, 'results from a basic binary division between the ordinary/everyday and the extraordinary'.[32] The notion of tourist 'departure' from 'normal society' bears a striking similarity to Henry's experience inside and outside Mafia circles:

> . . . the notion of 'departure', of a limited breaking with established routines and practices of everyday life and allowing one's senses to engage in a set of stimuli that contrast with the everyday and the mundane.[33]

Three of Urry's nine characteristics of tourism relate directly to the experience of the melancholic tourist. The inevitable association of leisure tourism with organised work suggests the fact that one cannot exist without the other.[34] We recall that Henry's narrative stages a strong critique of organised, nine-to-five work just as it frequently involves a mixing of Mob work and leisure activities, as when Paulie sends Henry to Florida with Jimmy. Henry's experience with the Mob, when considered within the tourist framework as fun, enjoyable and outside organised work, must inevitably suggest the potent and regulating existence, somewhere, of the opposite of all this. Urry stresses the 'short term and temporary nature' of the tourist's 'residence elsewhere', which clearly depends upon an 'intention to return "home" within a relatively short period of time'.[35] As we see both in Henry and other Scorsesean melancholics, the experience of that place beyond home is merely a place to visit. This experience is always predicated on an eventual return home, whether it be to the middle-America of *GoodFellas*, collaboration with the Mob in *Raging Bull* or the tribal community of families in *The Age of Innocence*. Finally, in Urry's assertion of the role of daydream and fantasy in the anticipation of 'intense pleasure', we can make a connection to Henry's youthful yearning to visit Mob culture. So, too, in the nostalgia and fantasy he demonstrates throughout the narrative, Henry further suggests a yearning and an anticipation of experiencing those pleasures again.[36]

Like the male melancholic performance, travel, or the role of the tourist, is intimately bound to the issue of status. Urry reads travel as being as important an accoutrement to comfortable, modern society as owning a car or 'nice house'.[37] If Henry belongs in a middle-class milieu this notion of status is important. The status he achieves in middle-class society is largely derived from that which assists his melancholic desire to be a man apart. His experience of being a tourist is much higher up in the hierarchy of destinations. Like Jake La Motta performing his loss at the Barbizon Plaza, Henry lures us in to hear of his experience because, as he has been on such an exciting and unusual journey, we consider it and him fascinating. Like the tourist who has returned from some far-flung and dangerous destination, the male melancholic loves to boast of it and bask in the extra status it gives him in his dull home community.

The dubious claims by the melancholic tourist as to the authenticity of their experience is further undermined by theoretical formulations of tourism which have emphasised the falseness of the tourist 'event'. Urry considers the importance of Daniel Boorstin's 'pseudo event', that is, the event as presented to tourists, often in groups, which is especially constructed for easy consumption. This is the world of 'photo-stops' and attractions brought to the tourist within easy reach of coach depots and public conveniences. Such attractions stand in for 'real' cultural experience while being conspicuous for the way they dilute those experiences to cater to the tastes and requirements of mass tourism. The male melancholic always distances himself from the crowd, but nevertheless shares a similarly constructed and diluted experience with his coach tour counterpart. For all the 'action' that Henry sees, his inability to be privy to the undisclosed world of the Mafia and his ignorance and separation from vital information and events in the text suggests the extent to which his experience of the Mafia event is largely mediated and 'circumscribed'.[38]

Finally, through the work of Dean MacCannell, Urry links the tourist's quest for authenticity with a modern expression of the pilgrim's quest for the sacred.[39] This provides us with a useful comparison for understanding the male melancholic's journey. As Urry paraphrases Victor Turner's analysis of the pilgrim's journey:

> Important rites de passage are involved in the movement from one stage to another. There are three such stages: first, social and spatial separation from the normal place of residence and conventional social ties; second, liminality, where the individual finds him/herself in an 'anti-structure . . . out of time and place'—conventional social ties are suspended, an intensive bonding 'communitas' is experienced, and there is a direct experience of the sacred or supernatural; and third, reintegration, where the individual is reintegrated with the previous social group, usually at a higher social status.[40]

For present purposes, the key to Turner's analysis lies in the third stage, marked by the notion of 'reintegration'. For the Scorsesean melancholic the 'direct experience of the sacred or supernatural' is never an end in itself. Rather, the sacred is nearest when it is lost. Henry's experience of 'communitas' has more in common with the pilgrim than the tourist, in that it is more substantial. Like the tourist, however, Henry is telling his story from the safety and comfort of his home environment. It is a 'true story' bathed in the selected memory of nostalgia. For its audience it paints a picture of Henry Hill as a gangster—foreigner and outsider to mainstream society. But the label of 'tourist' reads as a far more accurate description of the melancholic's self-estrangement. He may lecture on the customs of the foreigner at length and with anthropological detail, but the more he does, the less convincing is his disguise. Seeing him as he really is, as tourist, the male melancholic's strategy of estrangement is exposed as another approach to hiding his profound sense of loss with a ruse of difference and empowerment.

CHAPTER SIX

Cape Fear:

the white trash angst

> You're gonna learn about loss.
>
> *Max Cady*

*Cape Fear* is framed at beginning and end as Danny Bowden's (Juliette Lewis) family holiday reminiscence. It concerns the return of 'ex-con' Max Cady (Robert De Niro), into the life of his former lawyer, Sam Bowden (Nick Nolte). Cady stalks Sam and his dysfunctional family, kills the family dog, rapes Sam's colleague, cum mistress, Lori (Illena Douglas), and confronts both Sam's wife, Leigh (Jessica Lange), and his daughter, Danny. Despite his articulated desire for Leigh (and Danny), Max's deeper motives are obscure. In his frequent encounters with Sam, however, Max tells Sam that he is 'gonna learn about loss'. Max has become a lawyer ('to all practical purposes') while in prison for an aggravated sexual battery conviction and knows Sam's secret. While acting as Max's lawyer, Sam withheld a report on the promiscuity of Max's victim which might have helped him in obtaining a lesser sentence. Having endured fourteen years of imprisonment as a result, Max has returned to teach Sam the meaning of loss.

Despite his actions, Max now seems to be immune from prosecution. With residence and legal tender, Max avoids the usual police persecution of white-trash. Lori, a clerk of the court, has seen the harassment of female victims in rape cases and refuses to testify against Max. When Sam engages a private dick, Kersek (Joe Don Baker), to follow Max and have him beaten-up in a so-called hospital job, Max not only discovers he is under surveillance, but powerfully out-manoeuvres Kersek's hired goons. Finally, Max engages Lee Hiller (Gregory Peck)—'the best criminal lawyer in the state'—to represent him only a day before Sam attempts to do the same. With Lee Hiller's representation, Max has Sam's original restraining order reversed. Legally, Sam becomes the threat and Max is considered 'beyond reproach'.

Without recourse to the law, Sam must deal with the continued threat from Max outside it. With the help of Kersek, Sam arranges a stake-out, set up to induce Max to break into the Bowden home so that he can be shot. The plan fails, however, and Max further demonstrates his ability to slip in and out of the house by murdering Kersek and the Bowden family maid. The Bowdens flee New Essex for the site of their once idyllic family houseboat holidays, Cape Fear. On the river the family believe themselves to be safe until Max appears and proceeds to rape both Leigh and Danny. Danny manages to set Max alight causing him to leap from the boat and the family to think him gone, once again. Max reappears, however, takes the family hostage and enacts a mock trial of Sam, accusing him of betrayal and condemning him to the ninth circle of hell. As the houseboat is on the verge of destruction, however, Sam manages to handcuff Max to it. Speaking in tongues and singing hymns, Max sinks to the bottom of the river with the house boat just as Sam and the family emerge from the mud.

'I aint no white trash piece of shit . . .'

Cape Fear is a tale of white bread mainstream Anglo-America. Like *The Age of Innocence* its Scorsesean mob is once again the urban middle class. The film's melancholic, Sam Bowden, is not part of a socio-cultural sub-group like Jake La Motta, Travis Bickle or Henry Hill. As with Newland Archer, Sam is a member of the American white Anglo-Saxon upper-middle classes. As lawyers, both Sam and Newland professionally embody their connection not only to the law, but also to the institutions of authority and privilege in their respective communities. Furthermore, both Newland and Sam are represented in relation to their families and, by implication, the wider network of families which make up middle-class society. Accordingly, Sam and Newland are located much closer to the centre of political and civic authority in the community than Scorsese's wiseguys and urban loners. In this sense, the narratives of Sam and Newland suggest wider implications for melancholia within the Scorsesean body politic. When the male melancholic is represented at the apex of authority in his community, we may consider the extent to which his melancholia becomes a dominant factor in the ideology of that community. Through the narratives of Sam and Newland we may better assess the relationship, in Scorsese's films, between male melancholia and the body politic of the Scorsesean melancholic world.[1]

Scorsese's *Cape Fear* represents an illness of the body politic through its articulation of crisis at the heart of the law and the family, both perverted and contaminated by middle-class liberal notions of morality and the democratic state. More so than in any of the films discussed so far, *Cape Fear* demonstrates the extent to which the male melancholic, Sam, is complicit is creating this illness. Like his fellow melancholics, Sam is similarly ambivalent about the decadent values and crumbling institutions of the community around him. What *Cape Fear* emphasises, however, is the way in which the melancholic's ennui actively contributes to the general malaise which he pretends to despise.

Outside the body politic of *Cape Fear* lies another social strata, embodied by Max Cady, which rises up in the midst of the general crisis. The Scorsesean narrative of the male melancholic has always concerned itself with an object of desire outside the mob or tribal group. In Max Cady, however, *Cape Fear* presents Scorsese's most forceful assertion of that outsider. The film pays its major attention to Max as representative of the social under-class which it designates as 'white trash'. Through Max's excesses of performance and bodily discourse, the white trash element is represented as a forceful and attractive spectacle. As white trash, Max has been victim of Sam's exploitation. Like Ellen Olenska, Joey and Vickie, Max's past contains an experience of victimisation at the hands of the melancholic's perverse notion of desire. In this case, that perverse desire is Sam's liberal, middle class conscience. Unlike the quiet resignation of Ellen and Joey, Max Cady powerfully embodies the vengeance of the male melancholic's victim. He has endured loss—real loss as opposed to the male melancholic's play loss—and takes it upon himself to teach Sam the true nature of loss. Despite the force of violence with which Max enacts this lesson, however, it makes no lasting challenge to melancholic authority. The articulation of this victim-other in *Cape Fear* merely increases the terms of melancholic desire and the pursuit of loss. The narrative plays out in a familiar fashion. The male melancholic, Sam, pursues the object of his perverse desire, Max, to the fullest extent before destroying his nemesis and returning safely to the family at the end of the film, as producer, Steven Spielberg, required.[2]

In this chapter I consider the way Max Cady represents a white trash challenge to the traditionally empowered, but fast decaying, middle class mob of the Scorsesean world. Max articulates the discontent and the feelings of rejection experienced by the male melancholic's victim in class terms; that is from the perspective of a white, working class, conservative rural minority—the white trash of the middle class body politic. Max's rhetoric complains of the loss of the sturdy, old-time values suffered at the hands of an increasingly professional, middle-class, liberal, urban-centred and atheistic society. *Cape Fear* expresses this class and socio-political discontent through Max Cady as a figure of white trash angst. Cady embodies the fear and threat of an ultra-conservative revolt against the inequities and perversions of the body politic. Not immediately eradicated, this revolt is permitted to perform for Sam and the body politic. It is this performance of loss which the male melancholic and body politic love to watch. It ignites their common desires and anxieties over the fear of loss, just as it enables them to master that fear. As a narrative which incites common fears over the disruption of order and authority, *Cape Fear* is an experience of that which Julia Kristeva has termed 'abjection'—a site of horror and loathing which is at once a sign of life.[3] Max Cady and his white trash challenge, thus stands as a potent reminder to the Scorsesean tribe that fears that it is itself white trash.

The law in crisis

The first time we see Sam in *Cape Fear* he is coming out of court with his colleague, Tom. We learn that Sam has done some legal work for Tom's daughter who, evidently, is involved in a complex divorce and property settlement. Tom is happy with the outcome and thanks Sam. Momentarily the legal system appears to be working. What the film uncovers however, as this first scene demonstrates, is that if the law is perceived to be working, it is working on behalf of a minority middle-class legal fraternity, those who have direct access to it and the resulting protection of their own middle-class property and values. The crisis of the law presented in *Cape Fear* is described as a threat, not to abstract notions of the law as provider of 'justice for all', but to the law as pro-tector of the rights and privileges of the few. Sam's original crime, withholding the promiscuity report, has compromised any claims of the law he represents to signifying itself in absolute and universal terms. Sam's act of hypocrisy has enabled the crisis. In *The Age of Innocence* and Scorsese's Mafia films we have noted the decline in strict observation of rules and codes of behaviour. Similarly in *Cape Fear* the law is rendered as an arbitrary and relative system of empowerment which, as a result of Sam's act, may now be questioned, challenged and opposed by alternative, or in this case, ultra-traditionalist philosophies.

Max Cady—and the inability of the authorities to prosecute him for the crimes he commits—represents the greatest crisis for the law. There is already sufficient indication of corruption and compromise surrounding the legal system in Sam's community. These are not so much created by Max as they are demonstrated as pre-existing and merely brought out into the open upon his return. The minority-serving law seems to be working well when, on Sam's whim, the police officer (Robert Mitchum) is able to arrest and body search Max on a trumped-up charge.[4] However, later in the film, the policeman has to resort to advising Sam to 'take the law into his own hands', by setting up Max in a break-and-enter situation where he can be shot, legally. When Sam challenges this improper suggestion, in one of his many performances as noisy upholder of the law, the policeman has to back-track and assert the correct ethical position—for the record. What is made clear here is that the legal system is impotent when challenged by a figure like Max and unable to protect its own citizens even through proper legal channels. As Kersek suggests:

> this system is set up to handle generalized problems like burglary and robbery. But if some lone creep out there targets you for some obscure reason, the system is slow, skeptical, it's pathetic even.

The very existence of Kersek as private dick, a staple of the noir/crime thriller genre, highlights the weakness and inadequacy of the law at this level of enforcement.

Lori's unwillingness to testify to her own rape by Max is a chilling reflection on the general picture of legal decay in *Cape Fear*. Lori is a clerk of the court and knows the procedure. As she tells Sam, she will be asked to explain what she was doing alone in a bar, what she was wearing and, furthermore, she will be grilled about her relationship with Sam. Lori is well aware that rape cases highlight the gender and sexual inequality of women before the law. As an experienced legal worker, she has seen the way women who are the victims of rape easily become subject to accusations by clever and unfeeling legal sharks. It might be argued that such cases demonstrate the prejudicial nature of patriarchal law as operating at the height of its powers—protecting itself from the threat of dangerous and sexually active women. The crisis is felt at the heart of that law in this case, however, when patriarchy, and Sam, require the law to protect itself by giving justice to Lori. The law is so used to punishing minorities (women in this case) that it cannot be stopped from doing the same when its traditional beneficiaries require it. *Cape Fear* thus demonstrates the way in which the law can turn upon its makers.

If the return of Max Cady is symptomatic of this weakening of the law, 'Slippery Sam' as Leigh calls him, the legal eagle, is seen as the cause of the impending crisis. Leigh and Danny are continually reminding him of his career of legal manipulations. Following the ethical disaster of Sam's hospital job, Tom expects him to act on behalf of Tom's daughter in such a way that Sam will risk perjury. Tom describes the hospital job as 'stupid' but his own request, in terms of legal ethics, as 'no big deal'. Once Sam has been seen to disregard legal ethics, it is expected that he will continue to act with dubious professionalism. As Sam becomes further embroiled with Max Cady, however, he develops an increased consciousness as to his legal code of responsibilities. Twice the policeman, played by Robert Mitchum, reminds Sam, 'You're a lawyer Mr. Bowden, you oughta know that'. When Kersek first suggests the hospital job, Sam shuns the suggestion by saying 'I can't operate outside the law, the law's my business'. Nevertheless, he has already gone outside the law, as we understand it through the narration of his original encounter with Max fourteen years before.

The origin of the crisis of the law in *Cape Fear* is thus located within the actions of Sam and his original, arbitrary decision to conceal the evidence which might have gained Max a lesser sentence. Nobody watching the film could deny that Sam had just cause. Indeed, his action of personally denying the validity of the question of promiscuity directly addresses the concerns raised by Lori following her rape. The action was, however, directly in violation of the sixth amendment granting every individual the right to counsel for his/her defense. Moral outrage at the actions of a rapist is thus placed up against the sixth amendment—a central tenet of freedom and liberal democracy. The spectator's sympathy with Sam's original actions places both parties in a hypocritical position of denying Max's constitutional rights. As Tom quips, 'Some folks just don't have the right to the best defence, eh Sam?' The crisis of the law is thus coloured both by politically correct notions of what should and should not be allowed as evidence in rape cases, and social/moral distinctions based around the relative rights of a suspected rapist. Sam's original action has demonstrated that the law is not a fixed system of justice but an arbitrary set of rules designed to protect privilege according to the dictates of fashion and contemporary morality. Thus revealed, if the law can reflect the morality of the empowered democratic left, why not the morality of the white trash conservatives on the right?

The family in crisis

The crisis *Cape Fear* reveals in the law is that, although it is set up to serve the needs of those in power, observance of the law *to the letter* can damage the interests of its traditional beneficiaries. As Lesley Stern points out, it is just this *letter of the law* that Max Cady is insistent upon.[5] Sam's abandoning of the letter of the law, for all its inequalities, has turned it against him. Similarly the crisis in Sam's family is cast as the result of his abandoning his traditional role as patriarch in favor of a liberal and equivocating attitude towards family life. Just as Sam thinks he can serve the law according to his own bleeding-heart conscience, he also considers that he may exercise his role as patriarch with varying severity. From this perspective, the crisis at the heart of Sam's family is not a consequence of his infidelities, his disrespect for Leigh nor his incestuous desire for Danny.[6] As Freudian psychoanalysis tells us, these fantasies and indulgences are constitutional to the family and ought to be subject to its repressive authority. The crisis has arisen from his unwillingness to assert the traditional responsibilities of the patriarch to maintain order and to regulate sexuality within the family. Just as the crisis of the law comes about with his weakness as law maker so, too, the crisis of the family lies in Sam's weakness as patriarch.

Sam's lack of authority is obvious from the way Leigh and Danny ridicule him throughout the film. A comic example of this contempt is found in the scene when Sam and Leigh argue over his philandering. As their arguing subsides and they concentrate on the threat posed by Max, Sam articulates his fear and asks Leigh to stick with him in confronting it. It is a clichéd film strategy and we half expect it to end with Leigh acknowledging Sam's right and making a practical, if reluctant, reconciliation for the common good. No such reconciliation is made however, and Sam is seen in the next take bedding down for the night, not next to Leigh but on the couch.

Perhaps Sam's greatest crime against the semi-fascist code of authority evident in *Cape Fear* is that of fostering the culture of his melancholic ambivalence in his family. Intolerant of the decadent mob surrounding him, the male melancholic is always attracted to the performance of loss staged by his other. This performance of loss both incites and fuels the melancholic's feelings of rebellious hostility and his tendency towards conformity which Freud sees in the melancholic's constitutional ambivalence.[7] In this flirtation with loss the melancholic's ambivalence gleefully embraces the fantasy of escaping from or destroying the authority of his tribal group. Max Cady's performance of loss in *Cape Fear* offers Sam a similar fantasy of escape and destruction while, at the same time, emphasising the dire consequences for him should he give himself over to such a notion of loss. Max thus emerges in *Cape Fear* to excite, punish and correct the crime of ambivalence in Sam. It is to Sam's own family, however, that we should look first for the primary expression of loss and the desire for destruction fostered by the melancholic's own ambivalence.

Sam's ambivalence towards such notions of patriarchal authority is read through his experience of the loss, discontent and despair of Leigh and Danny. Much has been made of Danny as a problem child, and of the way she embodies the incestuous desires of her father. Here I want to focus on Sam's crime of ambivalence in so far as it engages with Leigh's profound sense of loss and developing feelings of ambivalence. In the closing sequences of the film, when Max finally confronts the family on the house boat, Leigh makes a speech about loss. Halting Max in his intention to rape her and Danny, Leigh speaks of her own loss, telling him of her experience of losing time, losing years. Comparing her loss to Max's, she begs him to do 'whatever' he had planned with her alone and not with Danny—'I could share this with you . . . because we have this connection.' The substance of this connection is, of course, the treachery and betrayal they have experienced at the hands of Sam. For Leigh, this took the form of Sam's infidelity which, as we discovered earlier in the film, played a major role in the onset of her nervous breakdown. These years were her lost years, a period of immense disenchantment and feelings of inferiority and insecurity. Importantly for Leigh, these years also bred the type of ambivalence in her own family and marriage that Sam has demonstrated in the legal and professional sphere.

A short scene during the stake-out sequence demonstrates the extent of Leigh's ambivalence and the extent to which Sam's perverse desires to allow his family to be exposed to Max's assault has become her own.

Late at night, Sam is reading in bed as Leigh tries to sleep next to him. He is reading the Book of Job from The Bible and Leigh surmises that, like her, Sam is looking for answers. Passing a cigarette back and forward between them, Leigh says:

> I'd like to know just how strong we are, or how weak. But I guess the only way we're gonna find that out is just by going through this.

Hardly acknowledge this comment, Sam summarises the Book of Job:

> Job was a good man, he believed in God. And God tested his faith and took away everything he had—even his children.

Looking on in a lazy wide-eyed manner, Leigh casually waves away the cigarette smoke and the sound track makes an eerie noise, like air being sucked through a lead pipe. Immediately the scene cuts to Danny, jumping up out of a bad dream as the camera fast tracks into a close up on her distracted face.

It is a highly disturbing scene. Spoken in little above a whisper, it has an intimacy about it which combines with a tired sensuality in alarming contrast to the terror of the thoughts and ideas expressed. The scene speaks not of fear but of desire. As the shot scale of the sequence gradually tightens-in on the faces of the actors, the camera gives strong emphasis on, what might well be described as Leigh's bedroom eyes. Similarly, her dragging on a cigarette places emphasis on her light red lips in addition to the misty atmosphere provided by the smoke and the traditional erotic connotations of the cigarette as a post-coital prop. Playing with her hair as she lies back on her pillow and contemplates the potential destruction of her family/marriage, her desire and her fear seem to have met to form a new perverse desire. Similarly, Sam, who previously has expressed concerns about the dog sitting on the table and Leigh making jokes about incest and necrophilia, seems strangely calm at the fate of his family as foretold by the prophet Max.

The ambivalence of Sam's feelings towards his family has become Leigh's. Just as Sam has so often demonstrated his willingness to sacrifice the well-being of his family, Leigh now embraces Max's attack as a welcome intervention. Whereas earlier in the film she guiltily wiped away the lipstick applied just before Max's first intrusion into the home, in this scene she lies back hungrily anticipating him. The luxuriant decadence of the scene summarises the mood. Abandoned by Sam, Leigh and Danny both look to Max for the sexual and emotional satisfaction that should be the responsibility of Sam. Violence and destruction at the hands of Max is preferable to the absentee authority of Sam. Such an encounter with fear, terror and the horror of family decay, is perhaps the only viable method of continuing. Only through the violent destruction, the result of ambivalence, can the life of the family be assured.

The family is shown in *Cape Fear* to be perverse. If Leigh and Danny welcome Max's attack it is due to Sam's confused response to the requirement of the role of patriarch. Sam's melancholic ambivalence has rendered him useless in the patriarch's task of the safe regulation of authority and sexuality within the family. In these terms, the crisis of the family in *Cape Fear* is that Sam's perversion of melancholia and ambivalence has led him to relinquish his responsibility as the primary agent responsible for the suppression of desire. The family is in crisis, according to the laws of patriarchy, because its woman and children are no longer subject to the forces of sexual repression.

Rather than playing the role of despotic patriarch, Sam's familial crisis is, in part, the result of his bleeding heart liberalism. Several factors help us construct a social profile of Sam which distances him from the

The family in crisis. Juliette Lewis, Jessica Lange and Nick Nolte in *Cape Fear*.

role of patriarch essential to the maintenance of traditional family order. Early in the film, when they are discussing Danny's suspension for smoking dope, Sam reminds Leigh that they 'smoked a lot of dope' in their younger days. We later learn that Sam worked in the Office of the District Attorney where he made, what has to be considered the political decision, of dismissing the evidence of promiscuity against his client's victim. Finally we learn that following one of Sam's affairs he agreed to go to marriage counselling. Sam is hardly presented as the traditional God and country family conservative, defender of the rights of the father. In the eyes of those, like Max, who call for traditional values and morality, Sam looks very much like an ex-dope-smoking hippy who has matured into a bleeding-heart, civil libertarian, public-defender type, commonly found in *Dirty Harry* films as protectors of the right of criminals and left-wing causes.

Beyond the body politic

Excluded from the spheres of law, order and family, Max is represented in *Cape Fear* as white trash, ex-con and Pentecostal cracker from the hills. He is thus drawn as a representative of that rural based, under-educated, socially conservative, and often religiously fundamentalist class popularly described as hillbillies or rednecks. The film frequently refers to Max as white trash, thus providing a social and class-based description of the origins of his complaint and the nature of his loss. As white trash, Max has no place in what the film's screenwriter, Wesley Strick, has described as the yuppified environment of the 'New South'.[8] When Max is confronted by Kersek and asserts his right to stay in New Essex, Kersek outlines the attitude towards the disenfranchised, criminal classes, by calling Max a 'white trash piece of shit' and telling him, 'I don't give a rat's ass about your rights'. Throughout the film Sam casually comments on Max being an ex-con, summarising the implications of this tag to Tom by saying 'you know as well as I do what that means'. Max's social status is thus determined as the key element in discrimination against him, particularly by the law as represented by Sam. Max's response is driven by his heightened awareness that Sam—and the community he represents—considers themselves socially superior.

In complaining about his loss, Max speaks for the white trash class which have similarly been disenfranchised by the social and political process. For Max it is this type of discrimination which is to blame for the loss of fourteen years of his life in prison, the loss of his family and the little sense of self-respect he once had. This has made him a victim of the law which refuses to recognise his citizenship under its rule. One scene in particular demonstrates the force of Max's complaint against his social and economic discrimination. During the stake-out sequence Kersek hears a suspicious noise in the kitchen. Looking into it with gun poised, he is relieved to find that the noise is merely that of the Bowden's maid, Graciella, preparing a midnight snack. Thinking nothing of the maid's inarticulate replies to his questions, Kersek sits down to pour himself a drink. Scarcely has Kersek embarked on a boring tale of past stake-out hi-jinks, when we discover the maid is not Graciella but Max, sporting a wig seemingly on loan from the set of Hitchcock's *Psycho*. Slitting Kersek's throat in one fluid gesture, Max laughingly berates his prey with the same taunts Kersek once taught him:

> I learned that in prison, you like? You white trash piece of shit!

As Pam Cook has pointed out there are strong inter-connections between class, gender and ethnicity made in this scene which place the episode of disguise and gender transformation beyond its obligatory reference to *Psycho*.[9] Like the Hispanic serving woman, Max is considered an unwanted alien in this community. He has no rights to a place of his own apart from that of serving the pleasure of the ruling elite. The spectator may be surprised to find that it is Cady not Graciella in the kitchen behind Kersek, but the symbolic significance of the exchange is clear. In the eyes of mainstream society the white trash and the alien trash are virtually interchangeable. It is a logical step that we should find Max aggressively denying his lowly status as white trash as he slits Kersek's neck with a piano wire.

In their first conversation, Max chats away to Sam about how the average man gains a pound a year, whereas he has lost a pound every year of his sentence. Two bodies are invoked in this early exchange, standing on either side of the law. One is the body in decay which enjoys privilege, an easy life-style, gaining weight, becoming softer and weaker. The other body has suffered, been punished and yet has resurrected itself, become harder and stronger. Max's strengthening body is thus compared with the weakening body politic signified by Sam. The former is a reconstructed body which makes a spectacle of itself, giving material form and newfound strength to the abstract concepts of law and justice which Max believes to be in decay. As such, it performs to excess, refusing to be the white trash of the decaying body politic. Through his newly virile and tattooed performing body, Max recognises this social stigma and rejects it violently.

Max Cady as spectacle of discontent

Max presents an unashamedly uncouth spectacle of excess. His performance, as Lesley Stern has pointed out, is heavily reliant upon the surface values of bodily enunciation.[10] Max's personal demonstration of loss, rage and a certain confused, resurgent redneckism is enacted by, and written across, what Stern aptly calls, his 'body too much'.[11] We are alerted to that text of Max's complaint by his loud and excessive sartorial regime. Among Max's wardrobe of retro white and brown short-sleeve shirts and faun slacks we also see him in an eye-catching array of Hawaiian sunset, white and scarlet red shirts matched with white shoes and white boating cap. In our frequent glimpses at Max's body underneath these clothes we are easily drawn to his excessively muscular and heavily tattooed torso. Furthermore we are invited to note the feats of physical excess staged by this body—the rape of Lori, the hospital job, the burning of Max's hand by the lighted torch—as well as the intrusive nature of Max's physical presence. It is in the use of this body that Max asserts his own aspirations and the aspirations and frustrations of a vocal and emerging underclass seeking political recognition. This body-in-performance also, more threateningly, can read as the fascinating spectacle expression of a repressed white trash angst within the body politic.

Max's tattoos, prominently displayed in our first sight of Max in his prison cell and later in the police strip-search scene, are an essential part of his performance. Decorating much of Max's upper body and arms the tattoos refer to a series of homilies and biblical quotations— yesterday's thoughts for today—such as 'Vengeance is mine', 'My time is at hand' and 'I have put my trust in the Lord, in him will I trust'. In addition we see a clown holding a smoking gun and a Bible, a crucifix balancing scales supporting 'truth' (a Bible) and 'justice' (a sword), as well as bolts of lightening, a portrait of 'Time the Avenger' and a broken heart for 'Loretta'. Lesley Stern and Helen Stoddart have made a number of excellent observations concerning Max's adornment. I want to highlight some of these in order to explain the ideology, the personal sense of loss and suffering, the social sense of disenfranchisement and the threatening aggression which lies behind the text of these tattoos as a summary of Max's discontent.

At the end of the hospital job scene, when Max is successful in withstanding and overcoming the attack by three goons hired by Sam, Max struts about triumphantly yelling:

> I ain't no white trash piece of shit, I'm better that you all. I can out run you, I can out read you, I can out think you, I can out philosophise you, and I'm gonna out last you. You think a couple of whacks to my good old bones is going to get me down? It's going to take a hell of a lot more than that, Counsellor, to prove you're better than me. 'I am like God and God like me. I am as large as God, he is as small as I. He cannot above me nor I beneath him be.' Salasius, seventeenth century.[12]

This is a powerful statement of the threat Max poses to Sam. At the moment when his rights as a citizen have been violated by Sam and an unofficial arm of the law, it also reads as an aggressive counter statement or assertion of Max's human rights. Max's performance demonstrates his ownership of a consistent and unswerving philosophy, an ideology to match and surpass the tenuous and shifting 'lifestyle' philosophy of Sam and the empowered upper-middle classes. It is a spectacle to show Sam that Max possesses these qualities because he enacts them in a physical way. In this performance Max seems to say, 'As I have (embody) a concrete philosophy you can't treat me as some sort of unreflective savage. I think, I read and I have a soul. You can no longer regard me as nothing. You, who show philosophical consistency in nothing.'

Lesley Stern places significant emphasis on Max's performance and it is through her reading that we can consider the way in which Max enacts this newly acquired philosophy through the idea of 'embodied reading'. Max has learned to read and write in prison and his tattoos are the functional expression of this new understanding. As he tells the prison guard on leaving, he has no need to take his books with him. He embodies their message both in word, tattooed across his chest, and in deed, through his violent actions of revenge. Stern extends the range of Max's textual consumption to the images of Stalin, a skewered oriental figure and various other cartoon and photographed super heroes which hang in his prison cell above his collection of books. Their message has become the text of his body: 'He sees words and images as instrumental and his attitude to reading and writing is, above all, functional.' Max has no more need of his book because he has taken their word 'into his own hands' and onto his own body. 'In this way he turns his body into a functional apparatus, an eloquent instrument of revenge.'[13]

Helen Stoddart describes our first sight of Max in his cell and how Max's exercising body almost swallows the texts and images on the walls and shelf, 'He *is* his books. It is their intelligence (mainly biblical) in the form of tattoos which makes his body spectacular.' Just as he embodies his reading of these works he also become a physical statement of that reading. As Stoddart puts it, 'He both demands to be looked at and yet he escapes decipherment because he cannot be fixed simply as the object of the man's gaze.'[14] Accordingly, we can read Max's tattoos as the bodily display of his social and political mobilisation. His attitude to these legal, philosophical and religious texts is, as Stern puts it, 'instrumental'. By translating them into material form, they demonstrate his readiness for action and his unwillingness to accept victimisation.

Beyond their appearance as text, illustration and decoration, tattoos should also be read as scars, wounds, marks of loss and suffering. This is particularly important to our reading of Max Cady and explains, to an extent, Sam's (and the spectator's) fascination with Max's body. Helen Stoddart considers the way in which bodily scarification in general inflects on formations of masculinity, when tattoos are read as self-imposed scars. According to this reading, male scarification marks the sado-masochism of the hero—his wounds acting as signs of the pain and endurance he has suffered in order to buy his heroism. Although marking his suffering and the trials he has endured in order to attain the heroism of ordinary men and women, these scars also emphasise his status as loner and outsider. They mark that aspect of the hero which divides and alienates him from other men and women.[15]

Further supporting this notion of the tattooed hero as loner/outsider is the idea of excessive tattooing as unfashionable and as representing as 'aggressive conservatism'. Drawing on the work of Ted Polhemus, Stoddart states how 'the adorning of a tattoo', might suggest 'a tactical defence or rebellion against the tide of fashion, mostly on the part of socially marginalised, eccentric, criminal or self-exiled groups and individuals because of its permanence'.[16] Accordingly she reads Max's tattoos in terms of a reaction:

> Cady is a confused and confusing figure whose tattoos func-
> tion anarchically as a statement of violent reaction against a
> diseased social order rather than as a pure commitment to
> Christian ethics. Like Travis Bickle in *Taxi Driver* (Martin
> Scorsese, US, 1975) who reverts to a more primitive Mohican

style to become an urban warrior with a mission, Cady's bodily decorations represent an attempt to throw himself into reverse gear against the flow of a society which he believes to be moving too quickly and in the wrong direction.[17]

The melancholic loves to watch

The hospital job scene provides a telling example of that perversion, common to all Scorsese's melancholics, that the melancholic loves to watch, an sometimes incorporate, the other's performance of loss and struggle to re-empower. Ellen, Joey, Vickie and, to an extent, Tommy are all marked by the notion of loss and all provide the melancholic with an attractive spectacle of struggle against the system which contains them. *Cape Fear*'s hospital job scene, therefore, can be considered as an exemplary performance of the male melancholic loss and re-empowerment containing within it much of the structure of male melancholic desire.

Following Max's greatest threat yet—his erotic confrontation with Danny in the school theatre—Sam takes Kersek's advice to 'go outside the law' and engages three hired hit men to 'do a little hospital job' on Max. Setting upon Max as he returns home, the three goons seem to be getting the better of Max, attacking him with kicks, punches, bicycle chains and lead pipes. Eventually, having sustained a series of punishing blows, Max turns on his attackers, sending one to the ground and the remaining two running off into the night. Puffed-up and strutting around quoting Salasius, Max perceives that which the audience already knows—that Sam is crouching behind some rubbish bins watching the encounter.

Sam's 'slumming'—literally hanging around the trash in a neighborhood markedly unlike his own familiar environment—is the highlight to date in the film of the many exchanges of looks between himself and Max. Max's original approach to the Bowden family was to watch them. He first stalks them on a family outing to the movies, then by keeping watch over Danny and Leigh in the family home and tailing Sam in his various movements outside it. Sam countered by looking back, as we have discussed in relation to the one-way mirror scene, during the hospital job and later in the film when, temporarily disabled, he watches Max raping Leigh and Danny on the house-boat. It is central to Sam's structure of desire to gain an element of voyeuristic mastery over Max to counteract the unsettling effect of Max's gaze, a bid for recognition, directed towards him. What Sam sees in the hospital job is that very cycle of dominance and mastery, repression and return which *Raging Bull*'s Jake La Motta makes manifest upon his own body in his 'playing possum' fighting style. Watching the spectacle enacted by his shadow, the melancholic Sam derives an equal pleasure of that initial punishment and eventual potency which is the melancholic's reward and an essential part of his privileged destiny. Indeed, Max's explosive performance— both in the hospital job and throughout the film—is Scorsese's most memorable representation of that mania, which Freud has identified as marking the end of 'oppressive compulsion' and the mastering of melancholia.[18] Thus, in Max's manic performance, Sam addresses his own loss and perceives what Julia Kristeva describes as the key to phallic identification and entrance to the symbolic which is the source of his re-empowerment and privilege.[19]

Unlike Jake and Travis and their wound-displaying acts of self-sacrifice, Sam does not enact a self-sacrifice but enlists Max as proxy to do it for him. As what we might call a socially evolved melancholic, Sam has come too far to stage his own sacrifice. Like the sophisticated Newland Archer, Sam lacks Jake La Motta's animal ambivalence essential to the act of self-sacrifice. What is more, Sam's perception of the extreme corruption surrounding him is such that his level of ambivalence towards the body politic is somewhat higher than that of Jake or Travis. For Sam, the world has become so sophisticated and corrupt that even were he inclined to be its saviour, such a gesture would be of negligible sacrificial efficacy. Just as Sam keenly reads the story of sacrifice in the Book of Job, Sam loves to watch Max in the role of the self-sacrificing god. It is the role which his melancholic fantasy scenario longs for. And yet he knows what a pointless gesture it would be in this world, drained of transcendence. Better to call upon the usual outsider or slave to take the role of sacrificial victim, a proxy for the god, in a perfunctory and de-sacralised ritual. For Sam the melancholic mob has become beyond redemption.

Max's performance thus demands the attention of the Scorsesean melancholic. It says that Max has an identity, a view of the world which he can articulate. It speaks also of its ability to threaten the corruption mainstream society. The threat is that Max shows he has a soul, that he has suffered and felt pain, known loss. It also speaks of his ennui—a reading of the world as diseased which brings on an aggressive nostalgia for the past and a melancholic refusal to let it go. Much of this view is shared by the Sam, which is partly why he finds the white trash spectacle so compelling. Essentially, however, it is a voyeurism based on the drive towards mastery—to identify, then overcome, lack and the fear of the maternal.

A fine tradition of savouring fear

During the stake-out, Kersek and Sam are hiding in the Bowden's marital bedroom when Sam expresses concerns about killing Max. Kersek attempts to reassure him by saying:

> You're scared. That's ok. I want you to savour that fear. You know the South evolved in fear. Fear of the Indian, fear of the slave, fear of the damn Union. The South has a fine tradition of savouring fear.

Why does Sam savour this performance and this fear? He loves to watch it because the spectacle of Max speaks of a profound experience of loss and an equally potent denial of loss. Although deeply attached to his own feelings of loss, the Scorsesean male melancholic must ultimately learn to fear this attachment if he is to affirm his tribal allegiance. *Cape Fear* places a central emphasis on just such an ambiguous denial of loss. Whereas Tommy offers Henry a model of loss as transgression in *GoodFellas*, in *Cape Fear* Max provides Sam with a model of manic reconciliation. Max teaches Sam the way to deny the fact of loss and thus aids him in renewing his contract with the middle-class mob of the Scorsesean world. Outside that world of comfort and privilege, a world perhaps closest to the world of the film's spectator, Max teaches that there is no maternal realm of bliss but only a place on the bottom of the heap—the fear of becoming poor. In *Mourning and Melancholia* Freud observes this fear as central to the condition of melancholia. Furthermore, he reasserts its importance by citing the example of 'winning a large sum of money' and the accompanying 'exultation' at being relieved of financial burden as a key example of a 'normal model for mania'.[20] Thus placed in the discourse of manic denial (the melancholic's resolution), Sam embraces a fine tradition of savouring fear.

Kristeva's notion of abjection tells us something of the cultural and psychological context of savouring fear and helps us read the way *Cape Fear* limits the scope of the male melancholic's world to the boundaries of symbolic patriarchy. As in any narrative of horror, the monster is inevitably the primary site of the abject and Max Cady forcefully bears this out in *Cape Fear*. As white trash, beyond the body politic, Max has been, and continues to be, subject to the discourse of radical exclusion which is central to the notion of abjection.[21] Now that the world has become corrupt through the actions of Sam and the social order her represents, Max pays no regard to notions of 'identity, system, order' which seek to hold the abject at a safe distance. Furthermore, like the deject/exile with a jocular confidence,[22] he refuses to respect those 'borders, positions, rules' which have hitherto contained him. As a 'criminal with a good conscience', a 'shameless rapist' and 'killer who claims he is a savior', Max patently enacts that force of abjection which Kristeva sees as flaunting the fragility of the law.[23] And yet, like *Cape Fear* itself, abjection is nothing if not ambiguous and ambivalent. For Max's performance to have any abject resonance it must address and expose those same qualities in the melancholic Sam. As in the case of bodily wastes, the site of abjection is a site of terror because it drops from us and assures us vitality. It is with this ambivalence that Sam confronts Max. As we have observed, Slippery Sam is no rapist nor killer, but like Max, he has demonstrated scant regard for law and order. In the mock court scene on the house boat at the end of the film, Max calls Sam 'traitor' and 'liar', which are among the very categories Krisetva employs in her discussion of abjection. Killer and rapist Max may be, but it is more to Sam and his crimes against Max and his own family that our thoughts are directed by Kristeva's sentence:

> Abjection, on the other hand, is immoral, sinister, scheming, and shady: a terror that dissembles, a hatred that smiles, a passion that uses the body for barter instead of inflaming it, a debtor who sells you up, a friend who stabs you . . .(sic.)[24]

For all the abjection of toothed vaginas and blood spurting monstrous women that Barbara Creed has located as central to the horror film,[25] Sam reminds us of, what Kristeva calls 'the socialized appearance of the abject'. In his moral and legal ambivalence Sam enacts abjection's 'most common, most obvious appearance', the hypocrite, the noisy upholder of law and morality who is, at the same time, their secret violator.[26] Thus Max may provide the fascinating spectacle of abjection for the willing male melancholic,[27] but it is Sam himself and his abject ambivalence which dominates the film's representation of abjection. This is what Kristeva refers to as the 'abjection of self', when the subject:

> weary of fruitless attempts to identify with something on the outside, finds the impossible within; when it finds that the

impossible constitutes its very being, that it is none other than abject. The abjection of self would be the culminating form of that experience of the subject to which it is revealed that all its objects are based merely on the inaugural loss that laid the foundations of its own being.[28]

When it comes to the male melancholic, the ambivalence and ambiguity of his experience of abjection should not confuse us at to where this version of the mean and melancholy history points us. Certainly, as Kristeva reads it, abjection carries within its discourse the constant danger of slipping back into that pre-symbolic realm which threatens it: 'Abjection preserves what existed in the archaism of the pre-objectal relationship'.[29] However, for all its fragility of signification, and its archaism:

> The abject is that pseudo-object that is made up before but appears only within the gaps of secondary repression. The abject would thus be the 'object' of primal repression.[30]

As Kristeva writes, 'to each superego its abject';[31] this experience of abjection, engaging perversely with prohibitions, rules and laws is, 'anchored in the superego', and its subject, Sam in this case, is 'firmly settled' there.[32] It may find its origins in 'our earliest attempts to release hold of the *maternal* entity even before existing outside of her,'[33] but the violence of its mourning is for an object which it acknowledges is already lost.[34] As John Lechte comments, abjection operates 'as a kind of background support for the symbolic and its attendant ego'.[35]

Thus, in relation to the notion of abjection, *Cape Fear* lays bare the phallic economy in which the Scorsesean melancholic really exists. While the male melancholic's ultimate conformism with the symbolic patriarchy of the Scorsesean mob is obvious, we have observed in Newland, Jake, Travis and Henry a healthy longing for a form of desire beyond the rule of the mob, beyond the symbolic. Sam, however, has no such outlook. In Sam the male melancholic has evolved to such a level of sophistication that the pre-symbolic realm of the mother is hardly even a dream for him. His willing engagement with the abject is a final confrontation with loss. It constitutes an abjection of the maternal and a violent attempt to modify and make safe the cycle of regression-melancholia-reconciliation-regression which pervades Scorsesean melancholia. When Sam looks back he can only see Max, a monster, not of the maternal pre-

'Two lawyers workin it out' Robert De Niro and
Nick Nolte in *Cape Fear*.

symbolic, nor of the anarchic id, but of the stern and moralising superego. The fear Max incites is, once again, the fear the melancholic has of not being a man apart. This fear, however, exists totally within the symbolic realm of the father. Should he follow Max's teachings, Sam does not face the prospect of transgression into a maternal order of desire, but a final denial of that order. Should he ignore Max's message and not be saved, as Max promises, he faces the fear of not being a man apart, but a man discarded. That is a fear of being lost on the other side of power and privilege as it is distributed in the masculine tribal order—the white trash of the Scorsesean melancholy body politic. Even this, however, is not the end to melancholia, the end of the cycle of melancholic loss and re-empowerment. In *Cape Fear* the Scorsesean melancholic tale has simply encountered the crisis of abjection with all its attendant fear, loathing and longing for the maternal. The melodrama of *The Age of Innocence* is insufficient to meet this fear in *Cape Fear* and horror has become the next genre for the Scorsesean hero's melancholic perversion.

CHAPTER 7

The melancholic momentum

> You will be born again and again.
>
> *Kundun*

 Since the *The Age of Innocence* was released ten years have passed and four more Scorsese features have been produced. An appraisal of the melancholic momentum of Scorsese's work since then is, therefore, highly desirable. Each of Scorsese's four narrative features since 1993 (*Casino* (1995), *Kundun* (1997), *Bringing Out the Dead* (1999), and *The Gangs of New York* (2002)) can be read in relation to the issues of melancholia and male desire. The influence of Scorsese's melancholic imagination on *Pulp Fiction*, *Bullets Over Broadway* (both 1994), *Donnie Brasco* (1997), *Analyze This* (1999), and *The Sopranos* (1999–) and on the newly celebrated Italian American Mob figure of contemporary media culture, the sensitive new age gangster, also warrants attention.

Kundun

As *Kundun* opens in 1937, the two-year-old Tenzin Gyatso, the yet-to-be-discovered Dalai Lama (Tenzin Yeshi Paichang), usurps his father's place at the table and, once again, demands to be told the story of his birth. The rest of the family groan as if preparing for another recitation of an interminable dinnertime tale. In a sense, they are. The two-year-old Kundun is the reincarnation of the ever-living Buddha of Compassion—and his tale is interminable and consistently reflective of his own past. The trial of object recognition to prove that the two-year-old Tenzin is the reincarnation and his constant possession of a photograph of his previous self make the point.

A number of amusing moments give a similar emphasis. When the five year old Kundun (Tulku Jamyang Kunga Tenzin) instantly knows how to use the Great Seal his instructor remarks, 'O, ho. Most auspicious 14th Dalai Lama.' Running about the Summer Palace he remembers where to find his old false teeth. Following his enthronement Kundun demonstrates something of his rejection of tradition and one of his ministers comments, 'He's a modern man, just as he was the last time.' All these examples emphasise the idea of looking back, and extend the idea of Scorsesean melancholic reflection, pushing the idea beyond its furthest limits, to a nostalgia for a previous incarnation.

Like Hamlet, Kundun has a potent 'mind's eye' vision. Removed from the traditional Scorsesean intra-tribal struggle, Kundun's struggle has, by the nature of these visions, moved Scorsesean resistance generally further inwards. The struggle with the Chinese thus appears as the Dalai Lama's internal and spiritual conflict to reconcile the impossible notions of Chinese military aggression with his own creed of universal harmony, peace and compassion. His visions are represented as the staged mindscape of a fantasy struggle between these opposites. They denote Kundun's difference, his self-assumed superiority and become the narrative plot-points and aestheticisations of his loss.

Scorsese has blurred the line between these visions and Kundun's reality, particularly in the marginal states of infancy and early childhood. The young Kundun's moments of St. Francis-like compassion and communication with rats and huge black spiders turn into a Christ-like pity for his Chinese persecutors. In a dream Kundun sees them telling him of China's own exploitation at the hands of the western opium trade. A dream montage describes the great cost of his vocation in his longing for the return of the childhood and the loved ones he has lost. As in the sight of a blood-splattered white horse at the Indian boarder, his visions become increasingly violent when the facts of the Chinese invasion become clear. In a scene, which details the Chinese demands on Tibet, we see Kundun's father's dead body dismembered and fed to devouring vultures. On hearing of the death and rape of his fellow monks and nuns, he conjures up images of children, forced to execute their parents. The fishpond of the Summer Palace, a source of his childhood joy, he now sees running with blood. At the height of the persecutions, he dreams of himself standing at the centre of a carpet of dead monks.

One of the most remarkable and disturbing ceremonies of *Kundun* is the consultation with the Nechung Oracle (Jumpa Lungtok). The Oracle dashes about, before Kundun's throne, divining the future in manic convulsions. The Oracle is consulted concerning the war with China and the manner of Kundun's escape to India. The future, in so far as it holds new variations on the past, is painfully extracted in this hypnotic ritual. Its revelations are painstakingly pulled from the violence and commotion of the Oracle's dance. Such divination contrasts with the things Kundun sees, born in the calm of personal meditation. The Scorsesean melancholic's mundane vision and the melodrama of his narrative operates to stress the melancholic's personal confinement through his lack of perspective. Kundun's visions contrast with those of the Oracle. It is not in his power to see the future. When he does, it is confined to that never-ending cycle of journeys that move, not towards some new future or some new site of desire, but merely towards, what the Oracle calls, a 'safe return.'

A desert argument in *Casino* between Nicky Santoro (Joe Pesci) and Sam Rothstein (Robert De Niro) ends with the rock-like Rothstein clamming up against the torrent of abuse he is receiving. It seems his powers of speech and movement have closed down when Santoro drives off leaving Sam surrounded by a cloud of desert sand. In this way Scorsese's melancholics have attempted to meet the struggle of their inner vision against the world around them with resignation and renunciation. It is in their inability to maintain this distance from the corruption around them that their satisfaction, and ultimate denial, of desire is measured. The visit of a Chinese deputation to the Dalai Lama's palace demonstrates Kundun's similar desire for resignation from contact with an oppressive force. The Chinese general sits before the callow Buddha of Compassion, formally presenting a treaty for his signature and glibly offering him every service. Kundun's ministers and councillors interact with the general but the Buddha himself says nothing, receives nothing, remaining impassive to the general's diplomacy.

The impact of this encounter, however, is not nullified in Kundun's mind by such a denial. Its resonance is indicated by the dream of the complaints of the Chinese soldier, which follows. The resignation assumed by Scorsese's melancholic is thus demonstrated as providing the visions, which are the mise-en-scène of potential transcendence. As

Jake La Motta sublimates his struggle with the Mob by effecting a self-sacrifice in the ring, Kundun internalises his own struggle with the Chinese and turns it into horrific and disturbing visions. However, the realities of external struggle are present and undeniable. Transcendence through resignation is shown in *Kundun* to be impossible, as even the Buddha of Compassion must enter the fray and involve himself in the struggle of the Chinese Government's choosing. Escape to India suggests, in one sense, the failure of Kundun's desire for transcendence and martyrdom through resignation. Looking back after his escape as we do, Tibet appears to be the place of transcendence for the Scorsesean hero. It is the desired and forbidden country of peace and harmony echoed in its mountainous landscape and the childhood delights of the Summer Palace. Crossing the boarder thus stands as defeat, failure and death. Chinese oppression does exist and Kundun must acknowledge that it has the power to enforce its authority on his own transcendent vision—the two cannot be kept apart.

Dominated by nostalgia for the past, and, in the case of *Kundun*, for a previous incarnation, the melancholic can never succeed in his desire to go from resignation to transcendence. Kundun is the logical extension of the Scorsesean corporal, earth-bound melancholic because, as his Regent Reting Rinopche (Sonam Puntsok) tells him, he is undying—'you will be born again and again.' Each of Scorsese's melancholics moves through a cycle of tribal disruption, sacrifice, restoration and longing, inevitably moving towards a recommencement of the cycle again and again. Similarly, Kundun keeps satisfying his own corporal deprivation. He represents his own cycle of plenitude and satisfaction, a comforting self-sufficiency but one which never transcends the struggle for individuation from a repressive external force.

Transcendence is a false narrative goal for Scorsese's men. To look back and to look out is to risk a glimpse of that abhorrent abject space outside the male world and the Scorsesean mob, which is forbidden and unconscionable. If melancholic reflection in Scorsese has taken his heroes dangerously close to that point, before the male world, the dynamics of re-incarnation in *Kundun* work at the disavowal and denial of that abject space. When the Dalai Lama looks back at origins, for the first time in Scorsese, there is an entity before the primal scene and before the maternal antecedent—the self. Unlike Oedipus, the re-incarnate Kundun does not look back to the primal scene or to Julia Kristeva's maternal bond, before language and before culture. He looks back to himself, to the pictures of himself on his desk or on the palace walls.

This is, perhaps, the end of the melancholic imagination in Scorsese. For the melancholic needs, at least, the prospect of desire beyond the tribal organisation or repressive force which claims him. With the eradication of the mother and the sublimation of the father in *Kundun*, it is Narcissus, not Oedipus, who is now fully revealed as the referent or model of the Scorsesean struggle.

The Gangs of New York

In the death-throes of *The Gangs of New York* a battle is taking place. In the middle of the fighting the leaders of the opposing forces, Bill 'the Butcher' Cutting (Daniel Day-Lewis) and Amsterdam Vallon (Leonardo DiCaprio), are desperately searching for each other. It is not just the melee which impedes their lonely search but the haze of gun smoke. And yet there are no guns allowed in this battle. Indeed, at the pre-battle parley Bill the Butcher commended his former protégé, Vallon, for excluding them. The gun smoke and the accompanying cannon fire have nothing to do with Bill and Vallon and their little war over control of Lower Manhattan's Five Points district. Outside that tiny world the island of Manhattan is engulfed by the draft riots of 1863 and beyond New York the Union itself is tearing apart in civil war. As the constant stream of immigrants pouring into New York throughout the film attests, there is a wide world beyond the inter-tribal struggles of Lower Manhattan. Nowhere in the film is the narrowness of the Five Points world made more explicit than here, when the opposing tribes are caught off-guard by troops diverted from Gettysburg and canons firing from the river to quell the general upheaval. In this form, national events and the myths of progress and the future come literally crashing in on the hitherto closed and petty ghetto cultures of Vallon and his defiantly conservative rival, Bill the Butcher. As they continue to seek each other out in the lonely mists however, their struggle, a tribal rite of father worship, is rendered insular and cut off from reality.

In *The Gangs of New York* Scorsese focuses his anthropological lense on the gang cultures of mid nineteenth-century Lower Manhattan. The film begins in 1846 with a battle between Bill's 'natives' and a congregation of immigrant gangs lead by Vallon's father, Priest (Liam Neeson). In this prologue, which stands behind everything of importance in the Five Points world, Bill kills Priest as a young Vallon (Cian McCormack) looks on. Sixteen years later Vallon, now free of his orphanage, returns to the Five Points seeking a Max Cady-like revenge. Falling in with a gang of thieves, Vallon comes under the patronage of Bill who is unaware of his identity. In Vallon, Bill sees a worthy son and heir. Vallon realises the full Oedipal implications of Bill's paternalism by attempting to murder Bill at the annual celebrations held to commemorate Bill's triumph over Priest. Vallon fails in this attempt and is severely mutilated but spared by Bill, who knows his destiny. Recovering from his treatment by Bill, Vallon gathers together the immigrant forces for one last showdown where Bill falls to Vallon's blade before being buried beside his nemesis, Priest.

With *The Gangs of New York*, what Scorsese has added to his own discourse of male melancholia is a kind of no-frills tale of loss. It is as if he has taken the totem meal from *Totem and Taboo* and simply staged it without the challenges and complications introduced into that scenario by *Raging Bull*. The initial, primal murder of Vallon's father by Bill thus becomes the site of origins, guilt and deferred obedience. Annually this deed is commemorated as much to celebrate and enforce the authority of Bill's regime as to appease the spirit of the dead warrior, Priest. As Bill's power threatens tyranny, however, it is inevitable that he should become the next sacrificial object, struck down by Vallon on behalf of all. Accordingly the narrative quite simply rehearses the ceremony of the totem meal in its most basic form. In Bill's self-aggrandisement there is only a ritualistic challenge to the stability of the social organisation and this is little more than a pretext for his murder. Jenny Everdeane (Cameron Diaz), who might have been the source of conflict and desire in the tribe, is as shared an object as any other. The message here in re-staging the totem commemoration in its most basic form, is that whatever layers of loss are applied by the melancholia of *The Age of Innocence, Raging Bull* or *GoodFellas*, the essential economy of loss portrayed in Scorsese's films is conservative. The celebration of loss in Scorsese is simply a deferral of an ultimate paternal obedience.

Melancholia has given way to the mania of revenge in *The Gangs of New York*. What both Bill and Vallon want is revenge for the death of their fathers. This clearly suggests the importance of loss to these protagonists. In neither case, however, is that loss deferred onto any beloved person or object, which threatens to draw away the melancholic from his ultimate identification with the Five Points tribal organisation. The taboo on Ellen Olenska and Joey La Motta, or the essential outsider status of Betsy and Max Cady, offered a realm of desire to the Scorsesean melancholic, at lest nominally, beyond the control of the Scorsesean mob. In *The Gangs of New York*, however, Scorsese has stripped away the pretence of such a deferral by locating desire solely in the sphere of the Five Points world. If the Scorsesean melancholic, despite his conformist nature, ever dreamt of something better than the tribal group controlling him, there is no such fantasy in *The Gangs of New York*. In fact, melancholia is impossible in this environment because there is no alternative point of desire to challenge obedience to the law of the father. The idea that Vallon might pursue some course of desire outside the course of deferred obedience to his father and a timely ritual slaying of Bill would be as surprising to him as the arrival of the first cannon shots from the river.

Bringing Out the Dead

The most obvious film, since *The Age of Innocence*, to attempt to offer an object of desire outside the Scorsesean mob is *Bringing Out the Dead*. *Bringing Out the Dead* is the story of a burnt-out paramedic, Frank Pierce (Nicholas Cage), whose nightly shift in the New York inferno is a hectic panorama of boozed, battered and bloodied bodies. Frank desperately needs a holiday, but his frequent attempts at resignation and excessive tardiness bring his attempts at escape to nothing. Begging to be fired he is given no release. Obsessed with his childhood Catholic hang-over of loss, sacrifice and redemption, Frank is trapped in the city of Travis Bickle's worst *Taxi Driver* nightmare. Similarly unable to escape his vocation, this Saint Francis is losing more souls than he is saving, and he is haunted by the ghosts of all those he has lost in the line of duty. All these phantoms of loss come together in the ghost of an Hispanic woman, Rose (Cynthia Roman), whom he also lost on the job. Throughout the film, in his most delirious moments, Frank sees Rose all over the city and in the face of every patient, hooker and angel who passes him by. At the beginning of the film, Frank brings about a miracle. With the help of Frank Sinatra's *September of My Years*, he brings Mr. Burke (Cullen Oliver Johnson) back from the dead and is given a glimpse of hope by meeting Burke's daughter, Mary (Patricia Arquette), who becomes his guide through the New York malaise. Saving the life of a drug dealer and mercy-killing Mary's father, Frank eradicates the ghosts of loss in his past, is forgiven by Rose's ghost and finally finds sanctuary in the arms of Mary.

Like *Taxi Driver*, *Bringing Out the Dead* presents its central pro-tagonist as not so much in the grip of an identifiable tribal organisation as in the clutches of New York City itself. Like the New York City of *Taxi Driver* and the middle seventies, the New York of the early nineties in *Bringing Out the Dead* has no clear power structure or centre of authority. No Mob boss pulls the strings or sets the codes of behaviour, and the structures of vested interest remain obscured. Dominated only by the many-headed beast of the drug trade, the city is awash with prostitution, corruption and vice. In this environment Frank, unlike Travis Bickle in *Taxi Driver*, has no delusions of finding a practical solution to the problems of the city or their devastating effect on him. There is no enemy or repressive group, which shows itself to be the clear agent of Frank's oppression. As indicated by the dissemination of the street junk, Red Death (a lethal and economically pointless cocktail of heroin and an amino acid), there is little point looking for logical and identifiable answers. All Frank can do, it seems, to assuage his feelings of loss is to treat the symptoms and, as he says, to 'bear witness'.

Whereas *Taxi Driver* is very much earth-bound in its picture of the city, *Bringing Out the Dead* (with the help of some drugs and excessive fatigue) is, for Frank, a city of spirits. In contrast to the comic magic show in which Frank's partner Marcus (Ving Rhames) pretends to save a Red Death victim, I. B. Bangin (Harper Simon), with the power of Jesus, Frank has some serious visions and hears haunting voices. It is out of this melange of the spirit world that Frank conjures Rose as his object of desire and release. A victim of the city and of its affect on Frank's ability to save her, Rose, the abject dead body wandering around his world, is the perfect object of loss. Frank's partners constantly remind him of the medical drama maxim to treat what he sees around him as merely part of the job. Unable to do this, Frank finds in Rose and in her living surrogate Mary, an object for the crypt-based conversation of loss, which defines his melancholia. Dedicated to pursing his vision of Rose, and desperately fighting her loss, Frank works hard to separate himself from the corruption around him. Maintaining his conversation with Rose, *Bringing Out the Dead* suggests that Frank has not given up the ghost of desire to a Scorsesean mob culture bent on forbidding desire outside its realm.

The film's final shot of Frank asleep in the arms of Mary is lit to create a marble like sheen over the image. In this far too serious, but not too subtle, parody of Michelangelo's *Pieta*, it is as if we are asked to believe in the final fulfilment of melancholic desire. It is as if we are now presented with an assertion of the Scorsesean melancholic's ability to master the ghosts of loss, to break the bonds of mob oppression and to seek something new. The problem here is that Scorsese has too often taught us to doubt such a scene. In the nightly cycle of violence and mayhem of *Bringing Out the Dead*, loss is demonstrated as the fundamental condition of the Scorsesean melancholic's being. The pervading cultural miasma is his natural state. As we see in *Taxi Driver* and *The Age of Innocence*, even when presented with the option of union and the chance to overcome loss and pursue desire, the Scorsesean melancholic will inevitably pass it by. This is not Frank's way. In giving himself over to the embrace of Mary, Frank suggests the possibilities of transcending the world that has hitherto contained his brother, Scorsesean melancholics. Thus presenting what looks like Scorsese's first Hollywood happy ending, *Bringing Out the Dead* ends on a note which has forgotten that, in the world of the Scorsese hero, unsatisfied desire and loss is not merely his destiny but also his pleasure. As the ghost of Rose concludes, just prior to giving him his manumission, 'No one asked you to suffer, it was your idea.' If *Bringing Out the Dead* is an attempt to break the melancholic's cycle of entrapment, longing and unsatisfied desire in Scorsese's films, it fails. This is because, both within this film and in the context of Scorsese's films generally, such a project has been rendered thoroughly untenable.

Casino

Early in *Casino*, having settled the kingdom, a self-satisfied Sam Rothstein is pressing for Ginger's hand in marriage. Ginger (Sharon Stone), a celebrated Las Vegas call girl and hustler, is reluctant to accept the offer and tells Sam that she does not love him. Almost on the point of tears and nervously dusting cigarette ash from his silk dressing gown, Sam becomes a sort of Scorsesean Snag. Swallowing his pride, Sam starts to babble on about his feelings and the way love can grow, as long as there is 'a mutual respect':

> You know, what is, what is love anyway? It's a mutual respect, its a devotion, its a caring from one person to another. And if we could set up some kind of a foundation based on that mutual respect, I feel that, eventually, you would care enough about me that I could live with that.

It is an effective pitch and clearly impresses Ginger, who looks on with the vaguely condescending air of one who has been moved by the eloquence of a child. But it is only with the matching offer of major cash and the promise of future security that Ginger agrees to the marriage. Sam emerges from the scene as a weak, vulnerable and naïve figure of romantic delusions and feelings—an impression confirmed in the middle of their wedding when Sam finds Ginger weeping down the phone to her ex-boyfriend, Lester Diamond (James Woods). In a previous scene Sam had the hands of a casino cheat smashed up with a hammer and backed up this by threatening to cut them off with a chainsaw. For such a character these hopeless romantic expressions appear almost mundane in comparison with the powerful figure he cuts as the Olympian god of Las Vegas gambling. This is what *Casino* is about—the merging of the worlds of gods and men. In Sam, Scorsese has demonstrated that melancholia is thoroughly grounded, and perhaps trapped, in the everyday world of the middle-classes—not unlike the world of the spectator watching it.

For all its anthropological detailing of the Las Vegas gambling business and its network of connections with government and organised crime, after Sam and Ginger's marriage, *Casino* becomes increasingly concerned with the domestic. As the film charts the tacky decline of the old, perhaps even romantic, Las Vegas, we observe an increasing emphasis on the details of the Rothstein home and marriage. While the million dollar empire surrounding them is breaking up, Sam and Ginger are sitting around in dressing gowns and designer track-suits, amongst the orange juice and cereal boxes, having breakfast fights over money, fur coats and the issue of mutual marital trust. When Ginger seems incapable of breaking with Lester, the Rothsteins move their conflict to the bedroom and they fight over booze and pills and the custody of their daughter, Amy (Erika von Tagen). Finally their battle, always bordering on Scorsese style screwball comedy, ends with an unseemly and very public shouting match on the front lawn of their respectable suburban Las Vegas residence. The neighbours are disturbed and the police are called, but in the middle of Ginger's rampage though the house, Sam, still in his dressing gown, stops to ask about the policeman's family and congratulate him on their forthcoming baby. All this time the core business of Casino Town is going on. Sam is fighting the Las Vegas County Commissioner over his dignity and his gaming licence. The Mob bosses 'back home' are keeping a watchful eye on their investments there. It is not that *Casino* has turned the world of the melancholic completely towards the bourgeois banal, as Nicky accuses Sam of doing. What has happened is that these elements of the mundane and the everyday have invaded the sphere of the gods, just like the bus loaded, track-suited slot-machine masses we see storming the new casinos in the film's regretful epilogue.

If melancholic desire in Scorsese's films since 1993 has shown itself as increasingly trapped within the self (*Kundun*) and within the ego-ideal of the father-obedient tribal organisation (*The Gangs of New York*), *Casino* has shown that desire to be thoroughly mundane. Scorsese explored the notion of the mundane world most clearly in *GoodFellas*, contrasting its ordinary suburban drudgery with the life of 'action', which Henry Hill finds in Mafia circles. In *GoodFellas* however, the mundane world is kept at bay from the world of action because Henry is only a visitor to that exciting place. For all its repressive energy, which Scorsesean melancholics such as Newland Archer and Jake La Motta have endured at the hands of their own tribal groups, the culture of the Mob in *GoodFellas* is depicted with an appealing element of danger and excitement. This representation of the Scorsesean mob allows the melancholic imagination to make the potentially radical association between the tribe and the idea of desire beyond its own boundaries. In such a context, although the Scorsesean mob is fundamentally conservative, the melancholic may keep alive the notion of a desire, which exists, beyond the patriarchal symbolic where he lives.

With *Casino*, however, that prospect of desire has been completely shut down. The idea that the Scorsesean mob can have any facilitating connection with the most radical melancholic desire is exposed as a myth. In the suburban soap opera of Sam's life we see that the oppression of the Scorsesean mob can result in nothing other than the triumph of the banal. In *Casino* the Mob and the mundane worlds, kept apart in the nostalgia of *GoodFellas*, have come together. The melancholic's object of desire—Ellen Olenska by the light house in *The Age of Innocence* or the life of a gangster in *GoodFellas*—once preserved as a treasured icons of loss, in the person of *Casino*'s Ginger has become the image of a drug-fucked hooker left to rot in a cheap hotel room. In *Casino*, melancholic desire has been all but eradicated from the land of Scorsese's men. Sam is left in the lonely semi-retirement of his San Diego study—a suburban crypt without its lost object—to make money for the bosses 'back home'. So often Scorsese has provided the spectator with a privileged view of his various tribal organizations. This has been to place the spectator in a world, like that of the Italian American Mob, beyond his or her own. Certainly Scorsese's melancholics have defined these groups as oppressive but this has not eradicated the air of excitement and glamour, which they impart. The melancholic's own ambivalence, his ultimately conformist reconciliation with his tribe has certainly not impeded the spectator from desiring something of that glamour. What *Casino* asserts, however, is that such a vision of the

Scorsesean mob can have no lasting appearance of glamour. In so easily merging with the spectator's own world, the world of the Scorsesean mob is rendered as not only oppressive but completely devoid of desire.

The sensitive new age gangster

In the first regular episode of the television series, *The Sopranos*, Christopher (Michael Imperioli)[1] and his girlfriend are queuing-up to get into a fashionable New York nightclub. Standing out among the beautiful people going into the club, Martin Scorcese (sic)[2] (Anthony Caso) makes for the door. Christopher calls after him, 'Marty! *Kundun*! I liked it'.

For all his films about gods on Earth, bourgeois lawyers or guilty saints, Martin Scorsese will always be popularly associated with the machismo and violence of the gangster picture. When considering the influence of Scorsesean melancholics on contemporary filmmaking, therefore, it is to the gangster genre that we should turn for perhaps the fullest picture of this influence. Clearly Scorsese's constant theme of male loss and impairment has had an enormous influence on contemporary male-centred dramas, such as *Thank God He Met Lizzie* (1997), *The Truman Show* (1998), *American Beauty* (1999), *Being John Malcovich* (1999), *The Sixth Sense* (1999), *Fight Club* (1999), *High Fidelity* (2000) and *The Man Who Wasn't There* (2001). However it is to the world of the American gangster in such films as *Pulp Fiction* (1994), *Donnie Brasco* (1997), *Analyze This* (1999) and the television phenomenon of *The Sopranos* (1999) that makes the strongest comment on the Scorsesean melancholic momentum.

In recent examples of the gangster narrative two characteristics are clear. The first of these is that, like Sam Rothstein in *Casino*, the gangster has been portrayed as eager to express his innermost thoughts and feelings. In Quentin Tarantino's *Reservoir Dogs* (1992) and *Pulp Fiction*, gangsters, restaurant robbers and stand-over men have show themselves expert at the sort of banal chatter popularised by the television sitcom, *Seinfeld* (1990–1998). One of the most striking things about Tarantino's films is the very fact of these demonstratively violent hoodlums discussing such everyday issues as the ethics of tipping and the socio-sexual politics of the foot massage. Such mundane matter and the lives of professional criminals seem incongruous. Even more striking and apparently incongruous is a scene in *Pulp Fiction* in which the gangster Jules (Samuel L. Jackson) is discussing his conversion to a new godly mission only hours after we see him coldly executing three boys eating burgers. Having escaped a similar death, Jules explains to his partner, Vincent (John Travolta), that they have been part of a miracle and that the experience has altered his outlook on life. Jules reveals his own vision to an incredulous Vincent with all the eloquence and emotional fanaticism of an Old Testament prophet. For Vincent, who is confined to the life of an urban gangster, Jules's intentions to 'walk the earth' appear impossible. Beyond that, his evangelical method of expression seems to deliver Vincent more information than he needed. Similarly in Woody Allen's *Bullets Over Broadway*, Cheech (Chazz Palminteri), a goon in the pay of a New York Mob boss, shows himself to be a sensitive and insightful playwright when ghosting for floundering author, David Shayne (John Cusack). Cheech's depth of feeling reaches its height when he sees that his boss's girlfriend, juiced-into the play, is massacring his dialogue. 'Every time I hear that voice it's like a knife in the fuckin heart', he says. His response to the casting dilemma is, of course, to bump her off. When he is himself slain in retribution, his last words are to tell David about a show-stopping alteration in the script.

In *Analyze This* and *The Sopranos* this tendency towards the expression of deep feelings has been formalised by turning the gangster into the analysand of the psychoanalytic exchange. Here the gangster narratives are completely intertwined with the psychoanalytic sessions where Paul Vitti (Robert De Niro) in *Analyze This* and Tony Soprano (James Gandolfini) have designated opportunities to air their most profound anxieties. Both characters are suffering feelings of loss related to their dead fathers. In *The Sopranos*, which has had multiple seasons to contemplate Tony's symptoms, a standard cocktail of maternal anxiety matched with a Madonna/whore complex further complicates these feelings of father-loss. These neuroses are played out across the characters of Tony's mother, Livia (Nancy Marchand), and his wife, Carmela (Edie Falco). For Paul Vitti, the plot moves through a series of blockages against freeing up his unconscious before his resistance finally breaks down. It is at this point, as befits its comic form, that Paul sees the light and withdraws from his gangster life. For Tony, however, even in the most recently screened episodes, despite his various important analytical breakthroughs and insights, in terms of his capability for violence, he remains effectively animalistic.

The second characteristic of the contemporary gangster narrative is that the gangster's environment has increasingly become infiltrated by the concerns of home, family and everyday life. In *The Sopranos*

Carmela centres these concerns and forces Tony to confront the fact of their family life. In more recent episodes these concerns largely revolve around the family's financial security in the event that Tony suffers the occupational hazard of being whacked. In the face of Tony's—again occupational—philandering, Soprano family politics also become concerned with the issue of marital fidelity. These take on even greater significance in the series given Carmela's own romantic longings involving Fr. Phil (Michael Santoro) and Tony's Neapolitan driver, Furio (Federico Castelluccio). Accordingly the domestic setting looms large in *The Sopranos* in the manner of the television comedy or melodrama. Like Sam in *Casino* and the faux gangster, Henry in *GoodFellas*, Tony is well aware that his Mob world of scams, unions, heists and mistresses must inevitably be considered among the kitchen coffee and the retirement community bingo concerns of everyday life.

In *Donnie Brasco* the merging of the Mob with the mundane is complete. Donnie (Johnny Depp) is constantly battling with his wife over his absence at Christmas, his inability to make it to their daughter's first communion and their general lack of family normality. Donnie is, of course, an undercover cop, but in a film, which operates to further

Tony (James Gandolfini) and Carmela (Edie Falco) and the pleasures of home and family in *The Sopranos*.

blur the distinction between criminal and cop, Donnie is as much gangster as anything else. Certainly he identifies with his mobster friends and his problem is that the further undercover he goes the less he is able to make the distinction himself. Thus identified as gangster to all practical purposes, we can see here that not only must the gangster be confronted with the banalities of everyday life, but also he must realise that these are the essence of his identity. The gangster is no longer an oppressed and marginalised working class figure longing for something beyond the authority of the Italian American Mob. The gangster is now the bourgeois Snag, sitting in front of his wide-screen television, immersing himself in the world of Mob action and longing for release from his daily corporate doldrums.

These two characteristics of the contemporary gangster narrative have been important to the gangster genre since *Scarface* (1932). The extent to which they have come to dominate the genre with *The Sopranos*, however, is notable. The greater domestication of the genre since *The Godfather* (1972) is a development which appears to be at pains to re-establish the old Hollywood trade category of 'gangster melodrama', which included classics such as the silent, *Musketeers of Pig Alley* (1912) and the talkie cycle of the 1930s including; *Scarface, Little Caesar* (1930) and *The Public Enemy* (1931). It is in the more recent gentrification of the Italian American gangster, through his turn to the bourgeois religion of psychoanalysis and his return to the domestic, that we can see the influence of Scorsese and the general spread of his melancholic vision.

In a recent interview, Scorsese speaks of being approached to direct *Analyze This*. He refused the offer because after *Casino* he could not add anything to what he had already said on this topic. Besides this, he considered that in *GoodFellas* he had already made a comedy in the style of *Analyze This*. It was this world that was blown up for him with the explosions at the end of *Casino*.[3] Scorsese's attitude in this interview to the end of the world of the Italian American gangster might well be read as reflective of the end of the melancholic imagination in his films. In the ten years since *The Age of Innocence* there has been an increased inward turning of the Scorsesean melancholic. This has been accompanied by his increasing domestication of desire within the confines of his tribal group.

Conformity to this group has always been the inevitable outcome of the melancholic's journey. Through the form of a particular object of desire, Ellen Olenska, Joey La Motta, and Betsy in *Taxi Driver*, the cyclical nature of melancholia has been maintained. In this way desire beyond the confines of the group may not be satisfied but it cannot be eradicated. As we observe in Scorsese's four most recent films, with the eradication of such an object however, not even the notion of external desire can be maintained. Like Christopher in *The Sopranos*, who loves *Kundun* and can only respond to his own subordination in Tony's family with the resignation of drugs and longing to write Hollywood scripts, the melancholic can have no option beyond the bleakness of self-love in the confines of the Scorsesean mob. Thus in the form of weekly television instalments beamed into homes all over the world, Scorsese's mean and melancholy history has found its bitter end. Liberated from the burdens of a threatening external desire, male melancholia can now finally operate, as Freud observed, under no authority other than its own narcissism.[4]

NOTES

INTRODUCTION

1 L. Mulvey (1989) *Visual and Other Pleasures*, Macmillan Press, London; K. Silverman (1992) *Male Subjectivity at the Margins*, Routledge, New York; G. Studlar (1988) *In the Realm of Pleasure: Von Sternberg, Dietrich and the Masochistic Aesthetic*, University of Illinois Press, Urbana and Chicago; B. Creed (1990) 'Phallic panic: Male hysteria and *Dead Ringers*', *Screen*, vol.31, no.2, Summer, pp.107–128; L. Kirby (1988) 'Male hysteria and early cinema', *Camera Obscura*, 17, May, pp.113–131; S. Bukatman (1988) 'Paralysis in motion: Jerry Lewis's life as a man', *Camera Obscura*, 17, pp.195–205.

2 Throughout this book I have used the word 'melancholic' in the term 'the male melancholic' according to its common use as a noun among writers on melancholia and as defined in both the Oxford English and Webster's dictionaries. As is common also among contemporary writers on melancholia, I have favoured the use of the word 'melancholia',

with its suggestion of psychiatric disease, over 'melancholy', which is a distinction particular to the English language suggesting a habitual sadness. I have used 'melancholy' to describe a mood or atmosphere in a specific film or group of films under discussion.

3 V. Lebeau (1995) *Lost Angels: Psychoanalysis and Cinema*, Routledge, London; K. Silverman (1988) *The Acoustic Mirror: The Female Voice in Psychoanalysis and Cinema*, Indiana University Press, Bloomington and Indianapolis; K. Fowkes (1998) *Giving Up the Ghost: Spirits, Ghosts and Angels in Mainstream Comedy Films*, Wayne State University Press, Detroit.

4 L. Stern (1995) *The Scorsese Connection*, BFI, London.

5 T. Modleski (1991) *Feminism Without Women: Culture and Criticism in a 'Postfeminist' Age*, Routledge, New York, p.7.

6 ibid.

7 P. Cook (1982) 'Masculinity in crisis', *Screen*, vol.23, pp.3–4.

8 T. Modleski (1988) *The Woman Who Knew Too Much: Hitchcock and Feminist Theory*, Methuen, New York, pp.95–96.

CHAPTER ONE

1 Kristeva, J. (1989) *Black Sun: Depression and Melancholia* (trans L. Roudiez), New York: Columbia University Press, pp.4–5.
2 Freud, S. (1984b) *Mourning and Melancholia*, A. Richards (ed) *The Pelican Freud Library volume 11, On Metapsychology* (trans J. Strachey), Penguin, Middlesex, p.252.
3 ibid, pp.254–255.
4 Both Freud (ibid, p.255) and Benjamin ((1977) *The Origin of German Tragic Drama* (trans. J. Osborne) NLB: London, p.158), to different effect, draw on the example of Hamlet for elucidation.
5 Schiesari, J. (1992) *The Gendering of Melancholia: Feminism, Psychoanalysis, and the Symbolics of Loss in Renaissance Literature*, Ithaca: Cornell University Press, pp.x-xi.
6 ibid, p.5.
7 ibid, p.5–6.
8 ibid, p.7–8.
9 ibid, p.10.
10 ibid, p.12.
11 ibid, p.13–14.
12 Benjamin (1977), op cit, pp. 145–146.
13 ibid, p.148.
14 Freud (1984b), op cit, pp. 254–255.
15 ibid, p.257.
16 ibid.
17 Schiesari, op cit, p.50.
18 ibid, p.51.
19 George Darley (1795–1846), 'It is not beauty I demand'.
20 Freud (1984b), op cit, pp. 253–254. Freud's gender specificity is undermined by his own misogyny—apart from his brief reference to Hamlet, like Dürer, he chooses to represent his melancholic as a female figure, e.g. the 'jilted bride' (253) and the nagging wife (257).
21 ibid, pp.257–258.
22 ibid, p.259.
23 ibid, pp.266–268.
24 N. Abraham & M. Torok (1994) 'Mourning or Melancholia: Introjection versus Incorporation', in N. Rand (ed) (1994) *The Shell and the Kernal: Renewals of Psychoanalysis*, Chicago: University of Chicago Press, pp.135–136.
25 'The patient represents his ego to us as worthless, incapable of any achievement and morally despicable; he reproaches himself, vilifies himself and expects to be cast out and punished. He abases himself before everyone and commiserates with his own relatives for being connected with anyone so unworthy.' Freud (1984b), op cit, p.254.
26 Schiesari, op cit, pp.42–43.
27 ibid, pp.47–48. In Freudian psychoanalysis, castration is a threatening idea or fantasy which occurrs to the young (male) child to account for the mother's lack of a penis. Bound up with notions of paternal power and threatening ideas of the child's own castration, it is an idea which is regularly denied by the child through the substitutuion of fetish objects standing in for any perception of a missing penis.

28 S. Sontag (1985) 'Introduction', *Walter Benjamin: One Way Street and Other Writings,* Verso, p.16. cf Heilman's definition of melodrama quoted in Mulvey (1989) op cit, 'In tragedy, the conflict is within man; in melodrama, it is between men, or between men and things'.

29 ibid, p.20.

30 ibid, pp.16–17.

31 Given the attention of Freud, Schiesari and Benjamin to Hamlet as melancholic, T.S. Eliot's reference in 'The Love Song of J. Alfred Prufrock' is not surprising. Eliot stresses the dangers Prufrock faces in the melancholy dialectic of becoming that very conformist he wishes to reject:

No! I am not Prince Hamlet, nor
    was meant to be;
Am an attendant lord, one that
    will do
To swell a progress, start a scene
    or two,
Advise the prince; no doubt an
    easy tool,
Deferential, glad to be of use,
Politic, cautious, and meticulous;
Full of high sentence, but a bit
    obtuse;
At times, indeed, almost
    ridiculous –
Almost, at times, the Fool.

T.S. Eliot (1917) 'The Love Song of J. Alfred Prufrock' in Allison, Barrows et al (eds) (1983) *The Norton Anthology of Poetry* (Third Edition), pp.994–997.

32 Pensky, M. (1993) *Melancholy Dialectics: Walter Benjamin and the Play of Mourning,* Amherst, University of Massachusetts Press, pp.26–28.

33 Kristeva (1989), op cit, pp.4–6.

34 ibid, pp.13–14.

35 Kristeva (1989), op cit, pp.19–23.

36 In Bertolucci's *Il Conformista* (1970) Marcello, the fascist collaborator, visits his father Antonio, politically imprisoned in a mental asylum. When he first sees Antonio the latter's straitjacket is untied allowing him to write and read out his deliberations:

I shall never tire of repeating—if the state cannot model itself on the image of the individual how can the individual model himself on the image of the state, et cetera, et cetera, et cetera . . . slaughter and melancholy . . . slaughter and melancholy.

37 Pensky, op cit, p.16.

38 ibid, p.6.

39 ibid, p.19.

40 Pensky describes Kästner as a quickly rising star (author-intellectual) of the Weimar left.

41 Pensky, op cit, pp.7–10.

42 ibid, p.11–12.

43 ibid, pp.13–19.

44 Sociologist author of *Melancholie und Gesellschaft.*

45 Pensky, op cit, p.34.

46 Freud (1984b), op cit, p.257.

47 Schiesari, op cit, p.5.

48 Benjamin (1977), op cit, p.16.

CHAPTER TWO

1 S. Freud (1961) *Totem and Taboo* (trans. J. Strachey), Routledge & Kegan, London, pp.1–17.

2 Freud (1984b), op cit.

3 Abraham & Torok, op cit.

4 Freud (1984b), op cit, p.253.

5 Lesley Stern (op cit, p.224) relates this notion of fantasy to both the

cyclical nature of melancholic
desire and to the extent to which it
relies upon the battle over every
last one of Wharton/Scorsese's
'arbitrary signs':

Age of Innocence is, in this respect,
like any old love story. It doesn't end
happily, it's true, but this is not
what's significant; what matters is
that it never really ends. Like all
obsessives Newland takes his time;
he counts time passing. It is a
condition of his love that loss and
memory are inscribed within the
circuit of desire, within the
palpability of the present. To be in
the grip of an obsessive and
transgressive love requires that he
construct a world to sustain that
obsession, to make it last—an
intricately detailed world.

6 See R.B. Heilmann's definition of
melodrama as 'a conflict between
men and things', from his *Tragedy
and Melodrama* as quoted by
Mulvey (1989) op cit, p.41.
7 'Introducing all or part of a love
object or a thing into one's body,
possessing, expelling or alternately
acquiring, keeping, losing it—here
are varieties of fantasy indicating,
in the typical forms of possession
or feigned dispossession, a basic
intrapsychic situation: the
situation created by the reality of a
loss sustained by the psyche',
(Abraham & Torok, op cit, p.126).
8 The nine scenes, the first seven of
which are considered in 'The crypt
of melancholia', are as follows: (1)
The van der Luyden dinner party
for Ellen; (2) Archer visiting her
the next day at 5pm; (3) Their late
night divorce discussion; (4) Their
meeting at the play; (5) Their
meeting at the Patroon House; (6)

Their love making leading to the
telegram from May; (7) Their first
meeting after Newland's marriage;
(8) The carriage ride after
Catherine's illness; and (9) The
meeting in the Art Museum in the
Park.
9 Beethoven Sonata No. 8 in C
Minor, Op. 13 'Pathetique'.
10 Freud (1984b), op cit, p.255.
11 In *A Portrait of The Film*,
Scorsese/Cocks quote Wharton to
this effect: 'Newland Archer
prided himself on his knowledge
of Italian art. But these pictures
bewildered him, for they were like
nothing that he was accustomed
to look at (and therefore able to
see) when he travelled in Italy'
(p.47).
12 Abraham & Torok, op cit, p.126.
13 S. Freud (1984c) *Beyond the
Pleasure Principle*, A. Richards
(ed) *The Pelican Freud Library
volume 11, On Metapsychology*
(trans J. Strachey), Penguin,
Middlesex, pp.269–338. The 18-
month old 'good boy' whom
Freud observes plays two games,
or at least two parts of the same
game, the first of which—the
throwing away of his toys—Freud
mentions as the one almost only
ever witnessed. Despite Freud's
assumption that the second act—
the retrieving of the toy (wooden
reel)—was of greater pleasure,
there is a significant emphasis on
the first game of 'gone'. Freud's
interpretation, relying on the
child's 'great cultural achievement'
of mother-renunciation, will bear
significance for the male
melancholic: 'He compensated
himself for this, as it were, by
himself staging this disappearance
and return of the objects within

his reach'. The enacting of the mother's departure is considered 'as a necessary preliminary to her joyful return', but, given the aforementioned frequency of observations of only the first part of the game, Freud cannot conclude on the purpose of the game without central consideration of the 'fort' aspect (pp.284–5).

14 Lechte discussed theories of rejection and anal-aggressivity in Kristeva by stressing the importance of the 'fort'—'da' story, which in its repetition not only symbolises the dissappearence/reappearence of the mother but also 'evidence of the subject's expulsion of/ separation from the mother' (p.136).

15 Kristeva (1989), op cit, p.13.

16 ibid, p.14.

17 ibid, p.13.

18 Primary identification initiates a compensation for the Thing and at the same time secures the subject to another dimension, that of imaginary adherence, reminding one of the bond of faith, which is just what disintegrates in the depressed person, ibid, p.13–14.

19 A. Martin (1994) *Phantasms*, McPhee Gribble, Ringwood.

20 A. Masson (1983) 'Martin Scorsese', in Coursodon & Sauvage (eds), *American Directors*, Vol. II, McGraw Hill, New York, p.329.

21 Christie, I. (1994) 'The Scorsese Interview', *Sight and Sound*, February, p.11.

22 Freud (1984b), op cit, p.253.

23 Kristeva (1989), op cit, p.8.

24 Speaking of his method of working with Scorsese in an interview in 1995, Saul Bass told me how Scorsese sees the Bass's titles as 'a film within a film' or 'mini-film'. Beyond the importance of establishing a mood for a film, Bass sees the title sequence as mainly concerned with setting a 'subtext', determining the 'theme . . . What it all adds up to'.

25 Charlie's entrance into the club in *Mean Streets* and Henry's three-minute long-take entrance to the Copacobana in *GoodFellas* are the two examples. The *GoodFellas* example bears comparison with the spa scene early in Fellini's *8 ½*.

26 In the Beaufort ballroom hang two large paintings by Tissot of salon-and-ballroom entertainment which reflect the diversions and mores of the day no less than the large gilt-framed mirrors which hang beside them. The extent to which old New Yorkers looked to paint and canvas to see themselves is echoed throughout the film in the proliferation of portraiture (such as those of Catherine Mingott and Louisa van der Luyden), genre subjects of daily life and photography. Catherine Mingott endlessly reflects her own gallery walls in a painting of Samuel Morse's *Gallery of the Louvre* (1831). As the narration continues, once again, accompanied by the roving camera to emphasise both the tribal nature of this group and the location of women within it, the camera settles on a scene of two 'natives' raping/assaulting a screaming woman.

27 As we see in the ball scene and also when Newland and Beaufort send Ellen flowers, the fashion for

calling cards is to include only the owner's name with no address. Calling cards in this period seem to correspond (in spirit) to that period before house numbering and its associations of urban control, as discussed by Benjamin ((1973) *Charles Baudelaire: A Lyric Poet in the Era of High Capitalism*, (trans H. Zohn), NLB, Bristol, p.47).

28 Stern, op cit, p.226.
29 ibid.
30 Benjamin (1973), op. cit., p.55.
31 McFarlane, B. (1996) '*The Age of Innocence*: Scorsese meets Edith Wharton', *Metro*, 105, p.39.
32 Scorsese uses this device in *GoodFellas*, *Casino* and, to a certain degree, *Mean Streets*.
33 P. Cook (1994) 'The Age of Innocence—review', *Sight and Sound*, February, p.46.
34 ibid.

CHAPTER THREE

1 *Casino* begins with Sam (Robert De Niro) being blown up by way of a car bomb; it then proceeds to relate the narrative of how this initial loss/suspected death came about. In this it relies on a similar narrative technique popularised by *Sunset Boulevard* (1950).
2 *Totem and Taboo* has been read with suspicion by anthropologists and ethnologists like Evelyn Reed and René Girard. However, Freud's interest in the psychology of the group, mourning and melancholia in *Totem and Taboo* make it relevant for my discussion. Although this book does not concern itself with the finer points of structural or evolutionary anthropology, Freud's successors in the field, Lévi-Strauss in particular, have raised some objections to his work which serve my argument well in its handling of *Totem and Taboo* as a problematic text. Freud's anthropology reads like a nineteenth-century myth rather than a scientific examination of the facts. Similarly Juliet Mitchell observes, 'On the whole it seems fair to say that Freud's work in *Totem and Taboo* must be read as mythology not anthropology' ((1975) *Psychoanalysis and Feminism*, Pelican, Penguin, Harmondsworth, p.366). However, it may be argued that the same myths that inform *Totem and Taboo* also underlie a range of texts within patriarchal culture, of which the films and pop anthropology of Scorsese may be included. In addition, the status of Freud's text is such that it has exercised a strong influence over representations of totemism in popular culture and the patriarchal imaginary.
3 Freud (1961), op cit, p.9.
4 C. Siri Johnson (1994) 'Constructing machismo in *Mean Streets* and *Raging Bull*', in S. Kellman (ed) (1994) *Perspectives on Raging Bull*, G.K. Hall & Co, New York, p.101.
5 Freud (1961), op cit, pp.141–144.
6 Scorsese has spoken of the money-making imperative of the Mob: 'People think gangsters kill people. Yes, of course they do. But the main purpose of the gangster, especially in *GoodFellas* is to make money. That's why, in *GoodFellas*, Tommy is killed. After a while, he was making more noise than money. He

started killing people for no reason. So they had to get rid of him. He was messing up the whole plan!' (M. Kelly (1991) *Martin Scorsese: A Journey*, Thunder Mouth Press, New York, pp. 262–263.)

7 Male members of the totem clan were all 'brothers', and female members all 'sisters', although not necessarily blood brothers as we may associate these terms in relation to the family.

8 Freud (1961), op cit, p.141.

9 ibid, p.19. In *Group Psychology and the Analysis of the Ego* ((1949) (trans J. Strachey), J. Hogarth Press, London) Freud compares the powers of the hypnotist 'in possession of a mysterious power which robs the subject of his own will' (p.95) with that of the kings and chieftains whose 'mana' is 'the source of taboo' and 'makes it dangerous to approach them' (p.96).

10 Freud (1961), op cit, p.41.

11 Scorsese's *King of Comedy* (1982) suggests a strong emphasis on the undesirable politics of kingly substitution. The scene in which Marcia is phoning Jerry at home alone, and another when he is walking down the street to the cheers and jibes of 'fans', suggests the dangers of kingship in tribal communities.

12 G. Smith (1990) 'Martin Scorsese interviewed by Gavin Smith', *Film Comment*, September/October, p.28.

13 L. Keyser (1992) *Martin Scorsese*, Twayne Publishers, New York, p.201.

14 Freud (1961), op cit, pp.141–148.

15 Mitchell (1975), op cit, p.395.

16 J. Mitchell & J. Rose (eds) (1982), op cit, p.79.

17 Mortimer (1989), op cit, pp.30–36.

18 Played by Scorsese's father Charles.

19 J. MacCannell (1991) *The Regime of the Brother: After the Patriarchy*, Routledge, London.

20 Freud (1961), op cit, p.125.

21 ibid.

22 Siri Johnson (1994), op cit, p.102.

23 Kristeva (1989), op cit, p.23.

24 Siri Johnson (1994), op cit, p.102.

25 S. Freud (1984a) 'Psychoanalytic Notes on An Autobiographical Account of a Case of Paranoia (Dementia Paranoides) (Schreber)', in *The Pelican Freud Library volume 9, Case Histories II,* (trans J. Strachey), Penguin, Middlesex, pp.131–223.

26 Both *GoodFellas* and *Casino* represent similar group stand-offs in bars and clubs, notably involving Pesci, De Niro and Frank Vincent in each. The *GoodFellas* example leads to the 'primal' murder of 'made man' Billy Batts (Vincent).

27 Wood (1982), op cit, p.66.

28 ibid, p.64.

29 This has been discussed by Mulvey (1989), op cit, as male 'play and fantasy', a narcissistic regression, a celebration of phallic nostalgia which resists exact integration into Oedipal symbolic (pp.33–34).

30 Wood (1982), op cit, p.62.

31 Freud (1984a), op cit, p.146.

32 Freud (1961), op cit, p.144; C. Pateman (1988) *The Sexual Contract*, Polity Press, Cambridge, UK, p.109. However, Jake's aggressive erotic desire for other men (Salvy, Janiro) can be seen in this more general context, especially in so far as Jake can be

seen as ultimately conforming to the wishes of the tribe and its homosocial organisation.

33 Freud (1961), op cit, p.144.
34 In a key scene in *GoodFellas*, Paulie and Jimmy confront Henry in order to convince him to return to his wife and children. 'What are you gonna do?' asks Paulie. 'You're not gonna get a divorce. We're not animali'.
35 Freud (1961), op cit, pp.144–150.
36 ibid, p.69.
37 ibid. pp.150–153; J. Campbell (1976) *The Masks of God: Occidental Mythology*, Penguin, New York, pp.54–61, 258–261.
38 Freud (1961), op cit, p.153.
39 J. Lechte (1990) *Julia Kristeva*, Routledge, London, p.149. In that he sees sacrifice as the method of checking the outbreak of violence, René Girard ((1972) *Violence and the Sacred*, John Hopkins University Press, Baltimore) is more concerned with the establishment of order rather than law, in a society that has never known either. In its attempt to highlight the 'societal conflicts' embodied within sacrifice, Girard's picture observes the group as preoccupied with protecting itself from its own violence, as opposed to the Kristeva/Freud position which sees sacrifice as instrumental in the foundations of symbolic law with order already established:

. . . there is a common denominator that determines the efficacy of all sacrifices and that becomes increasingly apparent as the institution grows in vigour. The common denominator is internal violence—all the dissension,

rivalries, jealousies and quarrels within the community that the sacrifices are designed to suppress. The purpose of the sacrifice is to restore harmony to the community, to reinforce the social fabric. Everything else derives from that (Girard, p.8).

40 R. Librach (1992) '*Mean Streets* and *Raging Bull*', *Film Literature Quarterly*, vol.20, no.1, p.20.
41 Keyser, op cit, p.121.
42 Freud (1984a), op cit, p.146.
43 TV playwright who wrote, among others, *Requiem for a Heavyweight (Blood Money)* (1963).
44 Kristeva (1989), op cit, p.10.
45 J. Kristeva (1984) *Revolution in Poetic Language*, (trans M. Waller), Columbia University Press, New York, p.76.
46 Cook (1982), op cit, p.46.
47 Pam Cook uses 'alibi' to describe Ellen in her *The Age of Innocence* review (1994).
48 Freud (1984b), op cit, p.257.
49 Schiesari, op cit, p.50.

CHAPTER FOUR

1 Tester, K. (ed) (1994) *The Flâneur*, Routledge, London; Gilloch, G. (1992) 'The heroic pedestrian of the pedestrian hero? Walter Benjamin and the flâneur', *Telos*, 91 Spring, pp.108–116; Shields, R. (1994) 'Fancy footwork: Walter Benjamin's notes on *flânerie*', in K. Tester (ed) (1994) *The Flâneur*, Routledge, London, pp.61–80.
2 Ferguson, P. (1994a) *Paris as Revolution: Writing the Nineteenth-Century City*, University of California Press, Berkeley, p.83.
3 Benjamin (1973), op cit, p.37.

4 Tester, op cit, p.6.
5 Ferguson, P. (1994a), op cit, p.81ff.
6 Tester, op cit, p.1.
7 Wilson, E. (1992) 'The invisible flâneur', *New Left Review*, no.191, pp.90–110.
8 Benjamin (1973), op cit, p.41.
9 ibid, pp.36–37.
10 Freud (1984b), op cit, p.257.
11 Jake La Motta is similarly conservative. His horde posturing is a longing for a regime of authority which has passed.
12 Robert Ray, in *A Certain Tendency of the Hollywood Cinema, 1930–1980* (1985), discusses *Taxi Driver* as 'Right Cycle' movie, attributing to Travis certain characteristics of the conservative right such as distrust of the law, the belief in locatable centres of evil and the efficacy of captivity rescue (pp.349–360).
13 Jacobs, D. (1977) 'Martin Scorsese', in *Hollywood Renaissance*, Barnes and Co, New Jersey, p.126.
14 Benjamin (1973), op cit, p.55.
15 ibid.
16 Engels quoted in ibid, p.58.
17 MacCannell, op cit, p.32.
18 In his protection of Teresa and Johnny Boy in *Mean Streets*, Charlie casts himself in the role of St Frances of Little Italy. Sam Rothstein in *Casino* plays redeemer to both the prostitute, Ginger, and also to the Mob regime running the gambling 'scams' by attempting to drag both into the legitimate world through his skill and the force of his personality.
19 Freud (1984a), op cit, p.146.
20 Keyser, op cit, p.72.
21 Tester, op cit, pp.5–6.
22 Buck-Morss, S. (1991) *The Dialectics of Seeing: Walter Benjamin and the Arcades Project*, MIT Press, Cambridge, Massachusetts, p.212.
23 Tester, op cit, pp.3–4.
24 Gilloch, op cit, p.109.
25 ibid, footnote 7.
26 ibid, p.110.
27 Buck-Morss, op cit, p.345.
28 Tester, op cit, p.5. This is the heroism of Balzac's vision of 'true' flânerie, as Ferguson (1994a, p.90) points out. The flâneur-artiste of the second quarter of the nineteenth century possessed a detachment which was required of his brand of creative and critical observation.
29 Benjamin (1973), op cit, p.35.
30 ibid, p.39.
31 ibid, p.41.
32 Tester, op cit, pp.4–7.
33 ibid, p.4.
34 Herbert, R. (1988) *Impressionism: Art, Leisure, and Parisian Society*, Yale University Press, New Haven and London, p.34.
35 The bohemian and dandy are obvious models for the male melancholic. The flâneur largely subsumes their critical function here, however. Where the dandy will become important in himself is in his gendering. His frequently perceived femininity will be discussed as another role central to his general construction of melancholia. It provides the male melancholic an entree for his brief journey in the realms of difference and alienation.
36 Ferguson (1994a, p.88) sees dandyism as irreconcilable to flânerie for the very reason of its conspicuous flamboyancy.
37 Shields, op cit, p.66.

38 ibid, p.68.
39 ibid.
40 ibid, p.69.
41 ibid, p.71.
42 ibid, p.72.
43 Schrader quoted in Keyser, op cit, p.75.
44 Watching *American Bandstand* on television after shooting an African-American man in the local store, Travis aims his gun at the middle-class African-American couples slow-dancing to a song which echoes his own psychological development. Its prominent lyric is 'How long have I been sleeping?' Later, after writing to his own parents, he repeats the action by aiming at a couple in a soap opera, fires at them without a bullet and finally, accidentally, tips the set over, causing it to blow out.
45 He is mistaken in this. Not only is he soon back in the group but his 'absence' has served the purposes of the tribe. It allows the tribe to vent its (and Travis's) violence as if this venting was perpetrated by a savage and foreign other. A member of the community could not do such things, but a 'savage' could.
46 Siri Johnson, op cit, pp.100–101.
47 ibid.
48 Gilloch, op cit, p.111.
49 ibid.
50 Benjamin (1973), op cit, p.97.
51 Gilloch, op cit, p.112.
52 Benjamin (1973), op cit, p.97.
53 Gilloch, op cit, p.112.
54 Tester, op cit, p.5.
55 ibid, p.2.
56 Brand (1991) picks up on this idea in *The Spectator and The City in Nineteenth-Century American Literature*: 'The classic flâneur is perfectly suited to serve the function of a specific type of pre-character, who is also represented by the narrator of "The Fall of the House of Usher" and by the fisherman in "A Descent into Maelstrom". He is someone who tries to orient himself in a world he cannot understand, by thinking that he can read its most superficial aspects' (p.81).
57 Gilloch, op cit, p.113.
58 ibid, p.115.
59 Adams, C. (1994) 'Raging Batterer', in S. Kellman (ed.) (1994) *Perspectives on Raging Bull*, G.K. Hall & Co, New York, p.119. This example also prompts the spectator to recall the Hall of Mirrors 'shoot-out scene' in another tale of male melancholia, Orson Welles's *The Lady From Shanghai* (1948).
60 Keyser, op cit, p.82.
61 Some prints of the film seem to have left it out and thus, I suggest, have radically altered the way we read the film.
62 Keyser, op cit, p.71.
63 Julian C. Rice (1976) is one of few critics to have picked up on this tense moment: 'Is Travis simply watching the traffic? Perhaps the sudden disturbed backward glance is meant to suggest that the audience will also take a disturbed backward glance at what they have witnessed. Travis' return to real life cannot culminate in the usual audience catharsis, because the film, as mirror, has forced the audience to speculatively see, as well as empathically experience, the collective fantasy of liberating violence' (p.122).
64 Keyser, op cit, p.83.

CHAPTER FIVE

1 Keyser, op cit, p.199.
2 Kristeva, J. (1991) *Strangers To Ourselves*, (trans. L. Roudiez) Columbia University Press, New York.
3 Italian for 'Are you from my town?'
4 There is an interesting echo of this notion of ethnic purity in Keyser's reading of Scorsese's stated justification for his ethnic casting criteria for *GoodFellas*. Quoting from a Joyce C. Persicio article entitled, 'De Niro and Scorsese on the Same Wave Length', Keyser comments that Scorsese wanted '[T]o ensure verisimilitude', by casting 'virtually all Italian American performers in *GoodFellas*'. He quotes Scorsese's justification:

You don't have to tell an Italian American how to hold a glass or sit down with the boys. Casting Italian Americans saves you time, and, on one level, gives you authenticity (201).

5 Caputo mistakes Billy Batts for 'Frankie Carbone'.
6 Caputo, R. (1990) '*GoodFellas*: An Afterword', *Cinema Papers*, 81, p.26.
7 Kristeva (1991) op cit, p.15.
8 ibid, p.16.
9 Scorsese has suggested that, in Mob circles, murder is of secondary importance to the making of money. It is only likely to occur when something or someone gets in the way of making money (Keyser, p.200).
10 The tension between Morrie and Jimmy is finally released with Morrie's murder by Jimmy as part of Jimmy's post-Lufthansa murder spree. Caputo has pointed out how the murder further emphasises Henry's lack of agency in the film (p.26). Henry knows Jimmy is planning to kill Morrie and is relieved to think that the planned murder has been given up. Jimmy continues with his plans, however, leaving Henry in the dark and excluding him from even the knowledge of violence.
11 Caputo, op cit, p.24.
12 The word *omertà* is never mentioned in Scorsese's films, to my knowledge. Its sense, however, proliferates. Although it has popularly been understood to indicate the Mafia code of silence, most analysis and definition suggests a far wider frame of cultural meaning. Abadinski (1981) *The Mafia in America: An Oral History*, Praeger, New York, refers to it as a southern Italian concept, derived from 'uomo' (meaning 'man'), suggesting values of manliness, 'which included non-cooperation with authorities, self control in the face of adversity, and the vendetta in which any offence or slight to family must be avenged, no matter what the consequences or how long it takes' (p.14).
13 Keyser, op cit, p.207.
14 Kristeva (1991), op cit, pp.9–10.
15 ibid, p.14.
16 Lechte, op cit, p.79.
17 Kristeva (1991), op cit, p.3.
18 ibid, p.7.
19 ibid, p.5.
20 ibid, p.9.
21 ibid, pp.21–22.
22 ibid, pp.6–7.
23 Ibid, p.7.
24 ibid, p.8.
25 ibid, p.10.

26 ibid, p.14.
27 Maas, P. (1997) *Underboss: Sammy the Bull Gravano's Story of Life in the Mafia*, Harper, New York, p.479.
28 Quart, L. (1990) 'GoodFellas', *Cineast*, p.45.
29 See Keyser, op cit, p.201, and M. Viano (1991) 'Reviews— *GoodFellas*', *Film Quarterly*, vol.44, no.3, Spring, p.48.
30 Keyser, op cit, p.201.
31 Murphy, K. (1990) 'Made men', *Film Comment*, (Sept/Oct), p.26.
32 Urry, J. (1990) *The Tourist Gaze: Leisure and Travel in Contemporary Societies*, Sage, London, p.11.
33 ibid, p.2.
34 ibid, pp.2–3.
35 ibid, p.3.
36 ibid.
37 ibid, pp.4–5.
38 ibid, p.7.
39 ibid, p.8.
40 ibid, p.10.

CHAPTER SIX

1 I am using the notion of the 'body politic' in terms of the power this notion has had since the fourteenth-century to evoke political, legal and religious—that its, institutionalised—power. In so far as the body politic has been seen as an artificial legal creation for the enjoyment of rights, power, property and privilege by church and state hierarchies, it also suggests the realm of those who lack a place within and stand outside that body. Indeed, the place of the unempowered individual in the body politic has been part of that discourse since the English civil wars of the seventeenth-century. This discourse is given a greater assertion in the bodily expression of Max Cady which plays such a significant role in *Cape Fear*.
2 Keyser, op cit, p.215.
3 Kristeva, J. (1982) *Powers of Horror: An Essay in Abjection*, Columbia University Press, New York.
4 Cook, P. (1992) 'Scorsese's masquerade', *Sight and Sound*, April, p.15.
5 Stern, op cit, p.183.
6 cf. Stern, ibid. and Capp, R. (1992) '*Cape Fear*: Whose Fantasy Marty?', *Metro* no, 90, Winter, pp.4–7, for detailed discussions of Sam's incestuous relationship with Danny.
7 Freud, S. (1961) op cit.
8 Kelly, M. (1991) *Martin Scorsese: A Journey*, Thunder Mouth Press, New York, p.287.
9 Cook (1992), op cit, p.15.
10 Stern, op cit, p.184ff.
11 ibid, p.207.
12 'Salasius' is most likely Max's confused invocation of the scholar Claudius Salmasius (Claude De Saumaise) (1588–1653). A celebrated French Calvinist, classicist and polyglot, with a history of anti-papal activism, during the English Civil War he wrote *Defense of the Reign of Charles I* (1649) which stood in apparent contradiction to his own earlier views on priests and absolute monarchies. Seen as a traitor to the Protestant cause, Salmasius became subject to a savage attack by John Milton. In his *Catholics, Anglicans & Puritans: Seventeenth Century Essays*, Fontana, London, 1989, p.267, Hugh Trevor-Roper points

out that Milton savaged Salmasius as 'a foreigner, a grammarian, a pedant, a hired pedagogue, a monster, a madman, a liar, a pimp, a parasite, a henpecked eunuch, a Circean beast, a weevil, a bug, a dunghill cock, a filthy pig,'. As a powerful scholar associated with radical views and such an abject reputation (via Milton), Salmasius is certainly a figure who might attract Max Cady.

13 ibid, pp.178–179.

14 Stoddart, H. (1995) "I Don't Know Whether to Look at Him Or Read Him': _Cape Fear_ and Male Scarification' in Kirkham & Thumim, *Me Jane: Masculinity, Movies and Women*, St. Martin's Press, New York, p.198.

15 ibid, p.195.

16 ibid.

17 ibid, p.200.

18 Freud (1984b), op cit, pp.263–264.

19 Kristeva (1989), op cit, p.23.

20 Freud (1984b), op cit, p.256 & 263.

21 Kristeva (1982), op cit, p.2.

22 ibid, p.8.

23 ibid, p.4.

24 ibid.

25 Creed, B. (1993) *The Monstrous-Feminine: Film, Feminism, Psychoanalysis*, Routledge, London.

26 Kristeva (1982), op cit, p.16.

27 ibid, p.9.

28 ibid, p.5.

29 ibid, pp.9–10.

30 ibid, p.12.

31 ibid, p.2.

32 ibid, pp.15–16.

33 ibid, p.13.

34 ibid, p.15.

35 Lechte (1990), op cit, pp.159–160.

CHAPTER 7

1 Michael Imperioli played the role of 'Spider' in *GoodFellas*.

2 The credit sequence spells the name in this way.

3 Christie, Ian. (2003)'Manhattan asylum', *Sight and Sound*, January, p.21.

4 Freud (1984b) p.259.

BIBLIOGRAPHY

Abadinsky, H. (1981) *The Mafia in America: An Oral History*, Praeger, New York.

Abraham, N and Torok, M. (1994) "Mourning or Melancholia: Introjection *versus* Incorporation", in Rand, N. (ed.) (1994) *The Shell and the Kernal: Renewals of Psychoanalysis,* University of Chicago Press, Chicago, pp. 125–138.

Adams, C. (1994) "Raging Batterer", in Kellman, S. (ed.) (1994) *Perspectives on Raging Bull,* G. K. Hall & Co., New York, pp. 107–121.

Allison, A., Barrows, H. et.al. (eds.) (1983) *The Norton Anthology of Poetry,* (third edition) W. W. Norton & Company, New York.

Benjamin, W. (1977) *The Origin of German Tragic Drama*, Osborne, J. (trans.) NLB, London.
— (1973) *Charles Baudelaire: A Lyric Poet in the Era of High Capitalism*, Zohn, H. (trans.) NLB, Bristol.

Bliss, M. (1985) *Martin Scorsese and Michael Cimino,* Scarecrow Press, London.

Brand, D. (1991) *The Spectator and the City in Nineteenth Century American Literature*, Cambridge University Press, New York.

Bratton, J., Cook, J. and Gledhill, C. (eds.) (1994) *Melodrama: Stage Picture Screen*, BFI, London.

Brooks, J. (1995) "Between Contemplation and Distraction: Cinema, Obsession & Involuntary Memory" in Jayamanne, L. (ed.) *Kiss Me Deadly: Feminism & Cinema For The Moment,* Power Publications, Sydney, pp. 77–90.

Brooks, P. (1991) "The Melodramatic Imagination", in Landy, M. (1991) *Imitations of Life,* Wayne State University Press, Detroit, pp. 50–66.

Bruce, B. (1986) "Martin Scorsese: Five Films", in *Movie*, 31/2 Winter, 1986.

Buck-Morss, S. (1991) *The Dialectics of Seeing: Walter Benjamin and the Arcades Project*, MIT Press, Cambridge, Massachusetts.

Bukatman, S. (1988) "Paralysis in Motion: Jerry Lewis's Life as a Man", in *Camera Obscura*, 17, pp. 195–205.

Burkert, W. Girard, R. and Smith, J. (1987) *Violent Origins: Ritual Killing and Cultural Formation*, Stanford University Press, Stanford, California.

Butler, J. (1990) *Gender Trouble*, Routledge, New York.

Butner, R. (1990) *Register of the Martin Scorsese Collection*, Louis B. Mayer Library, American Film Institute, Los Angeles, California.

Byars, J. (1991) *All That Hollywood Allows: Re-reading Gender in the 1950s Melodrama*, Routledge, London.

Campbell, J. (1976) *The Masks of God: Occidental Mythology*, Penguin, New York.

Capp, R. (1992) "*Cape Fear*: Whose Fantasy Marty ?", *Metro* no, 90, Winter, pp. 4–7.

Caputo, R. (1996) "In review: *The Scorsese Connection* ", *Cinema Papers*, June, 58–59.

— (1990) "*GoodFellas*: An Afterword", *Cinema Papers*, 81, 24–26.

Cavell, S. (1996) *Contesting Tears: The Hollywood Melodrama of the Unknown Woman*, University of Chicago Press, Chicago.

Christie, I. (1994) "The Scorsese Interview", *Sight and Sound*, February, pp. 10–15.

— (1996) "Martin Scorsese's Testament", *Sight and Sound*, January, pp. 7–11.

— (2003) 'Manhattan asylum', *Sight and Sound*, January, p.21.

Cocks, J. and Scorsese, M. (1993) *The Age of Innocence: A Portrait of the Film*, Newmarket Press, New York.

Cook, P. (1994) "*The Age of Innocence*—Review", *Sight and Sound*, February, pp. 45–46.

— (1992) "Scorsese's masquerade", *Sight and Sound*, April, pp. 14–15.

— (1989) "*Dead Ringers*", *Monthly Film Bulletin*, vol. 56, no. 660, January, pp. 3–4.

— (ed.) (1985) *The Cinema Book*, BFI, London.

— (1983) "Melodrama and the Women's Picture", in Landy, M. (1991) *Imitations of Life*, Wayne State University Press, Detroit, pp. 248–262.

— (1982) "Masculinity in Crisis", *Screen*, vol. 23, 3–4.

Connelly, M. (1991) *Martin Scorsese: An Analysis of His Feature Films, and with a Filmography of His Entire Directorial Career,* McFarland and Company Inc., Jefferson.

Creed, B. (1993) *The Monstrous-Feminine: Film, Feminism, Psychoanalysis,* Routledge, London.

— (1990) "Phallic Panic: Male Hysteria and <u>*Dead Ringers*</u>", *Screen,* vol 31, no. 2, Summer, pp. 107–128.

— (1978) "Structures of Melodrama", *The Australian Journal of Screen Theory,* 4, Waterwheel Press, Shepparton.

Easthope, A. (1986) *What a Man's Gotta Do: The Masculine Myth in Popular Culture,* Paladin, London.

Ehrenstein, D. (1992) *The Scorsese Picture,* Birch Lane Press, New York.

Elsaesser, T. (1986) "Tales of Sound and Fury", in Grant, B. (ed.) (1986) *Film Genre Reader,* University of Texas Press, Austin, pp. 278–308.

Ferguson, H. (1995) *Melancholy and the Critique of Modernity: Søren Kierkegaard's Religious Psychology,* Routledge, London.

Ferguson, P. (1994a) *Paris as Revolution: Writing the Ninteenth-Century City,* University of California Press, Berkeley.

— (1994b) "The *flâneur* on and off the streets of Paris" in Tester, K. (ed.) (1994) *The Flâneur,* Routledge, London pp. 43–60.

Fitzgerald, G. (1994) "Scorsese's Constraints of Desire", *Metro* #97, pp. 10–13.

Fowkes, K. (1998) *Giving Up the Ghost: Spirits, Ghosts and Angels in Mainstream Comedy Films,* Wayne State University Press, Detroit.

Freud, S. (1984a) "Psychoanalytic Notes on An Autobiographical Account of a Case of Paranoia (Dementia Paranoides) (Schreber)", in *The Pelican Freud Library volume 9, Case Histories II,* Strachey, J. (trans.) Penguin, Middlesex, pp. 131–223.

— (1984b) *Mourning and Melancholia,* Richards, A. (ed) *The Pelican Freud Library volume 11, On Metapsychology* , Strachey, J. (trans.) Penguin, Middlesex, pp. 245–268.

— (1984c) *Beyond the Pleasure Principle,* Richards, A. (ed) *The Pelican Freud Library volume 11, On Metapsychology* , Strachey, J. (trans.) Penguin, Middlesex, pp. 269–338.

— (1961) *Totem and Taboo,* trans. Strachey, J., Routledge & Kegan, London.

— (1949) *Group Psychology and the Analysis of the Ego,* (trans.) Strachey, J. Hogarth Press, London.

Friedkin, D. (1994) "Blind Rage and 'Brotherly Love': The Male Psyche at War with Itself in <u>*Raging Bull*</u>", in Kellman, S. (ed.) (1994) *Perspectives on Raging Bull,* G. K. Hall & Co., New York, pp. 122–130.

Friedman, L. (1997) *The Cinema of Martin Scorsese,* Continuum,
    New York.
Fuery, P. (1995) *Theories of Desire,* Melbourne University Press, Carlton.
Gabbard, K. and Gabbard, G. (1987) *Psychiatry and the Cinema,*
    University of Chicago Press, Chicago and London.
Gay, P. (1995) *Freud: A Life for Our Time,* Papermac, London.
Gilloch, G. (1992) "The Heroic Pedestrian of the Pedestrian Hero? Walter
    Benjamin and the Flâneur", *Telos,* 91 Spring, pp. 108–116.
Girard, R. (1972) *Violence and the Sacred,* John Hopkins University Press,
    Baltimore.
Gledhill, C. (ed.) (1987) *Home is Where the Heart Is: Studies in Melodrama
    and The Woman's Film,* BFI, London.
— (1986) "Melodrama", in Cook, P. (ed.) (1985) *The Cinema Book,*
    BFI, London, pp. 73–84.
Grant, B. (ed.) (1986) *Film Genre Reader,* University of Texas Press, Austin.
Halliday, J. (1972) "*All That Heaven Allows*", in Halliday and Mulvey
    (eds.) (1972) *Douglas Sirk,* Edinburgh Film Festival 72, National Film
    Theatre and John Player and Sons, Lancashire, pp. 59–66.
— (1971) *Sirk on Sirk,* Secker and Warburg, London.
Halliday, J. and Mulvey, L. (eds.) (1972) *Douglas Sirk,* Edinburgh Film
    Festival 72, National Film Theatre and John Player and Sons,
    Lancashire.
Haverkamp, A. (1996) "Mourning Beyond Melancholia: Kryptic
    Subjectivity", *Leaves of Mourning: Hölderlin's Late Work,* State
    University of New York Press, pp. 6–21.
Heilmann, J. (1968) *Tragedy and Melodrama,* University of Washington
    Press, Seattle.
Herbert, R. (1988) *Impressionism: Art, Leisure, and Parisian Society,* Yale
    University Press, New Haven and London.
Hodenfield, C. (1989) "Martin Scorsese: The Art of Noncompromise",
    American Film, March, pp. 46–51.
Jackson, K. (1990) (ed.) *Schrader on Schrader,* Faber, London.
Jacobowitz, F. (1988) "The Man's Melodrama: *Woman in the Window* and
    Scarlet Street", *CineAction!,* Summer, pp. 64–73.
Jacobowitz, F. and Lippe, R. (1989) "*Dead Ringers* : The Joke's On Us",
    CineAction, Spring, pp. 64–68.
Jacobs, D. (1977) "Martin Scorsese", in *Hollywood Renaissance,* Barnes
    and Co., New Jersey, pp. 122–148.
Jenkins, S. (1988) "From the Pit of Hell", *Monthly Film Bulletin,*
    December, 1988, vol. 55, n. 659.

Kehr, D. (1983) "The New Male Melodrama", *American Film,* vol. viii, no. 6, April, pp. 42–47.

Kellman, S. (ed.) (1994) *Perspectives on Raging Bull,* G. K. Hall & Co., New York.

Kelly, M. (1991) *Martin Scorsese: A Journey,* Thunder Mouth Press, New York.

— (1980) *Martin Scorsese: The First Decade,* Pleasantville, Redgrave, New York.

Keyser, L. (1992) *Martin Scorsese,* Twayne Publishers, New York.

Kirby, L. (1988) "Male Hysteria and Early Cinema", *Camera Obscura* 17, May, pp. 113–131.

Kirkham, P. (1996) "Bright Lights Big City", *Sight and Sound,* January, pp. 12–13.

Klinger, B (1994) *Melodrama and Meaning: History, Culture, and the Films of Douglas Sirk,* Indiana University Press, Bloomington and Indianapolis.

Kleinhans, C. (1991) "Notes on the Melodrama and the Family Under Capitalism", in Landy, M. (1991) *Imitations of Life,* Wayne State University Press, Detroit, pp. 197–204.

Kolker, R. (1980) *A Cinema of Loneliness,* Oxford University Press, New York.

Kristeva, J. (1991) *Strangers To Ourselves,* Roudiez, L (trans.) Columbia University Press, New York.

— (1989) *Black Sun: Depression and Melancholia,* Roudiez, L (trans.) Columbia University Press, New York.

— (1984) *Revolution in Poetic Language,* Waller, M. (trans.) Columbia University Press, New York.

— (1982) *Powers of Horror: An Essay on Abjection,* Roudiez, L (trans.) Columbia University Press, New York.

Kuhn, A. (1985) *The Power of the Image: Essays on Representation and Sexuality,* Routledge and Kegan Paul, London.

Lacan, J. (1982) "God and the Jouissance of the Woman", in Mitchell, J. and Rose, J. (eds.) (1982) *Feminine Sexuality: Jacques Lacan and The Ecole Freudienne,* Macmillan, London, pp. 137–148.

— (1982) "A Love Letter", in Mitchell, J. and Rose, J. (eds.) (1982) *Feminine Sexuality: Jacques Lacan and The Ecole Freudienne,* Macmillan, London, pp. 149–161.

— (1981) *The Four Fundamental Concepts of Psycho-Analysis,* Sheridan, A. (trans.) Norton & Company, London.

— (1978) "The Mirror Phase" in *Ecrits: A Selection,* Bristol, pp 1–7.

— (1953) "Some Reflections on the Ego", *The International Journal of Psychoanalysis*, vol. 24, pp. 11-17.

Landy, M. (1991) *Imitations of Life*, Wayne State University Press, Detroit.

Lapsley, R. and Westlake, M. (1992) "From *Casablanca* to *Pretty Woman* : the politics of romance", *Screen*, Spring, pp. 27–49.

Lebeau, V. (1995) *Lost Angels: Psychoanalysis and Cinema*, Routledge, London.

Lechte, J. (1990) *Julia Kristeva*, Routledge, London.

Lévi-Strauss, C. (1969) *The Elementary Structures of Kinship*, Bell, J. and Sturmer, J. (trans.), Needham, R. (ed.), Beacon Press, Boston.

Librach, R. (1992) "*Mean Streets* and *Raging Bull*", *Film Literature, Quarterly* vol. 20, no. 1.

Lourdeaux, L. (1990) *Italian and Irish Filmmakers in America: Ford, Capra, Coppola and Scorsese,* Temple University Press, Philadelphia.

MacCannell, J. (1991) *The Regime of the Brother: After the Patriarchy*, Routledge, London.

McFarlane, B. (1996) "*The Age of Innocence*: Scorsese Meets Edith Wharton", *Metro* 105, pp. 37–41.

Maas, P. (1997) *Underboss: Sammy the Bull Gravano's Story of Life in the Mafia*, Harper, New York.

Martin, A. (1997) "Sex, cars and death", *The Age* Saturday Extra, January 11, p.10.

— (1994) *Phantasms,* McPhee Gribble, Ringwood.

Masson, A. (1983) "Martin Scorsese", in Coursodon and Sauvage *American Directors,* Vol. II, Mc Graw & Hill, New York, pp. 326–329.

Mitchell, J. (1975) *Psychoanalysis and Feminism*, Pelican, Penguin, Harmondsworth.

Mitchell, J. and Rose, J. (eds.) (1982) *Feminine Sexuality: Jacques Lacan and The Ecole Freudienne*, Macmillan, London.

Modleski, T. (1991) *Feminism Without Women: Culture and Criticism in a "Postfeminist" Age,* Routledge, New York.

— (1988) *The Woman Who Knew Too Much: Hitchcock and Feminist Theory*, Methuen, New York.

Monaco, J. (1979) "The Whiz Kids", *American Film Now.* Zoetrope, New York.

Morawski, S. (1994) "The hopeless game of flânerie", in Tester, K. (ed.) op. cit. pp. 181-197.

Morrison, S. (1986) "Sirk, Scorsese and Hysteria: A Double(d) Reading", *CineAction,* Summer/Fall, pp. 17–25.

Mortimer, L. (1996) "Book Reviews: *The Scorsese Connection*", *Metro*, 105, pp. 77–80.

— (1994) "*The Age of Innocence*: A Bloodless Feast", *Metro,* 97, pp. 3–9.

— (1989) "Blood Brothers: Scorsese, Schrader and the Cult of Masculinity", *Cinema Papers*, September, no. 75, pp. 30–36.

Mulvey, L. (1998) "Review—*Written on the Wind*", *Sight and Sound,* February, p. 57.

Mulvey, L. (1996) *Fetishism and Curiosity*, BFI, London.

— (1994) "'It will be a magnificent obsession' The Melodrama's Role in the Development of Contemporary Film Theory", in Bratton, J. Cook, J. and Gledhill, C. (eds.) (1994) *Melodrama: Stage Picture Screen*, BFI, London, pp. 121-133.

— (1989) *Visual and Other Pleasures*, Macmillan Press, London.

Murphy, K. (1990) "Made Men", *Film Comment*, (Sept/Oct). pp. 25–27.

Naremore, James. (1993) *The Films of Vincente Minnelli,* Cambridge University Press, Cambridge.

Neale, S. (1986) "Melodrama and Tears", *Screen,* (December), pp. 6–22

— (1980) *Genre* BFI, London.

Nicholls, M. (1998) "Martin Scorsese's *Kundun*: A Melancholic Momentum", *Metro*, no. 116, pp. 11-14.

— (1997) "She Who Gets Slapped: Jane Campion's *Portrait of a Lady*", *Metro,* no. 111, pp. 43–47.

Nowell-Smith, G. (1977) "Minnelli and Melodrama", *Screen*, vol. 18, no 2, Summer, pp. 113–118.

Parker, J. (1995) *De Niro,* Cassell, London.

Pateman, C. (1989) *The Disorder of Women: Democracy, Feminism and Political Theory*, Polity Press, Cambridge, UK.

— (1988) *The Sexual Contract*, Polity Press, Cambridge, UK.

Pearce, L. & Stacey, J. (1995) *Romance Revisited,* New York University Press, New York.

Pensky, M. (1993) *Melancholy Dialectics: Walter Benjamin and the Play of Mourning*, Amherst, University of Massachusetts Press.

Pye, M. and Myles, L. (1979) *The Movie Brats: How the FilmGeneration Took Over Hollywood,* Faber & Faber, Boston.

Quart, L. (1990) "*GoodFellas*", *Cineast*, pp. 43–45.

Rand, N. (ed.) (1994) *The Shell and the Kernal: Renewals of Psychoanalysis,* University of Chicago Press, Chicago.

Ray, R. (1985) *A Certain Tendency of the Hollywood Cinema, 1930–1980*, Princeton University Press.

Reed, E. (1975) *Woman's Evolution: From Matriarchal Clan to Patriarchal Family*, Pathfinder, New York.

Rice, J. (1976) "Transcendental Pornography and *Taxi Driver*", in *Journal of Popular Film 5*, no. 2: pp. 109 -123.

Robbins, H. (1993) "'More human than I am alone': Womb Envy in David Cronenberg's *The Fly* and *Dead Ringers*" in Cohan, S. and Hank, I. (eds.) (1993) *Screening the Male: Exploring Masculinities in Hollywood Cinema*, Routledge, London, pp. 134–147.

Rowe, C. & Mink, W. (1989) *An Outline of Psychiatry*, ninth edition, Wm. C. Brown Publishers, Dubuque, Iowa.

Rowe, K. (1992) "Melodrama and Men in Post-Classical Romantic Comedy", Kirkham, P. and Thumim, J. (eds.) *Me Jane* St. Martin's Press, New York.

Schatz, T. (1983) *Old Hollywood / New Hollywood: Ritual, Art and Industry*, UMI Research Press, Michigan.

Schatz, T. (1981) *Hollywood Genres*, Random House, New York

Schiesari, J. (1992) *The Gendering of Melancholia: Feminism, Psychoanalysis, and the Symbolics of Loss in Renaissance Literature*, Cornell University Press, Ithaca.

Schowalter, E. (1988) *The Female Malady: Women, Madness, and English Culture, 1830–1980*, Virago, London.

Shields, R. (1994) "Fancy footwork: Walter Benjamin's notes on *flânerie*", in Tester, K. (ed.) (1994) *The Flâneur*, Routledge, London. pp. 61-80.

Silverman, K. (1992) *Male Subjectivity at the Margins*, Routledge, New York.
— (1988) *The Acoustic Mirror: The Female Voice in Psychoanalysis and Cinema*, Indiana University Press, Bloomington and Indianapolis.
— (1980) "Masochism and Subjectivity", *Framework*, Issue 12, pp. 2–9.

Siri Johnson, C. (1994) "Constructing Machismo in *Mean Streets* and *Raging Bull*", in Kellman, S. (ed.) (1994) *Perspectives on Raging Bull*, G. K. Hall & Co., New York, pp. 95–106.

Smith Jr., D. (1975) *The Mafia Mystique*, Basic Books, New York.

Smith, G. (1990) "Martin Scorsese interviewed by Gavin Smith", *Film Comment*, September/October, pp. 27–30, 69.

Sontag, S. (1985) "Introduction", *Walter Benjamin: One Way Street and Other Writings*, Verso, pp. 7–28.

Stern, L. (1995) *The Scorsese Connection*, BFI, London.

Stern, M. (1979) *Douglas Sirk*, Twayne Publishers, Boston.

Stoddart, H. (1995) "'I Don't Know Whether to Look at Him Or Read

Him': *Cape Fear* and Male Scarification" in Kirkham & Thumim, *Me Jane: Masculinity, Movies and Women*, St. Martin's Press, New York.

Studlar, G. (1988) *In the Realm of Pleasure: Von Sternberg, Dietrich and the Masochistic Aesthetic*, University of Illinois Press, Urbana and Chicago.

— (1984) "Masochism and the Perverse Pleasures of the Cinema", *Quarterly Review of Film Studies*, vol. 9, no. 4, pp. 267–282.

Taubin, A. (1993) "Dread and Desire" *Sight and Sound*, December, pp. 6–9.

Taylor, B. (1981) "Martin Scorsese" in Tuska, J. (ed.) *Close up: The Contemporary Director*, The Scarecrow Press, New Jersey, pp. 293–368.

Tester, K. (ed.) (1994) *The Flâneur*, Routledge, London.

Thompson, D. and Christie, I. (1989) *Scorsese on Scorsese*, Faber & Faber, London.

Urry, J. (1990) *The Tourist Gaze: Leisure and Travel in Contemporary Societies*, Sage, London.

Viano, M. (1991) "Reviews—*GoodFellas*", *Film Quarterly*, vol. 44, no. 3, Spring, pp. 43–50.

Wallace, E. (1983) *Freud and Anthropology: A History and Reappraisal*, International University Press, New York.

Warren, Nettlebeck and Kirsop (eds.) (1996) *A Century of Cinema: Australian and French Connections*, Department of French and Italian Studies, University of Melbourne, Parkville.

Weaver, D. (1986) "The Narrative of Alienation: Martin Scorsese's *Taxi Driver*", *CineAction!*, Summer/Fall, p.12.

Weiss, M. (1987) *Martin Scorsese: A Guide to References and Resources*, G.K. Hall & Co., Boston.

Wilson, E. (1992) "The invisible flâneur", *New Left Review*, no. 191, pp. 90–110.

Wollheim, R. (1979) "The Cabinet of Dr. Lacan", *New York Review of Books*, vol. xxv, nos. 21 & 22, January.

Wood, R. (1982) "The Homosexual Subtext: *Raging Bull*", *Australian Journal of Screen Theory*, 15/16, pp. 57–66.

Interviews

Ansen, D. (1987) "Directors: Redeeming Features: Martin Scorsese", *Interview*, January, pp. 49–51.

Biskind, P. and Linfield, S. (1986) "Chalk Talk", *American Film*, November, pp. 30–33, 69.

Carducci, M. (1975) "Martin Scorsese: Now They're Knocking at His Door", *Millimeter*, vol. 3, No. 5, May, pp. 12–16

Ebert, R. and Siskel, G. (1991) *The Future of the Movies,* pp. 1-36, Buena Vista Media Inc.

Fuller, G. (1991) "Profile: Martin Scorsese", *Interview,* November, pp. 16–18.

Goldstein, R. and Jacobson, M. (1976) "Blood and Guts Turn Me On", *The Village Voice,* April 5, pp. 69–71, 1976.

Harvie, J. (1977) "Interview With Douglas Sirk", (unpublished) Sirk File, Museum of Modern Art Film Study Centre, New York.

Howard, S. (1975) "The Making of *Alice Doesn't Live Here Anymore*", *Filmmakers Newsletter,* vol. 8, No. 5, March pp. 21-26.

Jacobs, D. (1976) "Martin Scorsese Doesn't Live Here Anymore", *Viva* March, pp. 87–89, 104.

Macklin, A. (1975) "It's a Personal Thing for Me", *Film Heritage,* vol. 3, no. 10, Spring, pp. 13–28, 36.

Morrison, S. (1986) "An Interview with Martin Scorsese", *CineAction,* Summer/Fall, pp. 3–11.

Nicholls, M. (1995) "Interview with Saul Bass", (unpublished) June 23, Los Angeles, California.

Rosen, M. (1975) "Martin Scorsese Interview", *Film Comment,* March-April, pp. 42–46.

Schrader, P. (1990) *Taxi Driver,* Faber, London.

Scorsese, M. (1975) *American Film Institute Seminar with Martin Scorsese, February 12 1975,* Seminar Collection, Louis B Mayer Library, AFI, Los Angeles, California.

Truman, J. (1987) "Martin Scorsese", *The Face,* February, pp. 76–80.

Special Collections

Braun, A. (1991) *The Martin Scorsese Collection,* Louis B. Mayer Library, Special Collections no. 38, American Film Institute, Los Angeles, California.

Butner, R. (1990) *Register of the Martin Scorsese Collection,* Louis B. Mayer Library, American Film Institute, Los Angeles, California.

Silver, C. and Megliozzi, R (1995) Article Files Museum of Modern Art, Film Study Centre, New York.

Video Collection, British Film Institute Library, London.

FILMOGRAPHY

After Hours	(Scorsese, 1985)
The Age of Innocence	(Scorsese, 1993)
Alice Doesn't Live Here Anymore	(Scorsese, 1974)
All That Heaven Allows	(Sirk, 1955)
Un Amour de Swann	(Schlöndorff, 1984)
American Beauty	(Mendes, 1999)
Annie Hall	(Allen, 1977)
Analyze This	(Ramis, 1999)
The Bad and the Beautiful	(Minnelli, 1952)
Being John Malcovich	(Jonze,1999)
The Big Shave	(Scorsese, 1967)
Bigger Than Life	(Ray, 1956)
Boxcar Bertha	(Scorsese, 1972)
Bringing Out The Dead	(Scorsese, 1999)
Bullets Over Broadway	(Allen, 1994)
Cape Fear	(Scorsese, 1991)
Casino	(Scorsese, 1995)
Cat on a Hot Tin Roof	(Brooks, 1958)
Champion	(Robson, 1949)
Citizen Kane	(Welles, 1940)
The Color of Money	(Scorsese, 1986)
Il Conformista	(Bertolluci, 1970)
Crash	(Cronenberg, 1996)
Dark Victory	(Goulding, 1939)
Dead Ringers	(Cronenberg, 1988)
Donnie Brasco	(Newell, 1997)

Dirty Harry	(Siegel, 1972)
La Dolce Vita	(Fellini, 1960)
The Fall of the Roman Empire	(Mann, 1964)
Fight Club	(Fincher, 1999)
The Gangs Of New York	(Scorsese, 2002)
Il Gattopardo	(Visconti, 1963)
Gilda	(Vidor, 1946)
The Godfather	(Coppola, 1972)
Gone With the Wind	(Fleming, 1939)
GoodFellas	(Scorsese, 1990)
Green Card	(Weir, 1990)
High Fidelity	(Frears, 2000)
Hiroshima Mon Amour	(Resnais, 1959)
The Heiress	(Wyler, 1949)
Home From the Hill	(Minnelli, 1960)
Imitation of Life	(Sirk, 1959)
Italianamerican	(Scorsese, 1974)
It's A Wonderful Life	(Capra, 1946)
It's Not Just You Murray!	(Scorsese, 1964)
The King of Comedy	(Scorsese, 1982)
Kundun	(Scorsese, 1997)
The Lady From Shanghai	(Welles, 1948)
The Last Temptation of Christ	(Scorsese, 1988)
The Last Waltz	(Scorsese, 1978)
Last Year at Marienbad	(Resnais, 1961)
Letter From an Unknown Woman	(Ophuls, 1948)
Life Lessons (from *New York Stories*)	(Scorsese, 1989)
Little Caesar	(Le Roy, 1930)
Long Hot Summer	(Ritt, 1958)
Lost Weekend	(Wilder, 1945)
The Magnificent Ambersons	(Welles, 1942)
Magnificent Obsession	(Sirk, 1954)
Manhattan	(Allen, 1979)
The Man in the Gray Flannel Suit	(Johnson, 1956)
The Man Who Wasn't There	(Coen, 2001)
Mean Streets	(Scorsese, 1973)
Mildred Pierce	(Curtiz, 1945)
Musketeers of Pig Alley	(Griffith, 1912)
New York, New York	(Scorsese, 1977)
The Night of the Hunter	(Laughton, 1955)

Now Voyager	(Rapper, 1942)
The Old Maid	(Goulding, 1939)
One Way Street	(Hughes, 1992)
On the Waterfront	(Kazan, 1954)
8 ½	(Fellini, 1963)
A Personal Journey with Martin Scorsese Through American Movies	(Scorsese, 1995)
Peyton Place	(Robson, 1957)
Picnic	(Logan, 1955)
The Portrait of a Lady	(Campion, 1997)
Psycho	(Hitchcock, 1960)
The Public Enemy	(Wellman, 1931)
Pulp Fiction	(Tarantino, 1994)
Raging Bull	(Scorsese, 1980)
Random Harvest	(Le Roy, 1942)
The Red Shoes	(Powell & Pressburger, 1948)
Reservoir Dogs	(Tarantino, 1992)
Le Samurai	(Melville, 1967)
Scarface	(Hawks & Rosson, 1932)
Scarlett Street	(Lang, 1945)
The Searchers	(Ford, 1956)
Seinfeld	(Seinfeld, 1990-1998)
The Sixth Sense	(Night Shyamalan, 1999)
Sleepless in Seattle	(Ephron, 1993)
Somebody Up There Likes Me	(Wise, 1956)
The Sopranos	(Chase, 1999)
A Star is Born	(Cukor, 1951)
Sunset Boulevard	(Wilder, 1950)
Tarnished Angels	(Sirk, 1958)
Taxi Driver	(Scorsese, 1975)
Thank God He Met Lizzie	(Nowlan, 1997)
There's Always Tomorrow	(Sirk, 1956)
The Trueman Show	(Weir, 1998)
Two Weeks in Another Town	(Minnelli, 1962)
Vertigo	(Hitchcock, 1958)
What's a Nice Girl Like You Doing in a Place Like This?	(Scorsese, 1963)
Who's That Knocking at my Door?	(Scorsese, 1969)
The Wizard of Oz	(Fleming, 1939)
Woman in the Window	(Lang, 1944)
Written on the Wind	(Sirk, 1957)
Zu Neuen Ufern	(Sirk, 1937)

INDEX

189